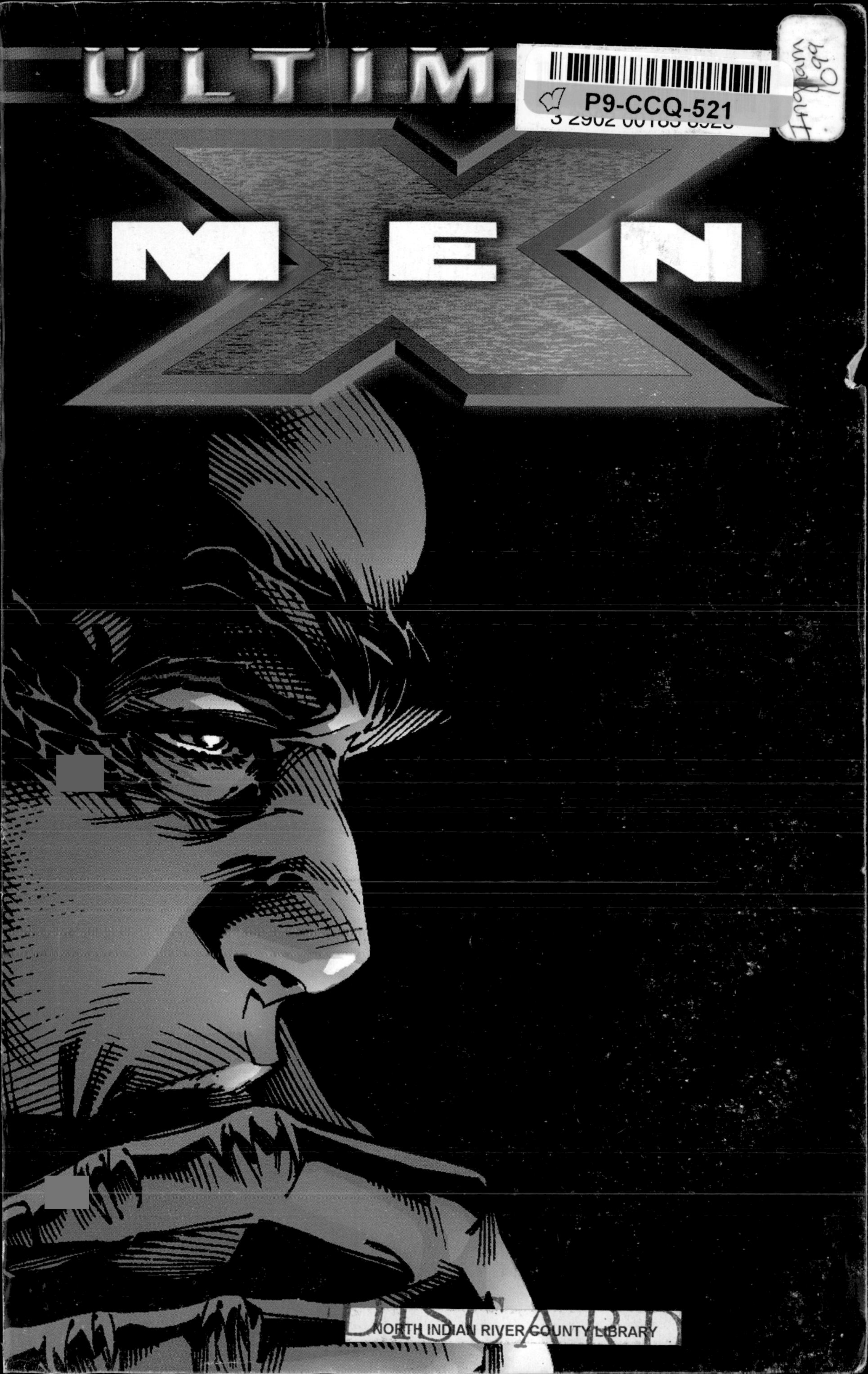
ULTIM
X
MEN

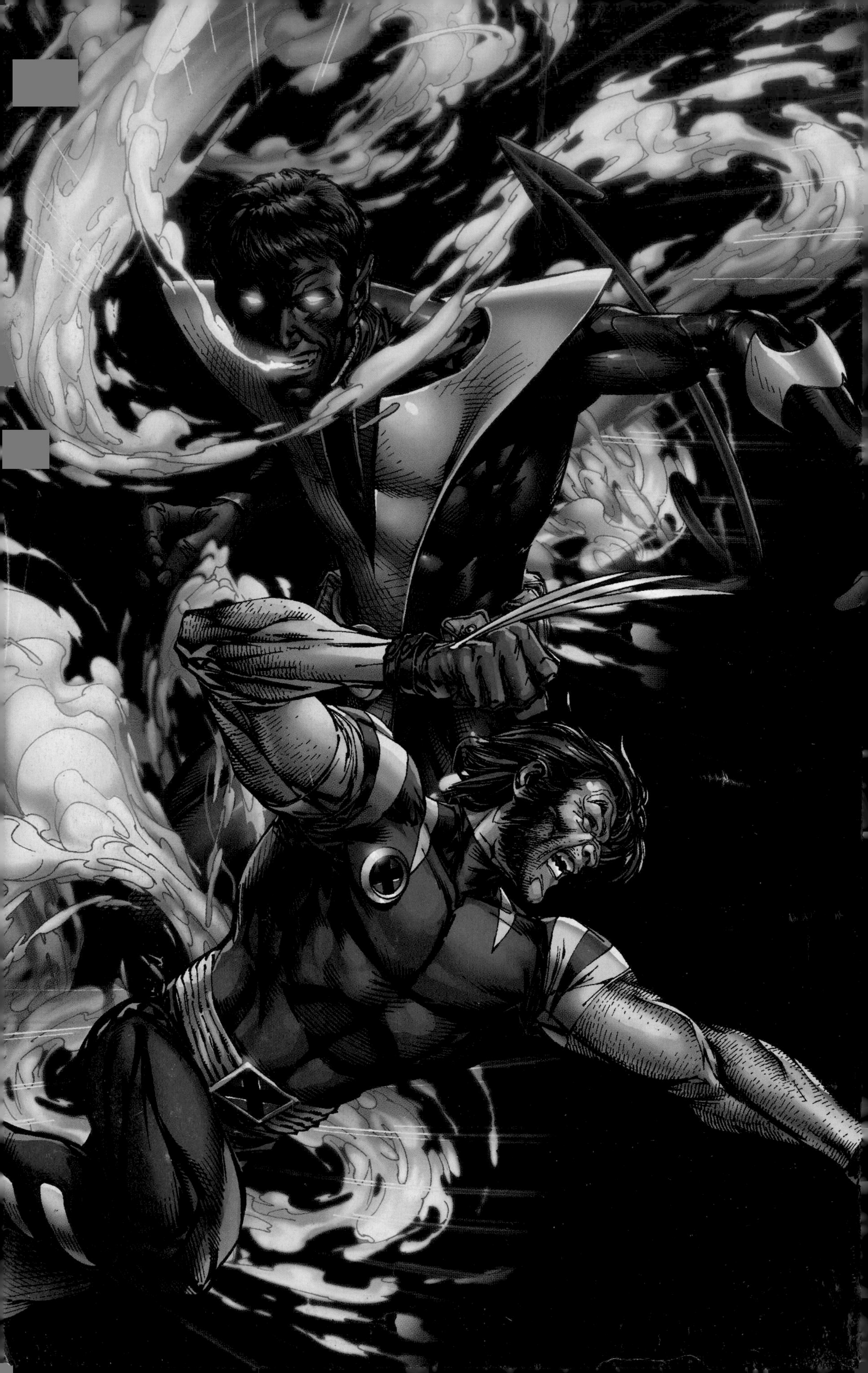

ULTIMATE X-MEN

writer
BRIAN K. VAUGHAN
artist
BRANDON PETERSON
colors
JUSTIN PONSOR
letters
CHRIS ELIOPOULOS

assistant editor
NICK LOWE
editor
RALPH MACCHIO
special thanks to
C.B. CEBULSKI

collections editor
JEFF YOUNGQUIST
assistant editor
JENNIFER GRÜNWALD
book designer
CARRIE BEADLE
creative director
TOM MARVELLI

editor in chief
JOE QUESADA
publisher
DAN BUCKLEY

THE TEMPEST

ULTIMATE X-MEN

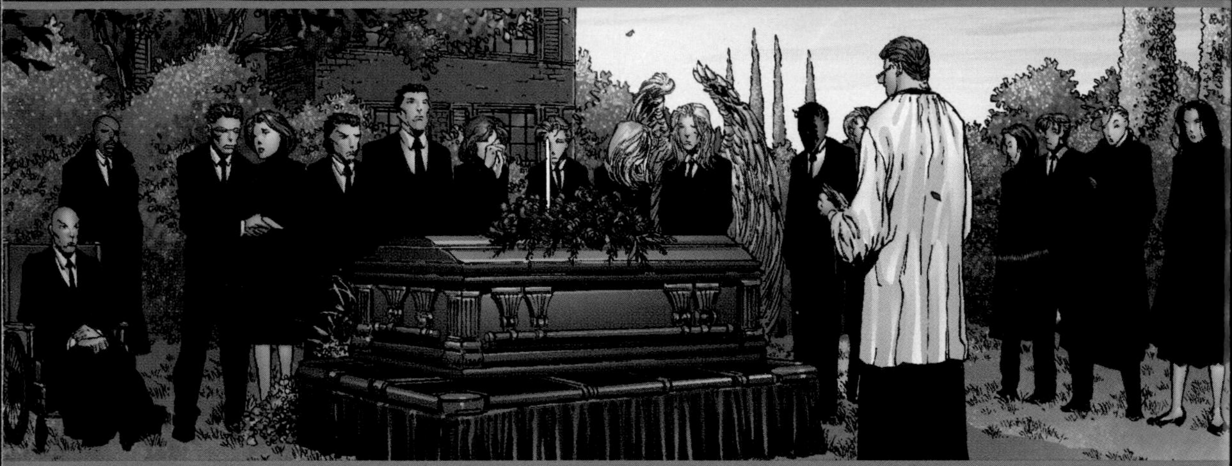

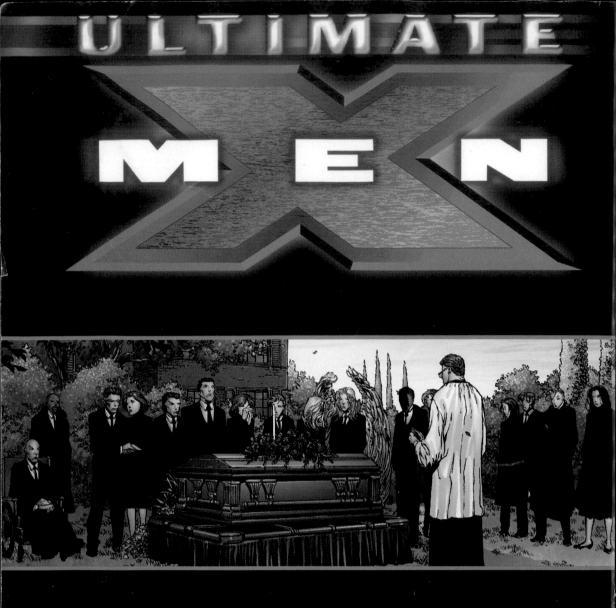

PREVIOUSLY IN ULTIMATE X-MEN:

Professor Charles Xavier brought them together to bridge the gap between humanity and those born with strange and amazing powers: Cyclops, Marvel Girl, Storm, Iceman, Beast, Colossus, and Wolverine. They are the X-Men, soldiers in Xavier's war to bring peace between man and mutant! But in every war, there are casualties. During their last battle, Hank "The Beast" McCoy was killed.

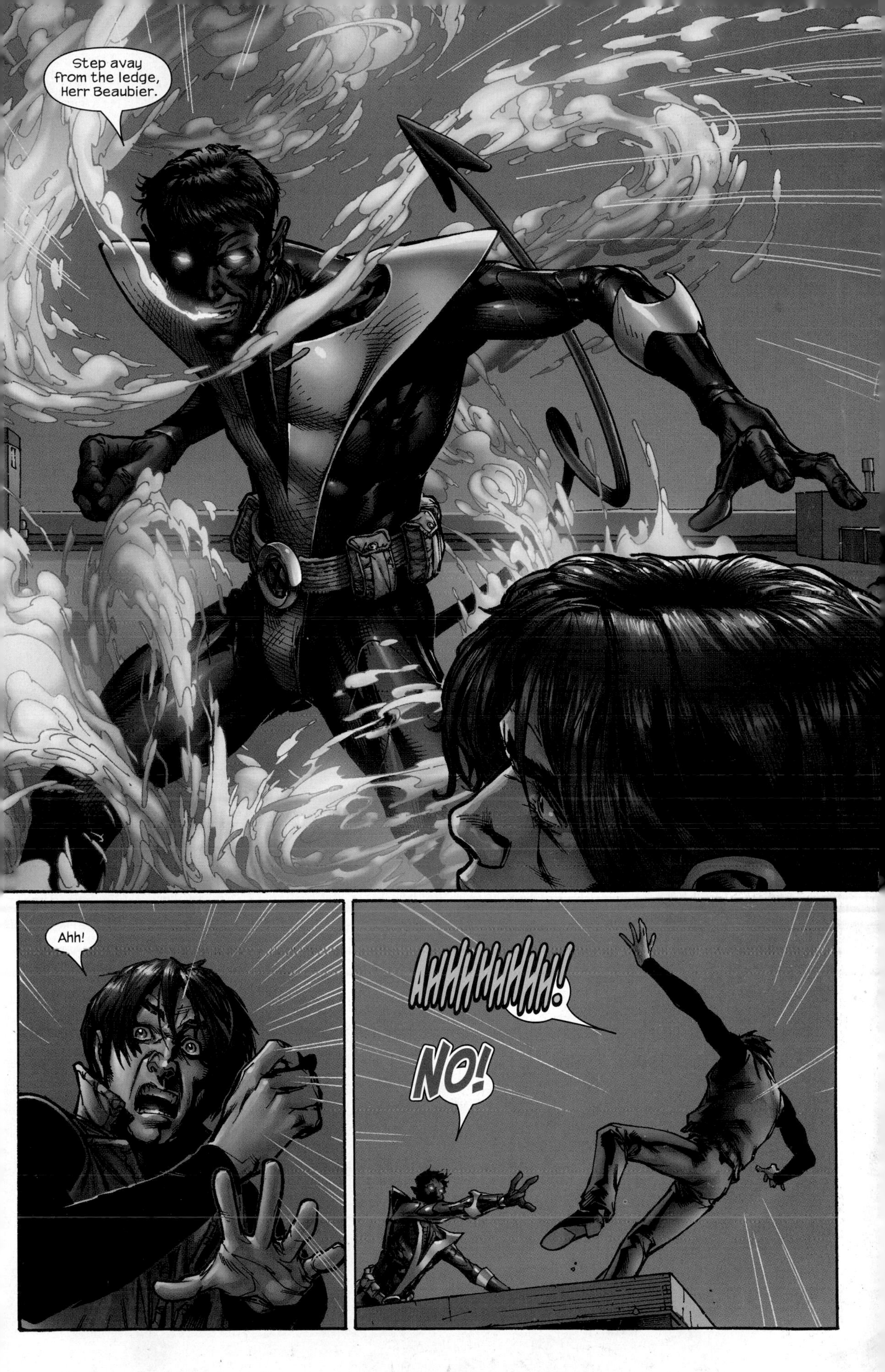
Step avay from the ledge, Herr Beaubier.
Ahh!
AHHHHHHHH!
NO!

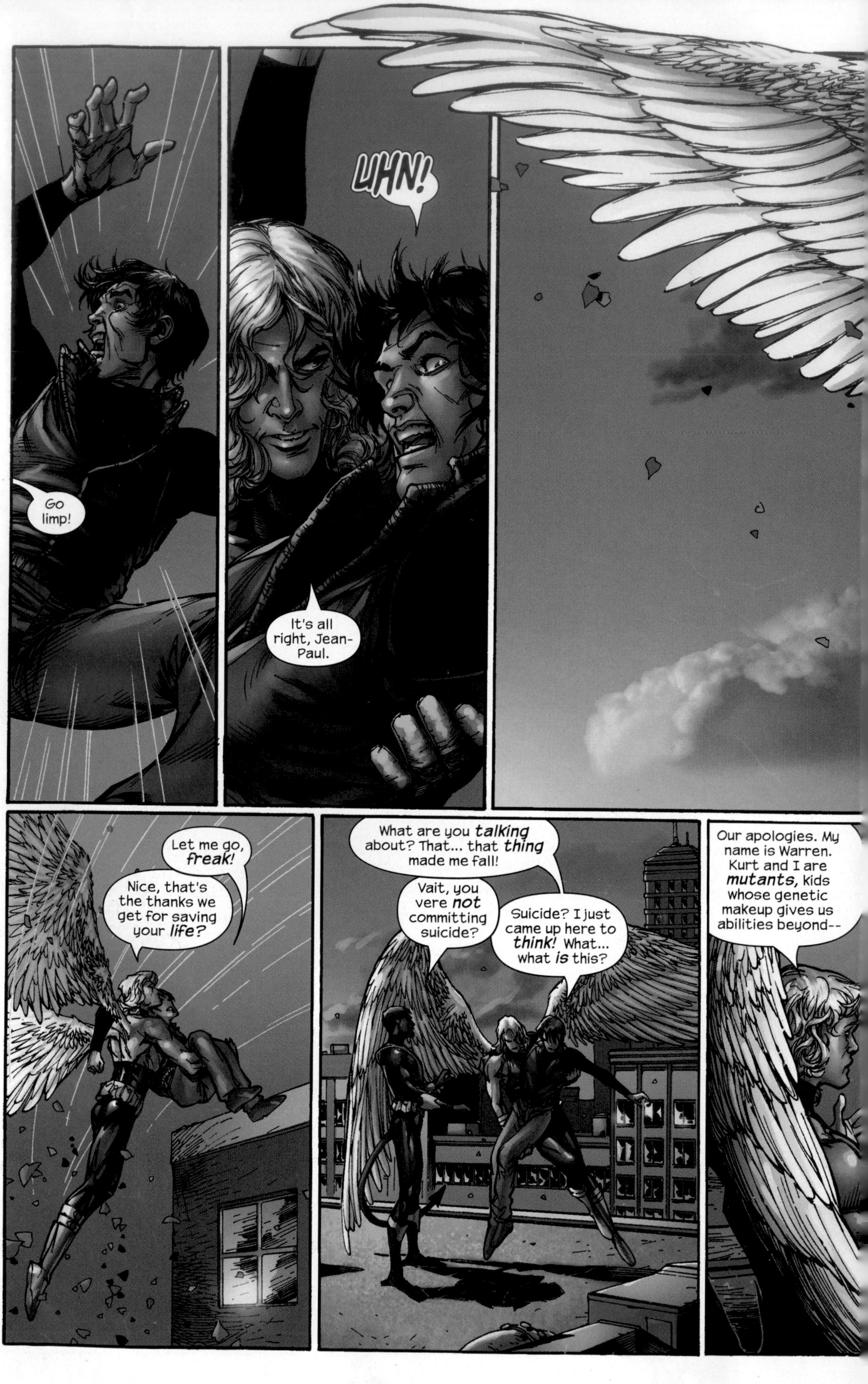

UHN!
Go limp!
It's all right, Jean-Paul.
Let me go, freak!
Nice, that's the thanks we get for saving your life?
What are you talking about? That... that thing made me fall!
Vait, you vere not committing suicide?
Suicide? I just came up here to think! What... what is this?
Our apologies. My name is Warren. Kurt and I are mutants, kids whose genetic makeup gives us abilities beyond--

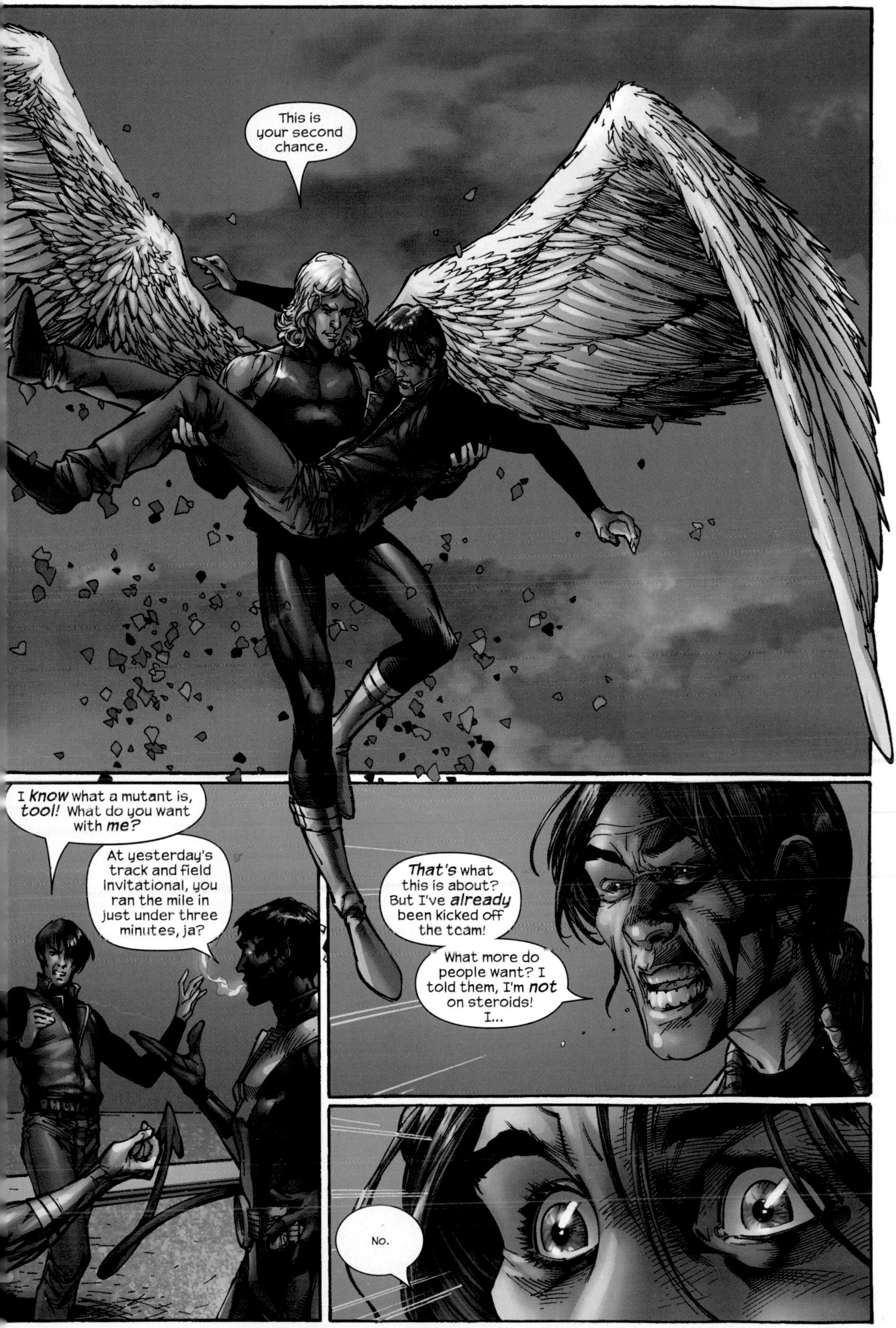
This is your second chance.
I KNOW what a mutant is, TOOL! What do you want with ME?
At yesterday's track and field invitational, you ran the mile in just under three minutes, ja?
That's what this is about? But I've already been kicked off the team!
What more do people want? I told them, I'm NOT on steroids! I...
No.

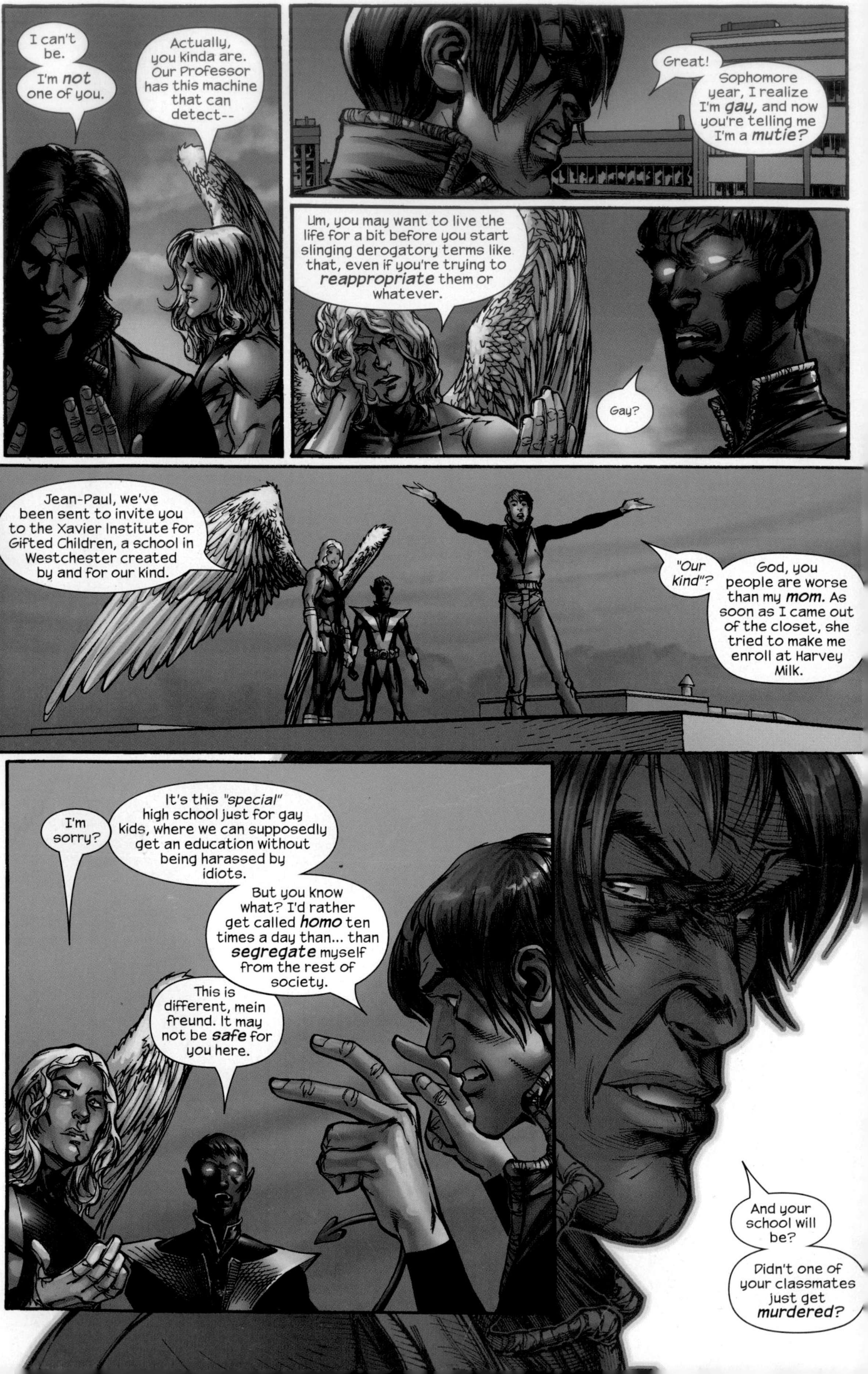
I can't be.
I'm *not* one of you.
Actually, you kinda are. Our Professor has this machine that can detect--
Great!
Sophomore year, I realize I'm *gay,* and now you're telling me I'm a *mutie?*
Um, you may want to live the life for a bit before you start slinging derogatory terms like that, even if you're trying to *reappropriate* them or whatever.
Gay?
Jean-Paul, we've been sent to invite you to the Xavier Institute for Gifted Children, a school in Westchester created by and for our kind.
"*Our kind*"?
God, you people are worse than my *mom.* As soon as I came out of the closet, she tried to make me enroll at Harvey Milk.
I'm sorry?
It's this "*special*" high school just for gay kids, where we can supposedly get an education without being harassed by idiots.
But you know what? I'd rather get called *homo* ten times a day than... than *segregate* myself from the rest of society.
This is different, mein freund. It may not be *safe* for you here.
And your school will be?
Didn't one of your classmates just get *murdered?*

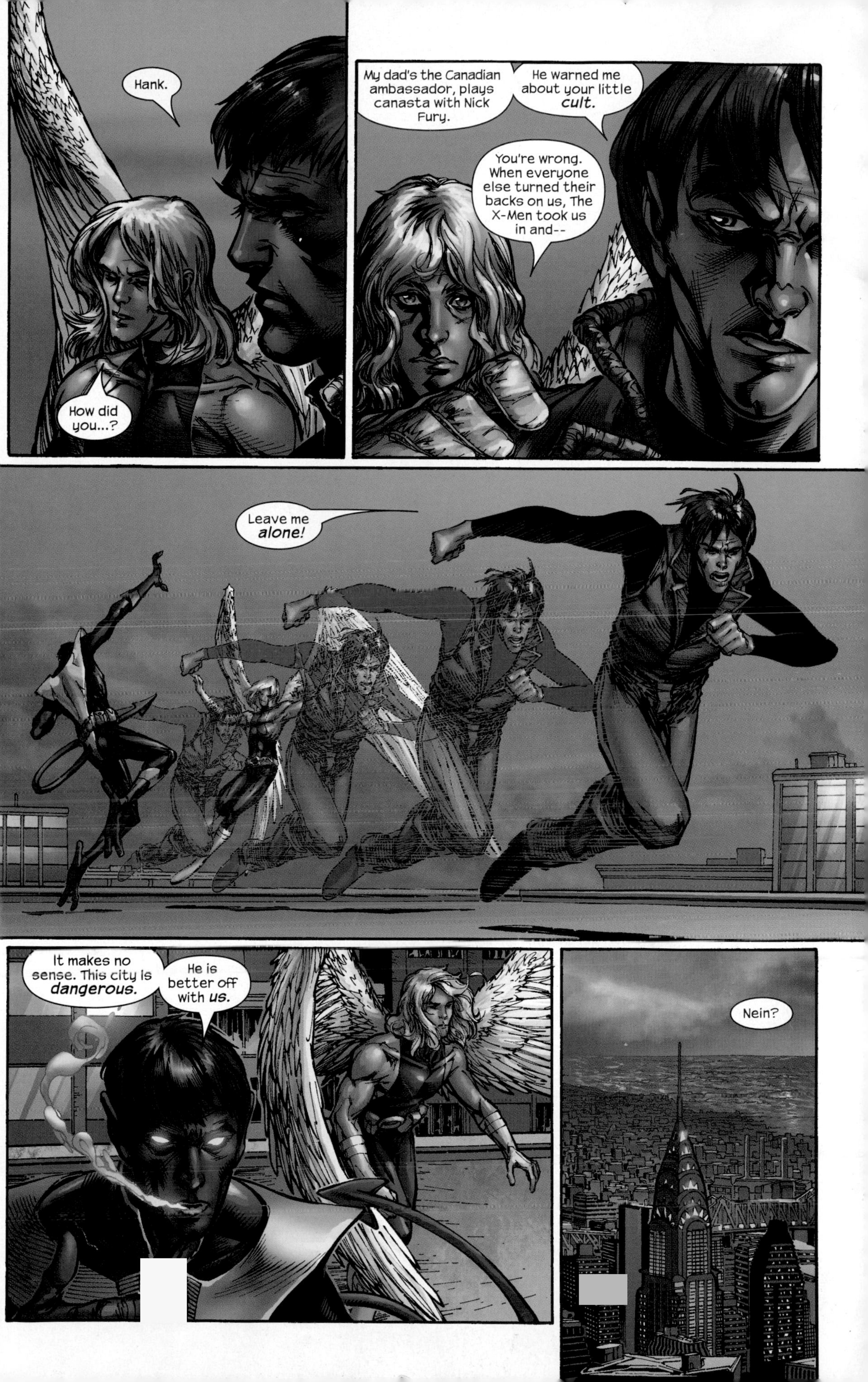
Hank.
How did you...?
My dad's the Canadian ambassador, plays canasta with Nick Fury.
He warned me about your little cult.
You're wrong. When everyone else turned their backs on us, The X-Men took us in and--
Leave me alone!
It makes no sense. This city is dangerous.
He is better off with us.
Nein?

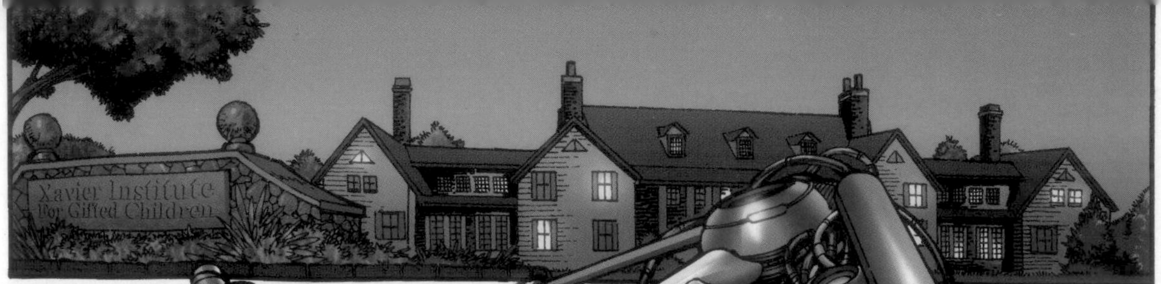
Xavier Institute
For Gifted Children

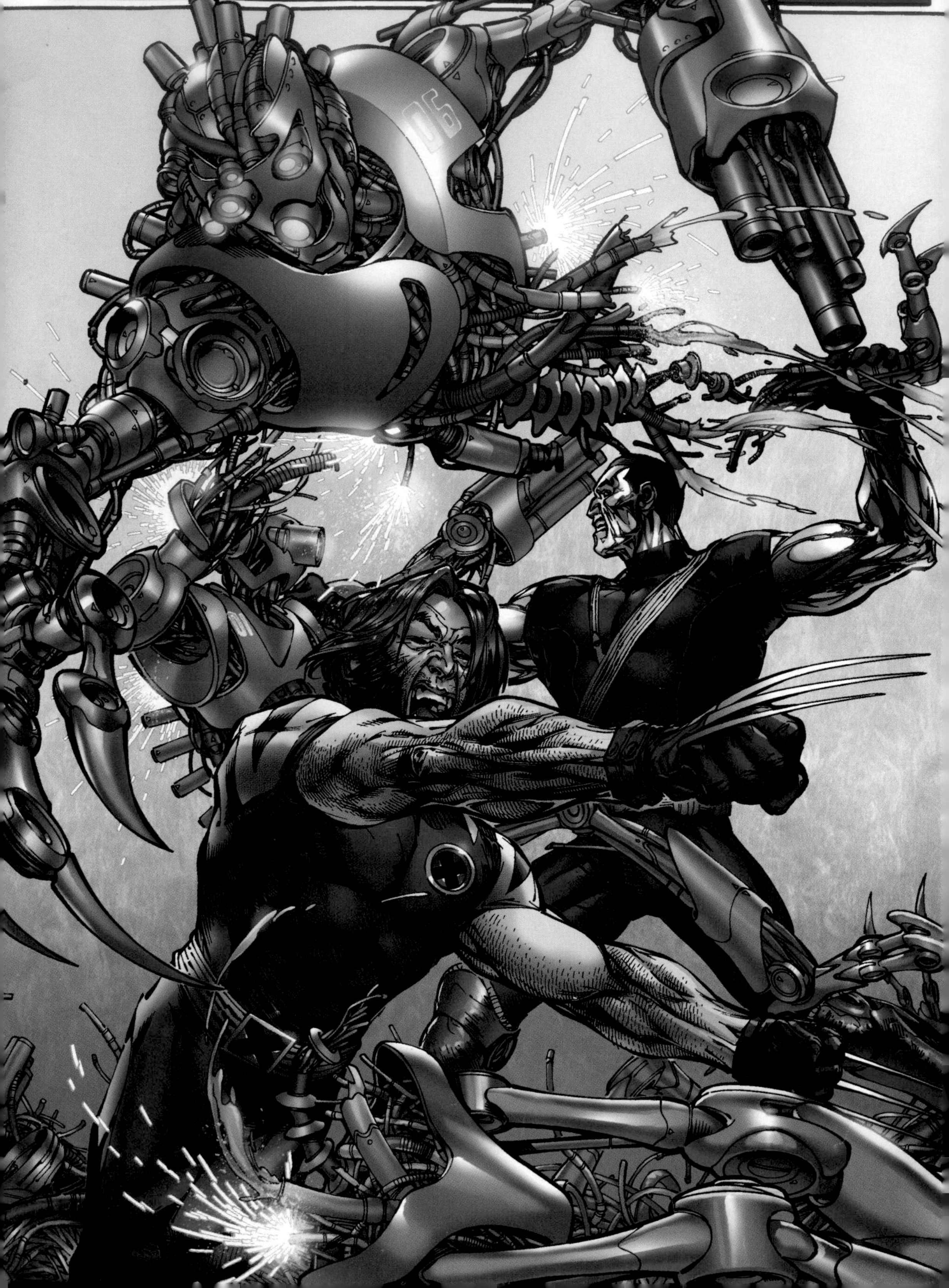

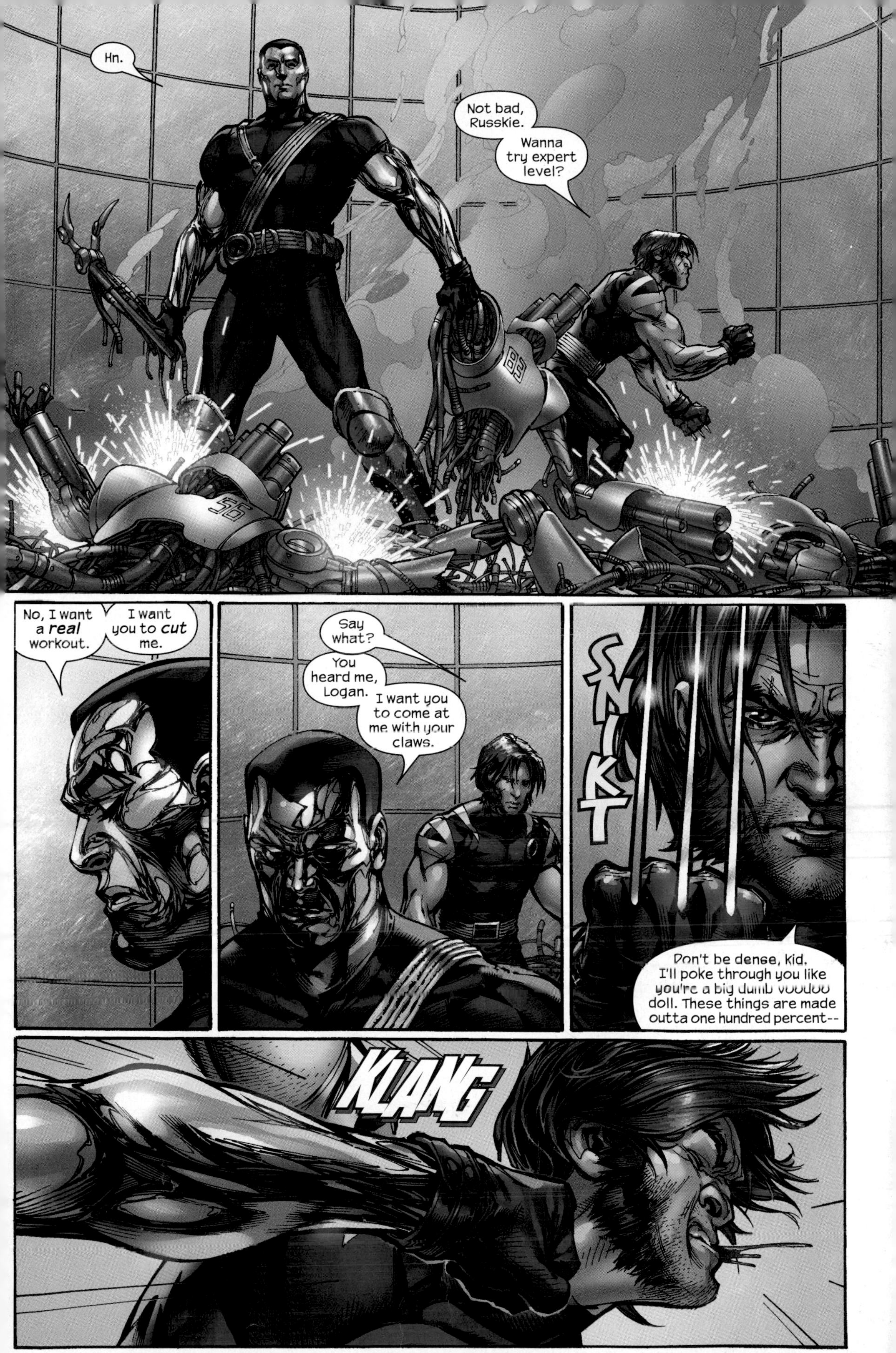

Hn.
Not bad, Russkie.
Wanna try expert level?
No, I want a real workout.
I want you to cut me.
Say what?
You heard me, Logan.
I want you to come at me with your claws.
SNIKT
Don't be dense, kid. I'll poke through you like you're a big dumb voodoo doll. These things are made outta one hundred percent--
KLANG

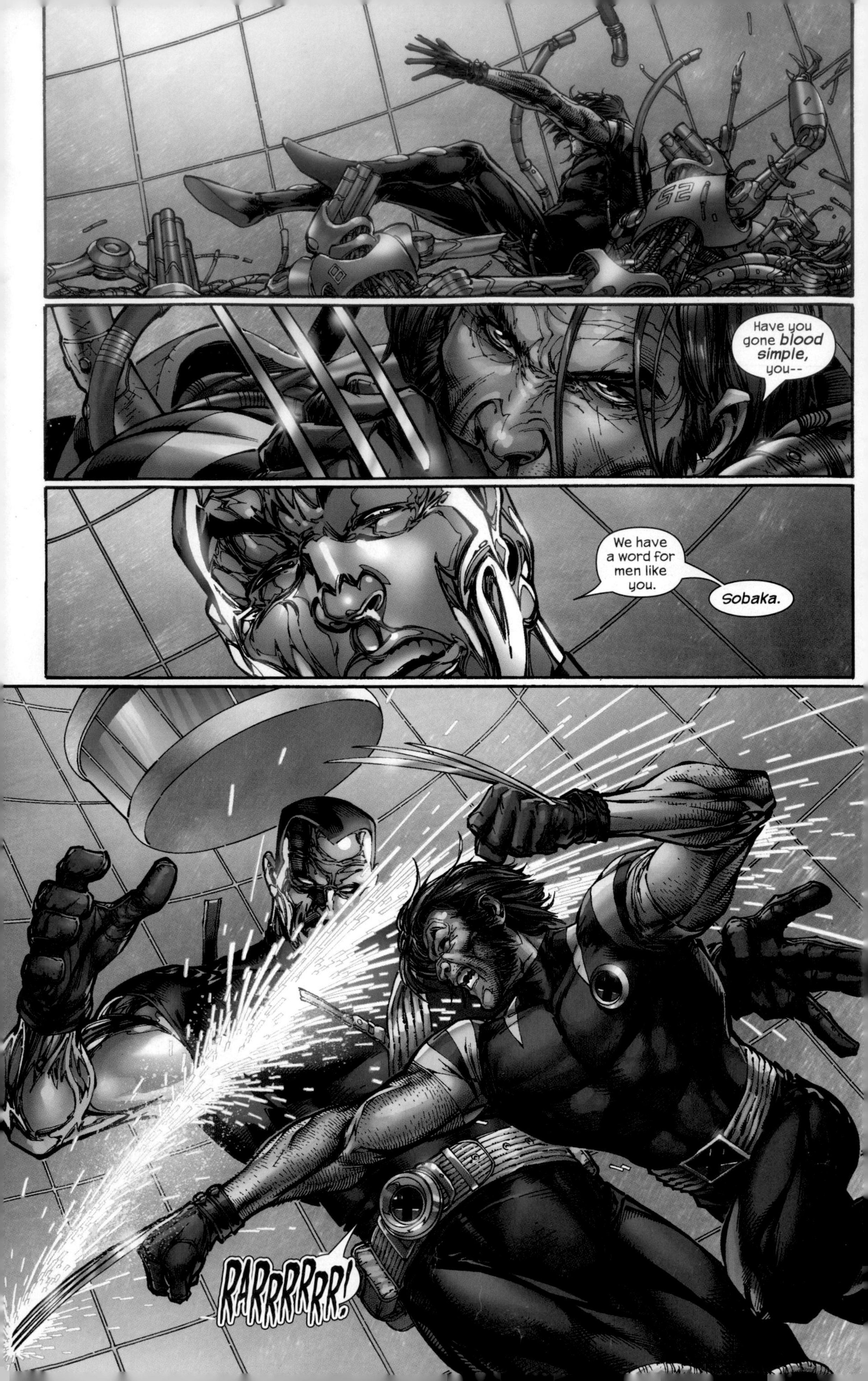
Have you gone *blood simple,* you--
We have a word for men like you.
Sobaka.
RARRRRRR!

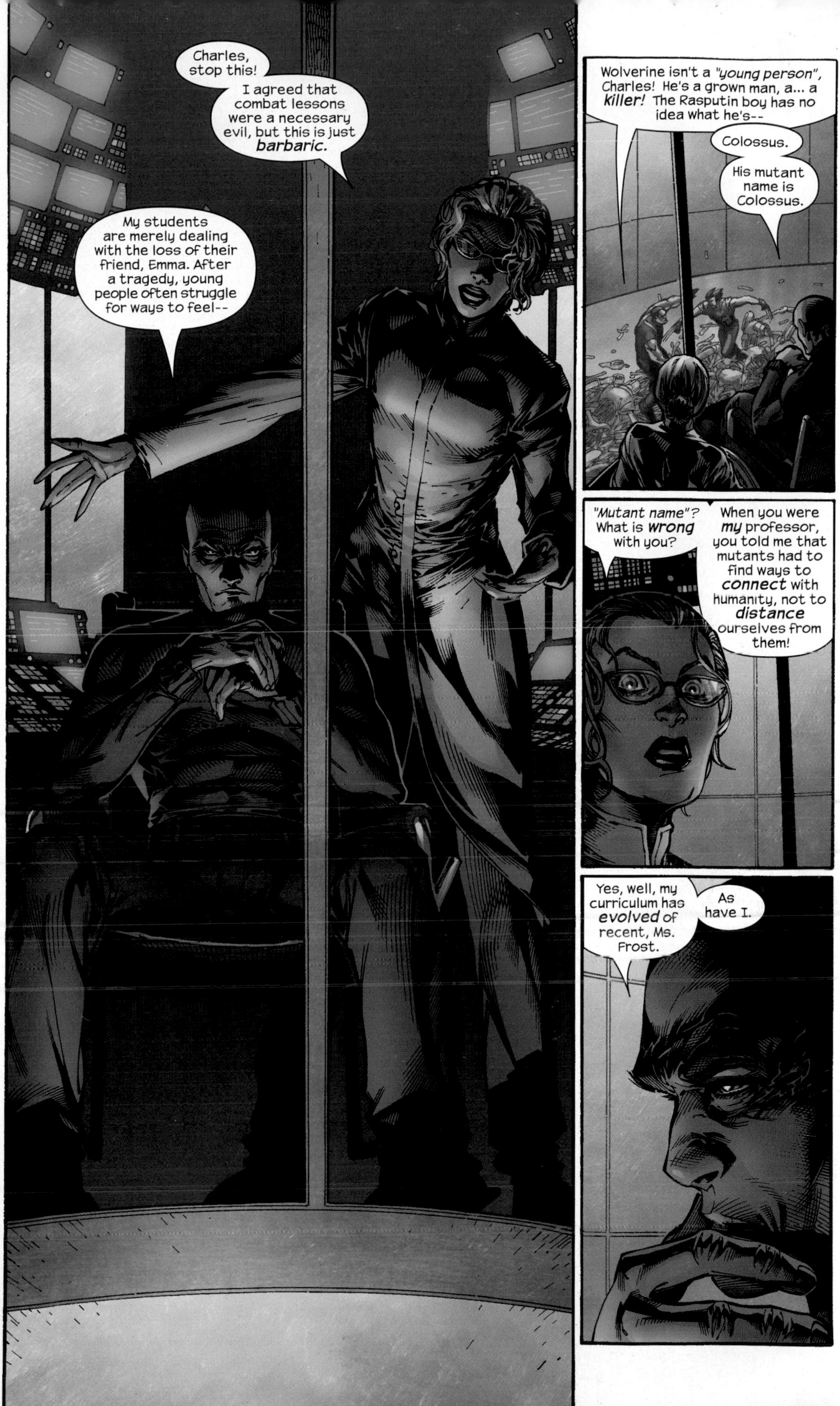
Charles, stop this!
I agreed that combat lessons were a necessary evil, but this is just barbaric.
My students are merely dealing with the loss of their friend, Emma. After a tragedy, young people often struggle for ways to feel--
Wolverine isn't a "young person", Charles! He's a grown man, a... a killer! The Rasputin boy has no idea what he's--
Colossus.
His mutant name is Colossus.
"Mutant name"? What is wrong with you?
When you were my professor, you told me that mutants had to find ways to connect with humanity, not to distance ourselves from them!
Yes, well, my curriculum has evolved of recent, Ms. Frost.
As have I.

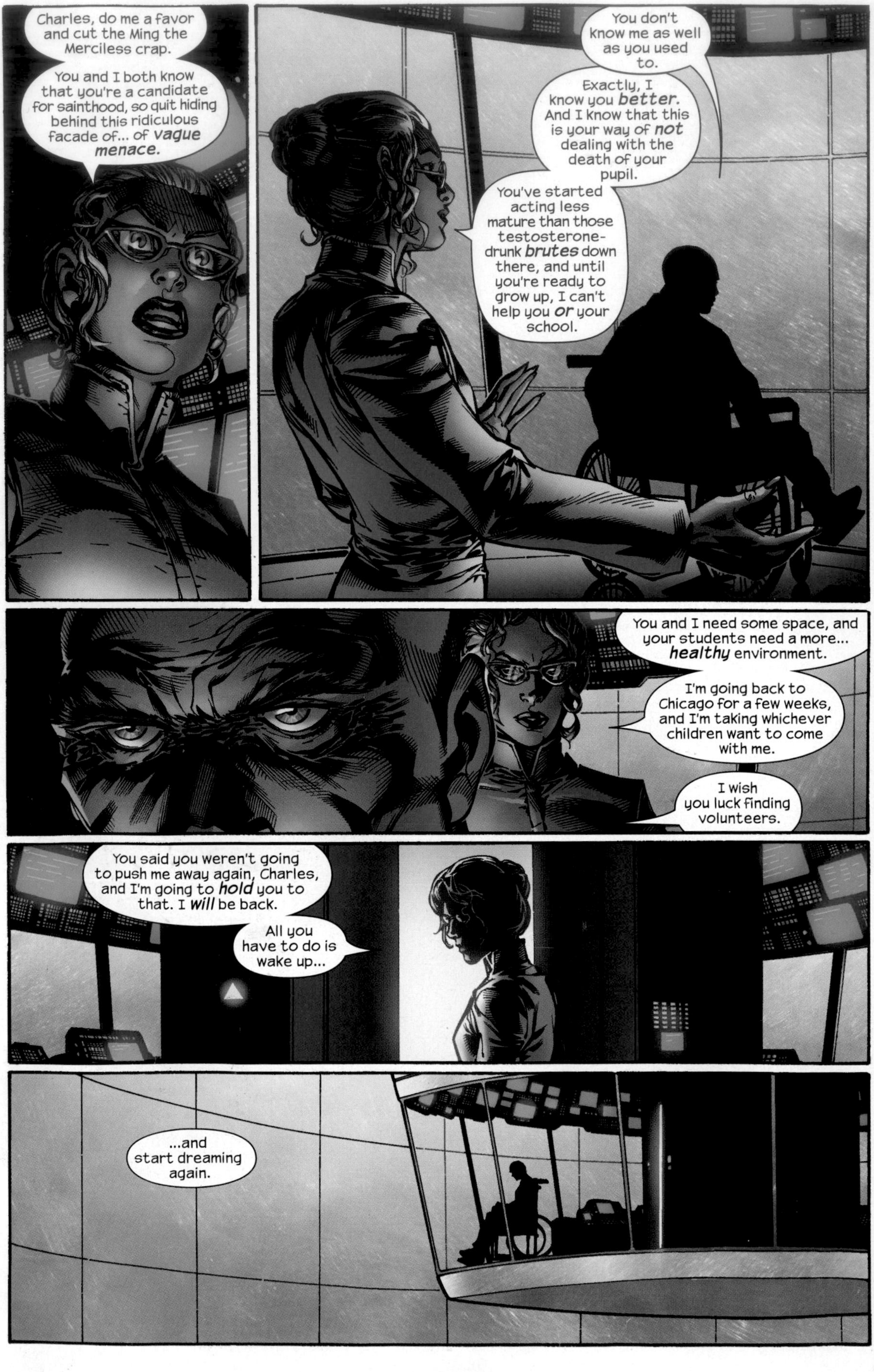
Charles, do me a favor and cut the Ming the Merciless crap.
You and I both know that you're a candidate for sainthood, so quit hiding behind this ridiculous facade of... of *vague menace.*
You don't know me as well as you used to.
Exactly, I know you *better.* And I know that this is your way of *not* dealing with the death of your pupil.
You've started acting less mature than those testosterone-drunk *brutes* down there, and until you're ready to grow up, I can't help you *or* your school.
You and I need some space, and your students need a more... *healthy* environment.
I'm going back to Chicago for a few weeks, and I'm taking whichever children want to come with me.
I wish you luck finding volunteers.
You said you weren't going to push me away again, Charles, and I'm going to *hold* you to that. I *will* be back.
All you have to do is wake up...
...and start dreaming again.

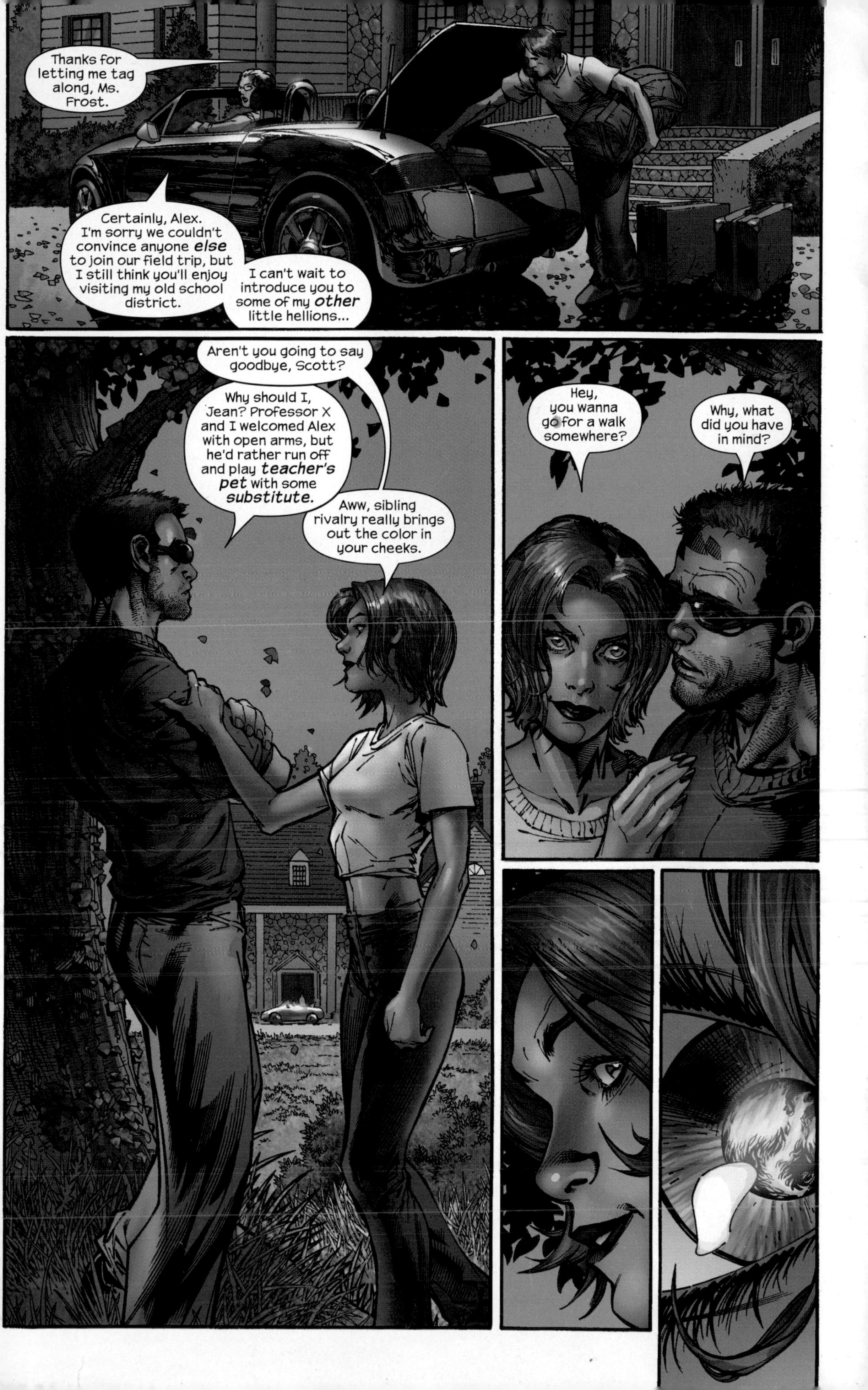
Thanks for letting me tag along, Ms. Frost.
Certainly, Alex. I'm sorry we couldn't convince anyone *else* to join our field trip, but I still think you'll enjoy visiting my old school district.
I can't wait to introduce you to some of my *other* little hellions...
Aren't you going to say goodbye, Scott?
Why should I, Jean? Professor X and I welcomed Alex with open arms, but he'd rather run off and play *teacher's pet* with some *substitute.*
Aww, sibling rivalry really brings out the color in your cheeks.
Hey, you wanna go for a walk somewhere?
Why, what did you have in mind?

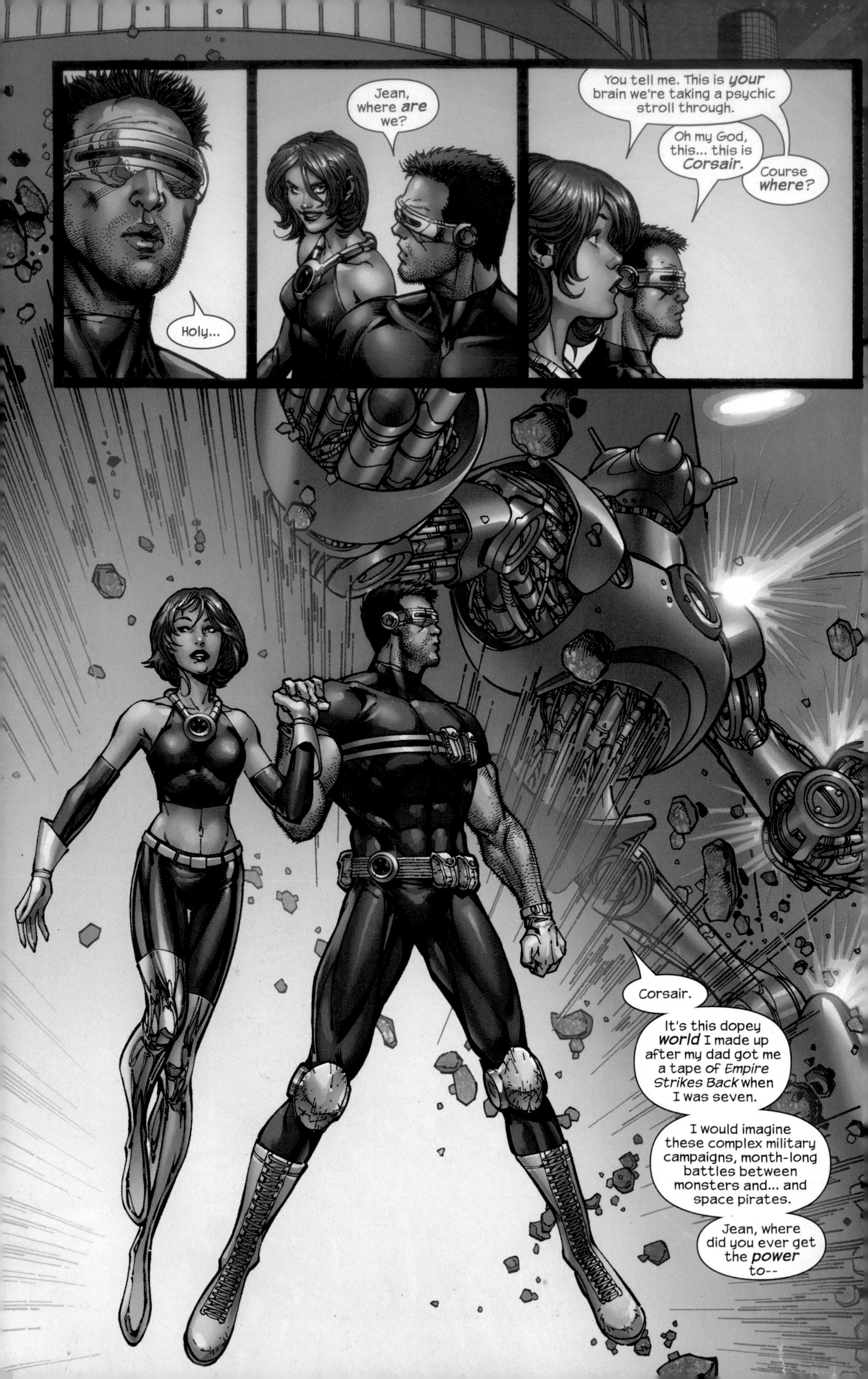

Holy...
Jean, where are we?
You tell me. This is your brain we're taking a psychic stroll through.
Oh my God, this... this is Corsair.
Course where?
Corsair.
It's this dopey world I made up after my dad got me a tape of Empire Strikes Back when I was seven.
I would imagine these complex military campaigns, month-long battles between monsters and... and space pirates.
Jean, where did you ever get the power to--

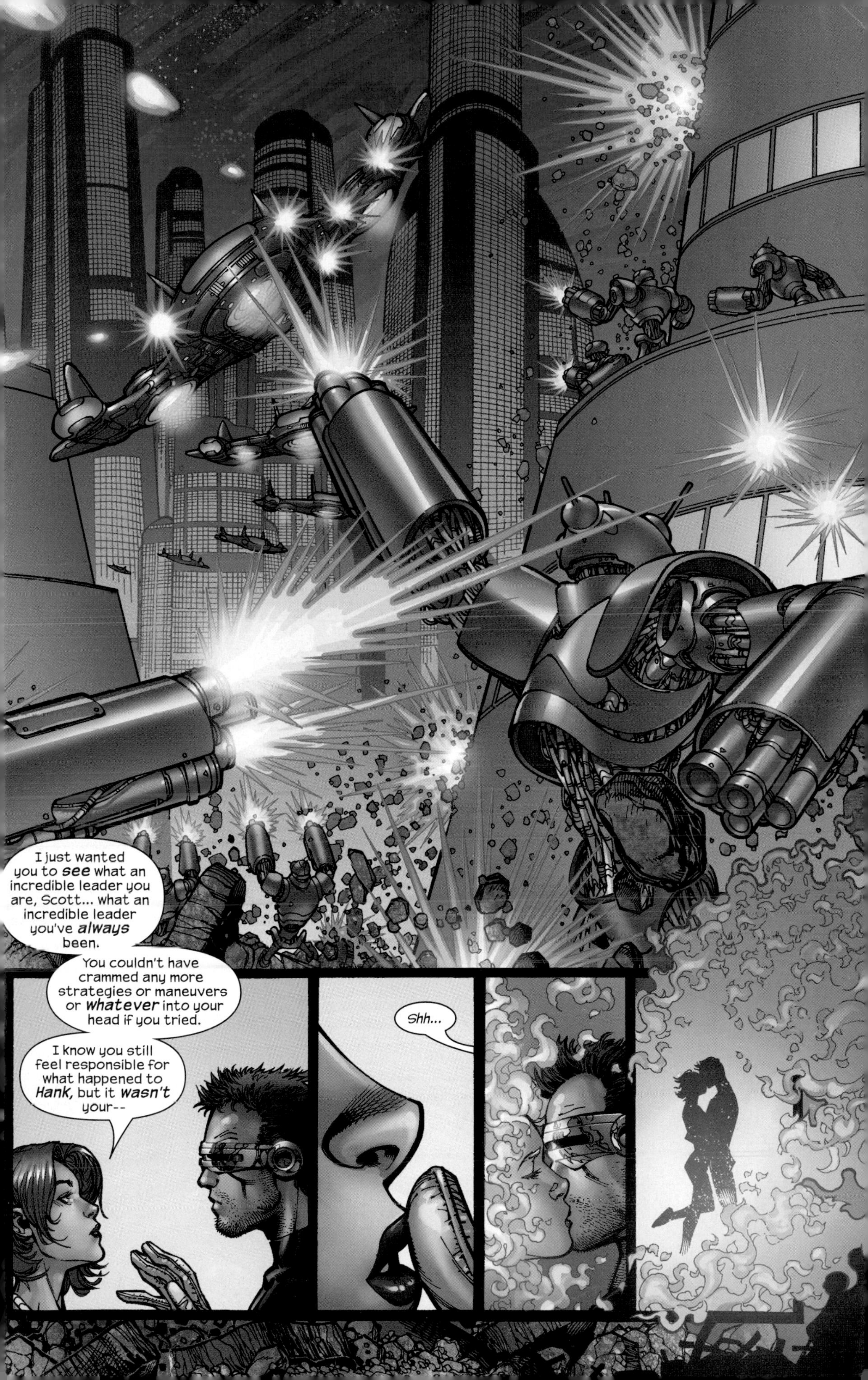
I just wanted you to see what an incredible leader you are, Scott... what an incredible leader you've always been.
You couldn't have crammed any more strategies or maneuvers or whatever into your head if you tried.
I know you still feel responsible for what happened to Hank, but it wasn't your--
Shh...

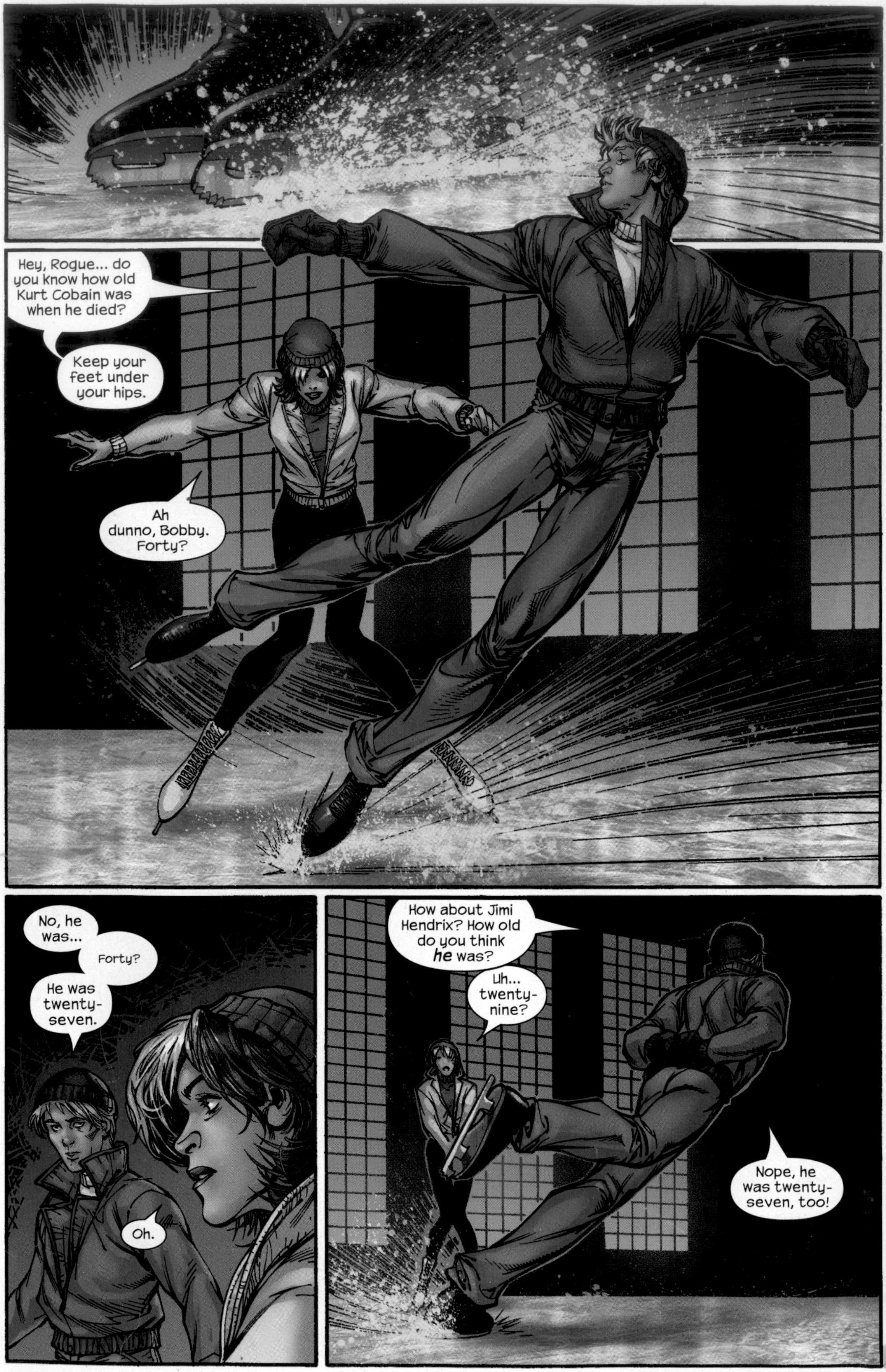
Hey, Rogue... do you know how old Kurt Cobain was when he died?
Keep your feet under your hips.
Ah dunno, Bobby. Forty?
No, he was...
Forty?
He was twenty-seven.
Oh.
How about Jimi Hendrix? How old do you think *he* was?
Uh... twenty-nine?
Nope, he was twenty-seven, too!

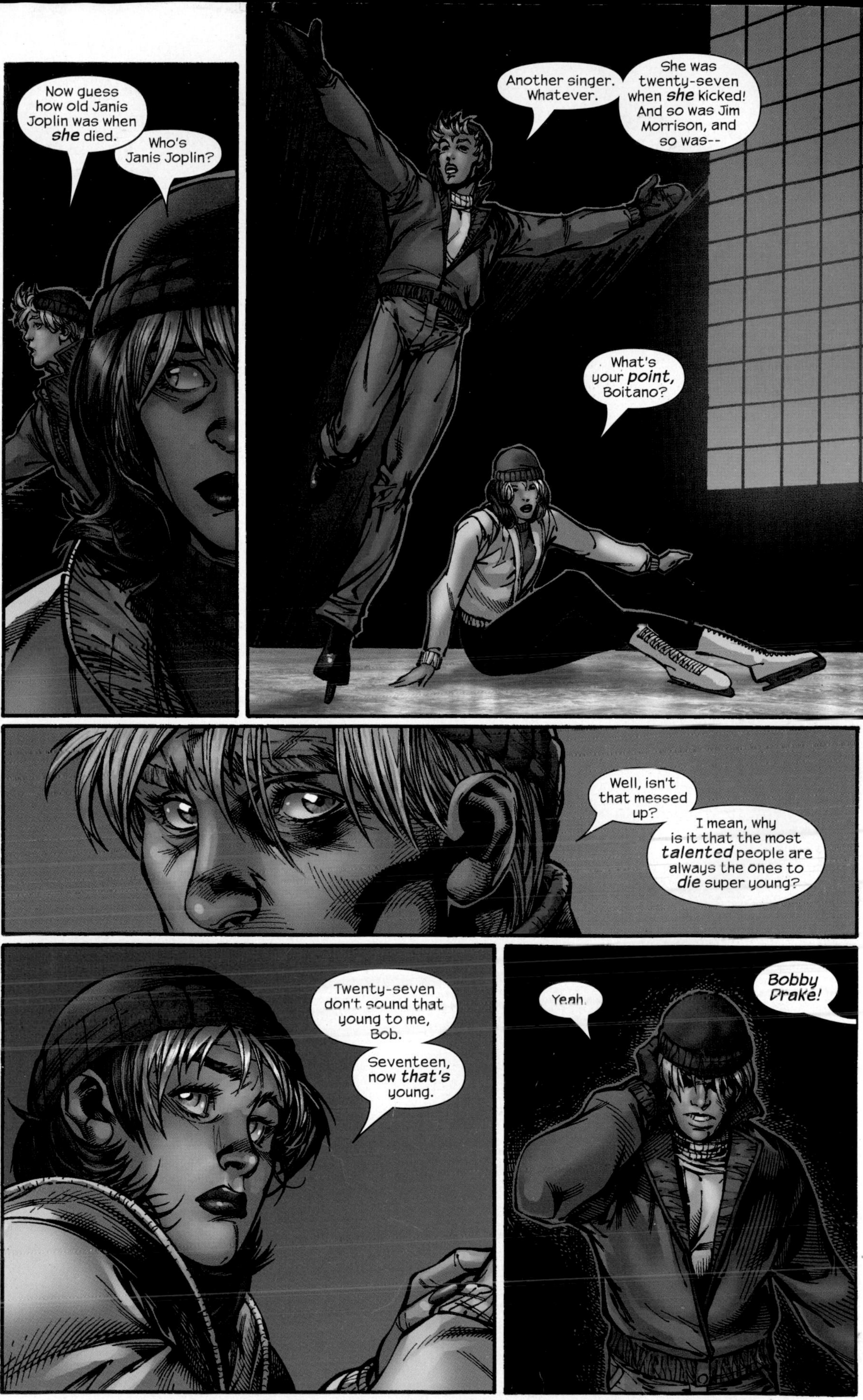
Now guess how old Janis Joplin was when *she* died.
Who's Janis Joplin?
Another singer. Whatever.
She was twenty-seven when *she* kicked! And so was Jim Morrison, and so was--
What's your *point,* Boitano?
Well, isn't that messed up?
I mean, why is it that the most *talented* people are always the ones to *die* super young?
Twenty-seven don't sound that young to me, Bob.
Seventeen, now *that's* young.
Yeah.
Bobby Drake!

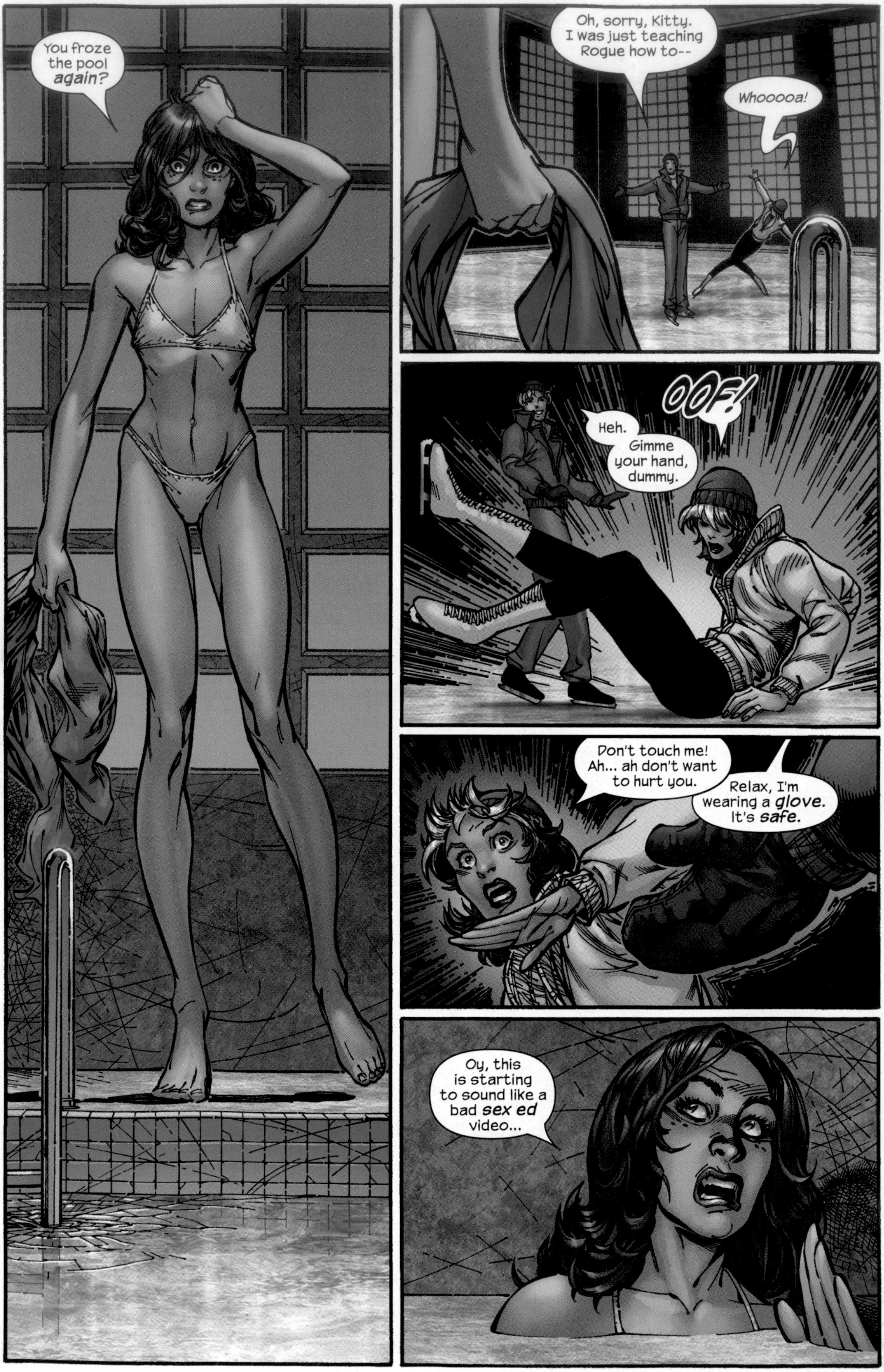
You froze the pool again?
Oh, sorry, Kitty. I was just teaching Rogue how to--
Whoooa!
OOF!
Heh. Gimme your hand, dummy.
Don't touch me! Ah... ah don't want to hurt you.
Relax, I'm wearing a glove. It's safe.
Oy, this is starting to sound like a bad sex ed video...

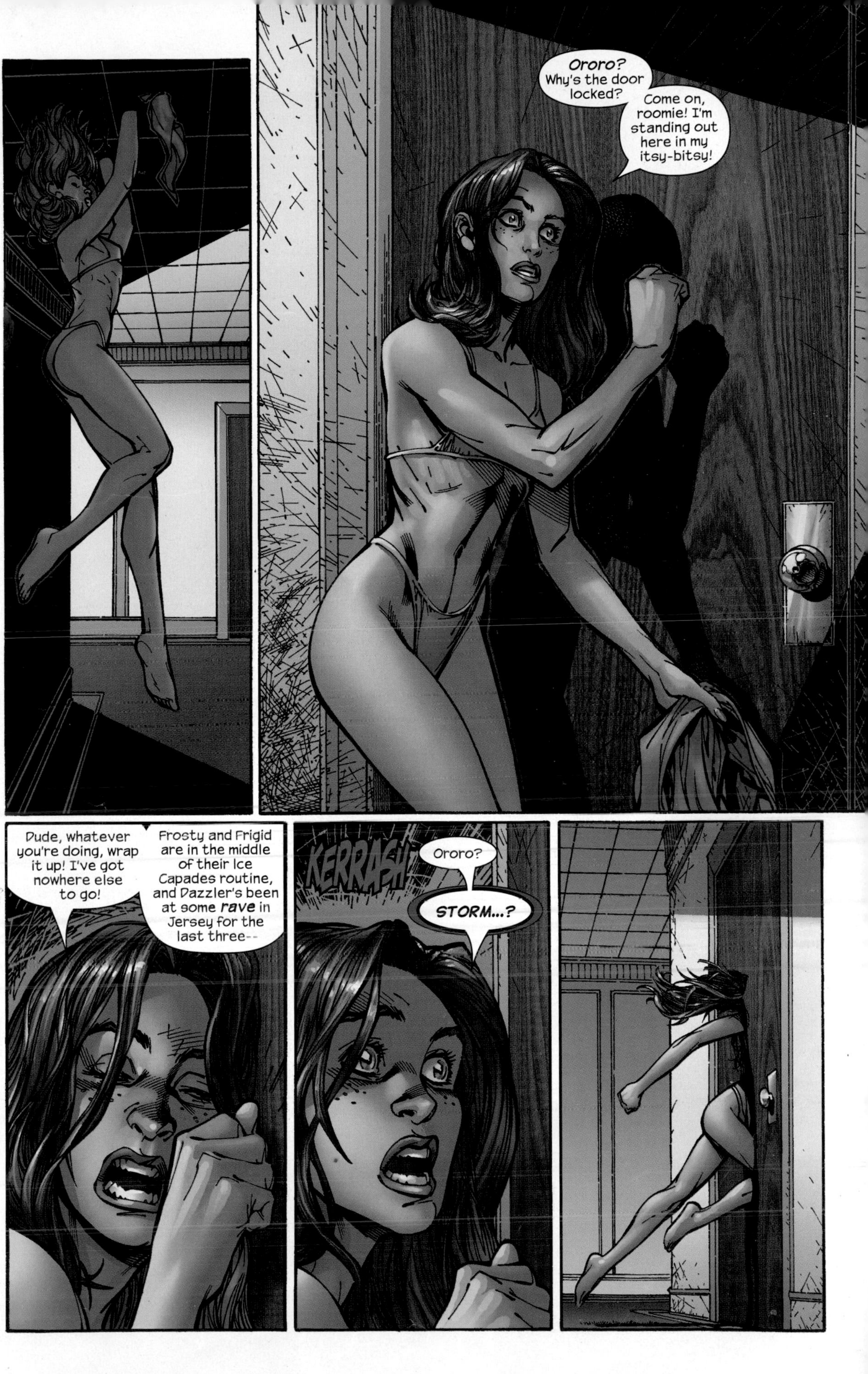

Ororo? Why's the door locked?
Come on, roomie! I'm standing out here in my itsy-bitsy!
Dude, whatever you're doing, wrap it up! I've got nowhere else to go!
Frosty and Frigid are in the middle of their Ice Capades routine, and Dazzler's been at some rave in Jersey for the last three--
KERRASH
Ororo?
STORM...?

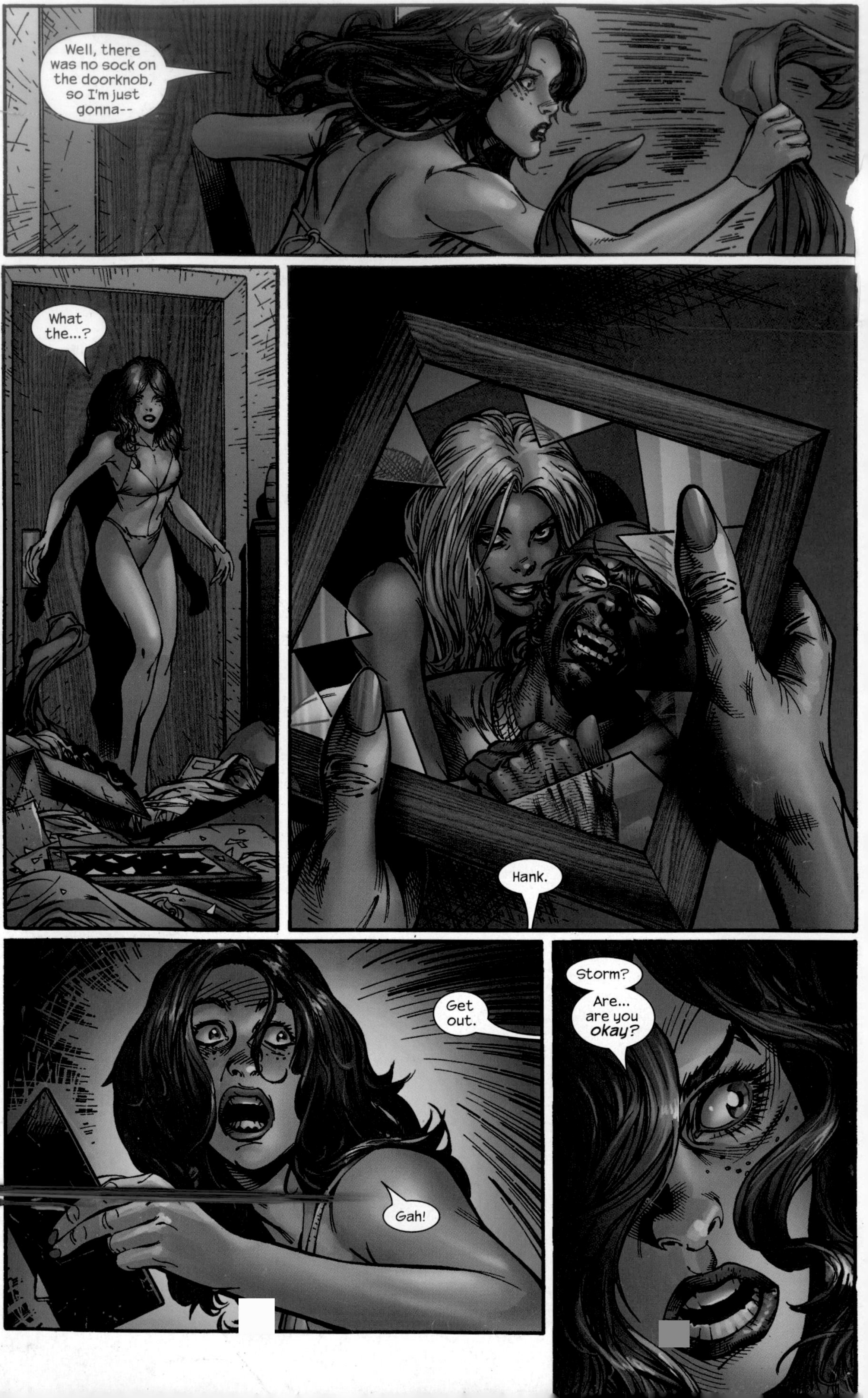
Well, there was no sock on the doorknob, so I'm just gonna--
What the...?
Hank.
Get out.
Gah!
Storm?
Are... are you *okay?*

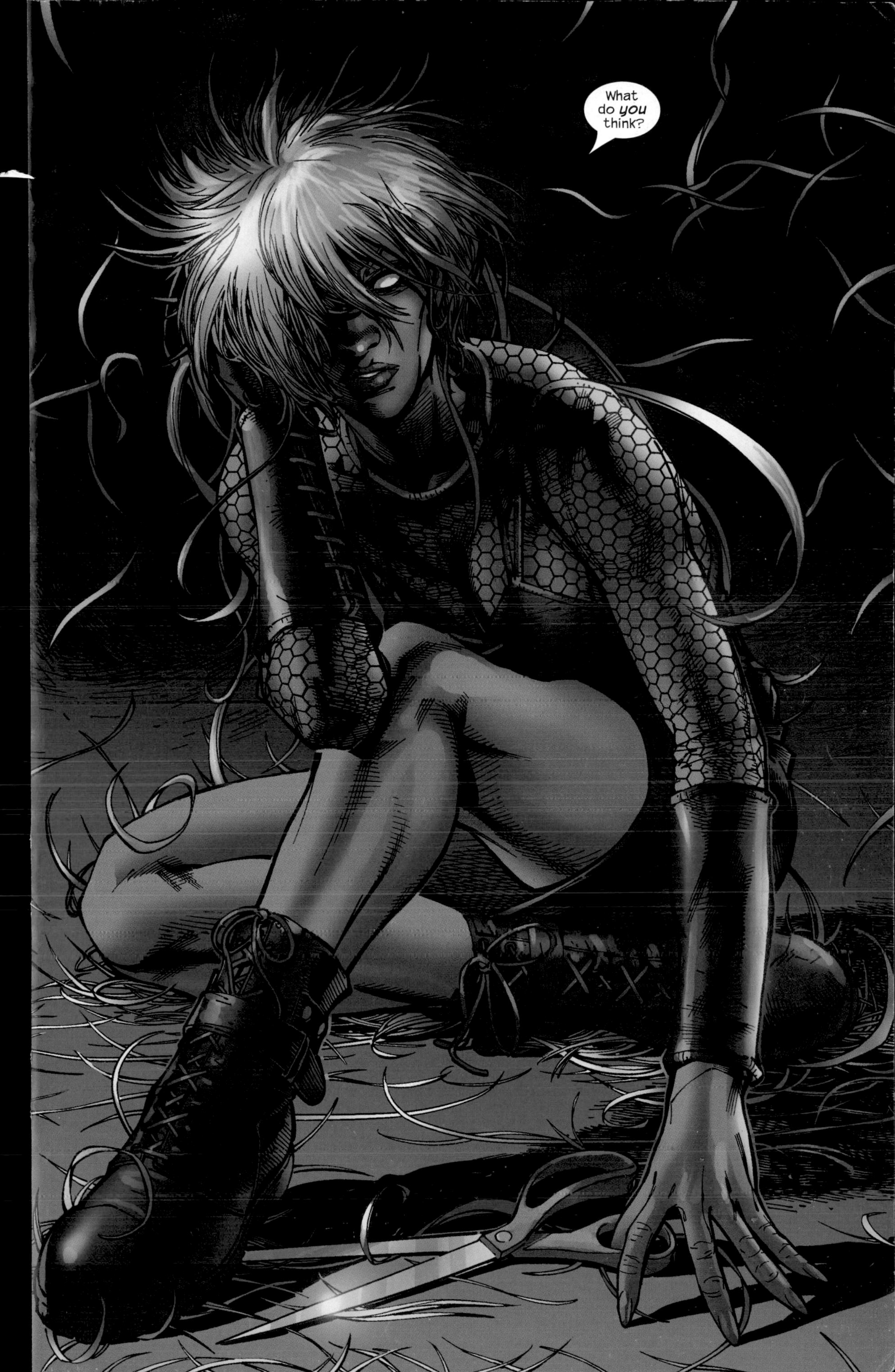
What do *you* think?

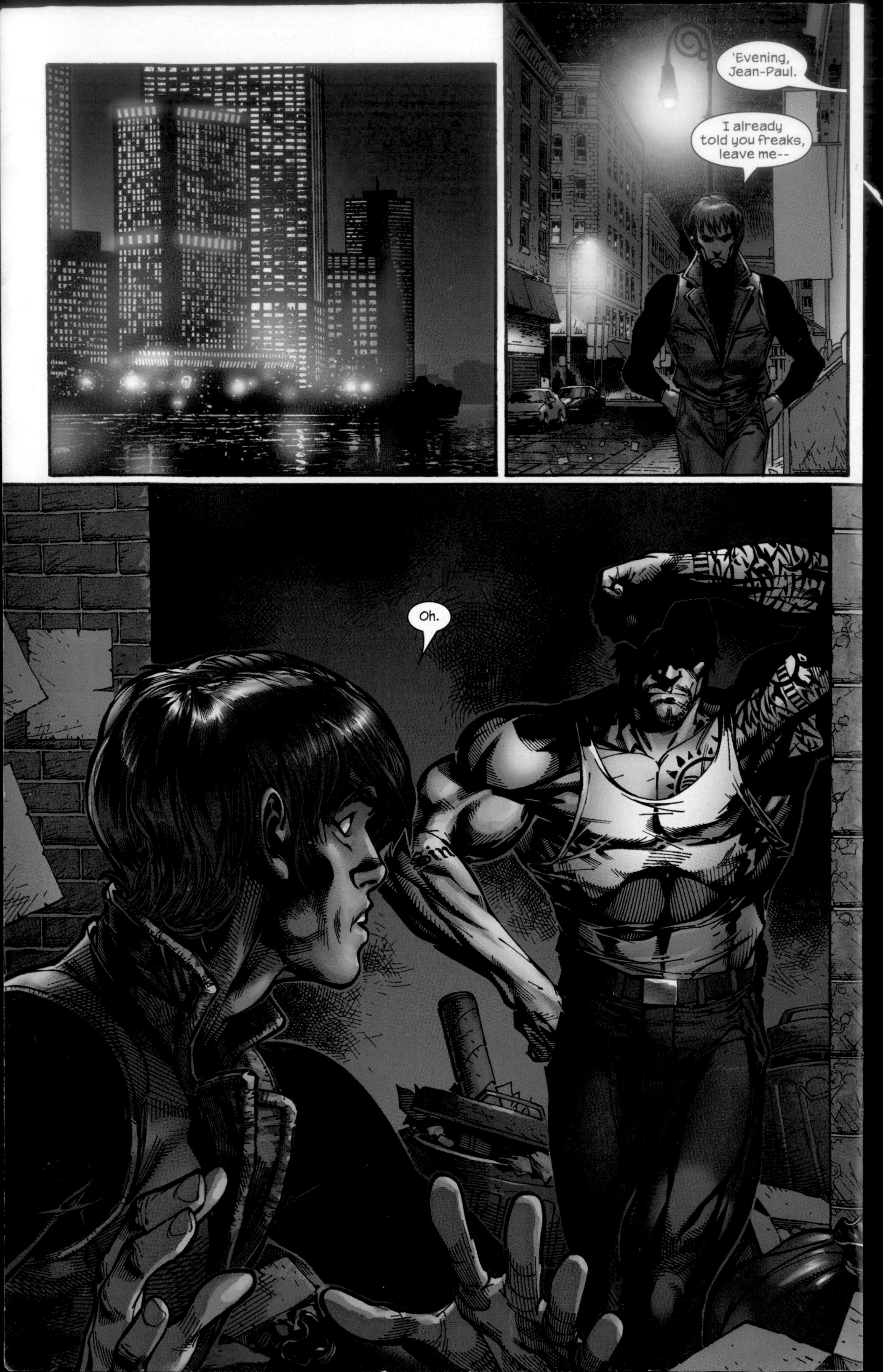
'Evening, Jean-Paul.
I already told you freaks, leave me--
Oh.

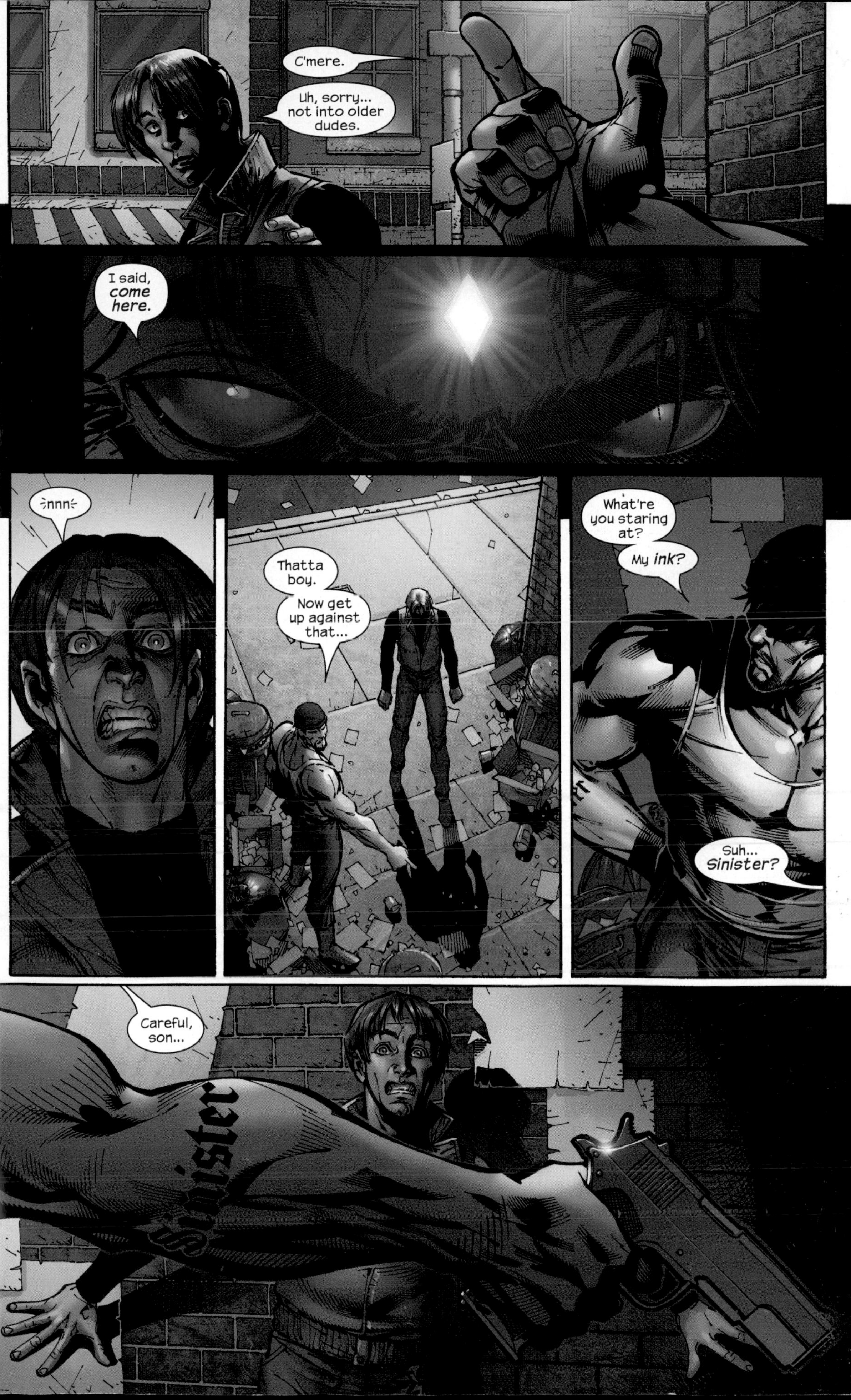
C'mere.
Uh, sorry... not into older dudes.
I said, *come here.*
nnn
Thatta boy.
Now get up against that...
What're you staring at?
My *ink?*
Suh... *Sinister?*
Careful, son...
Sinister

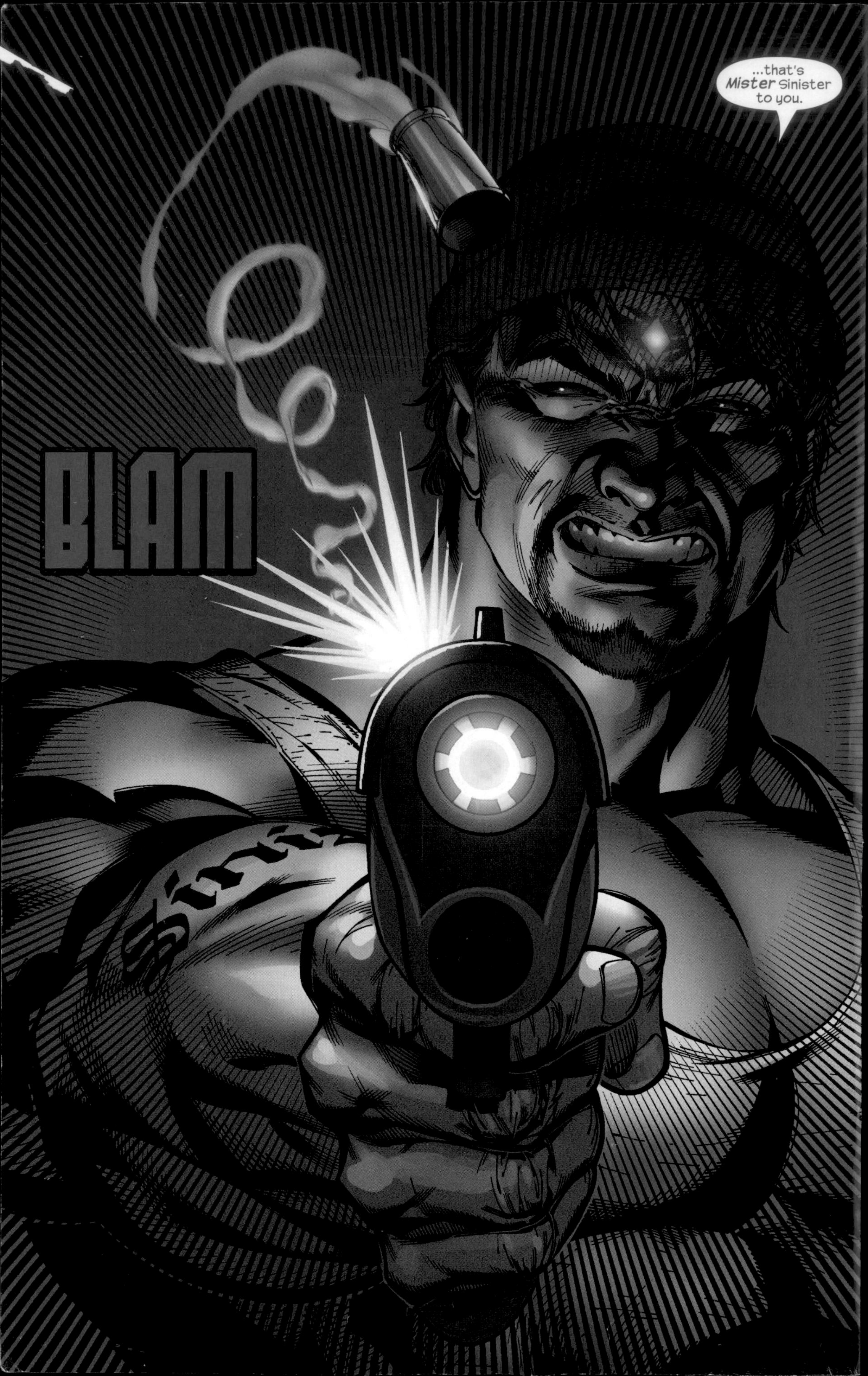
...that's Mister Sinister to you.
BLAM

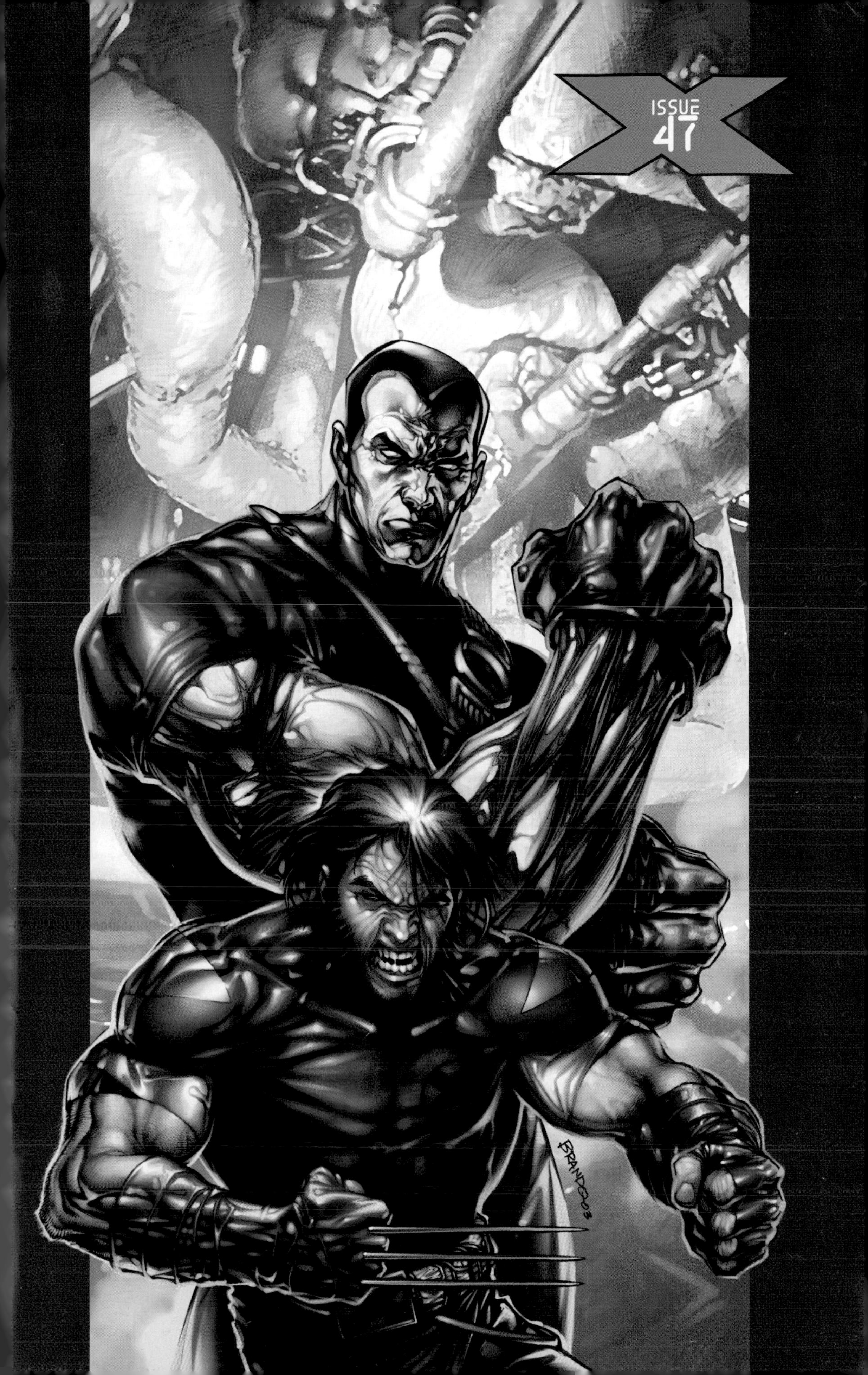
ISSUE
47

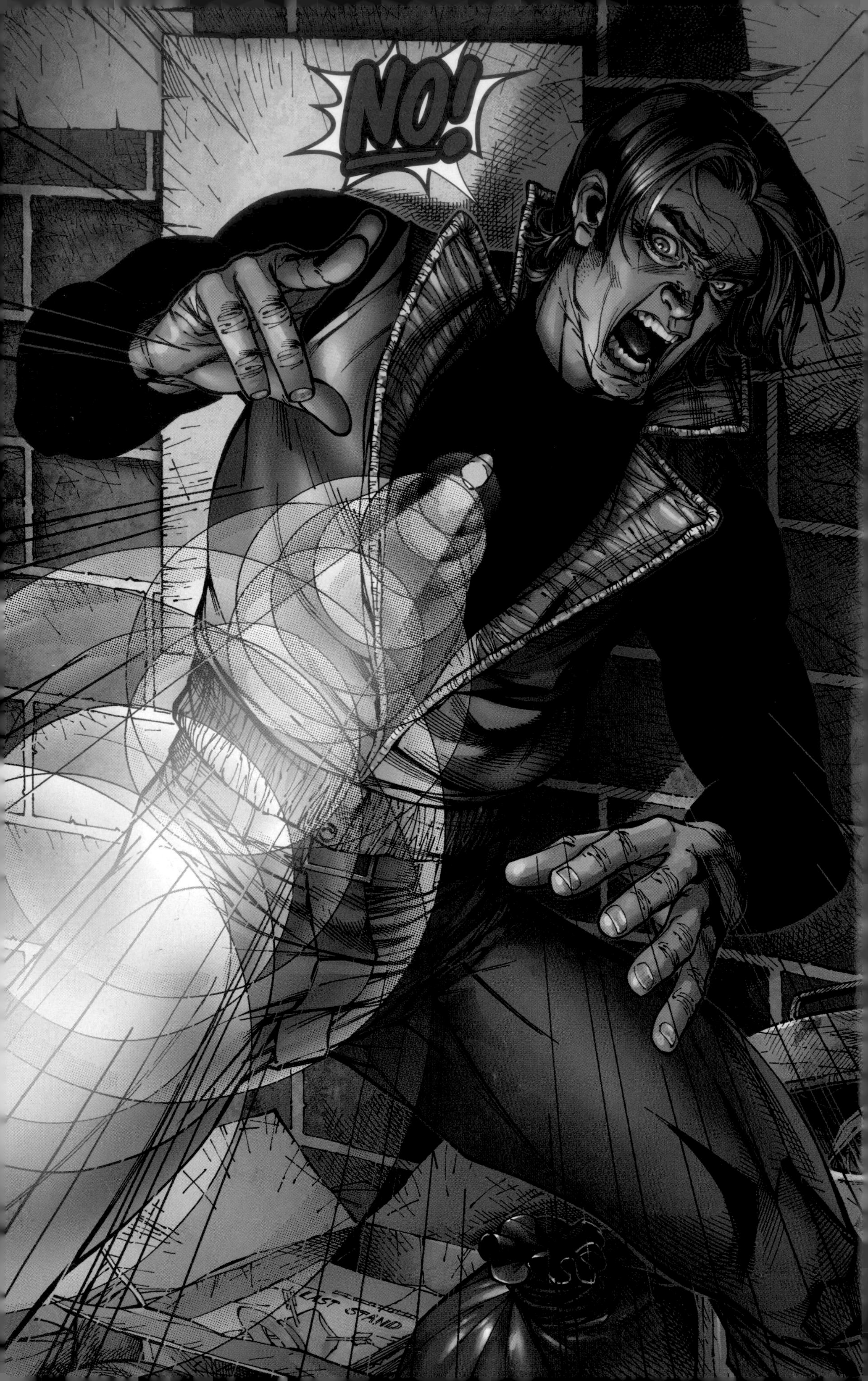
NO!
LAST STAND

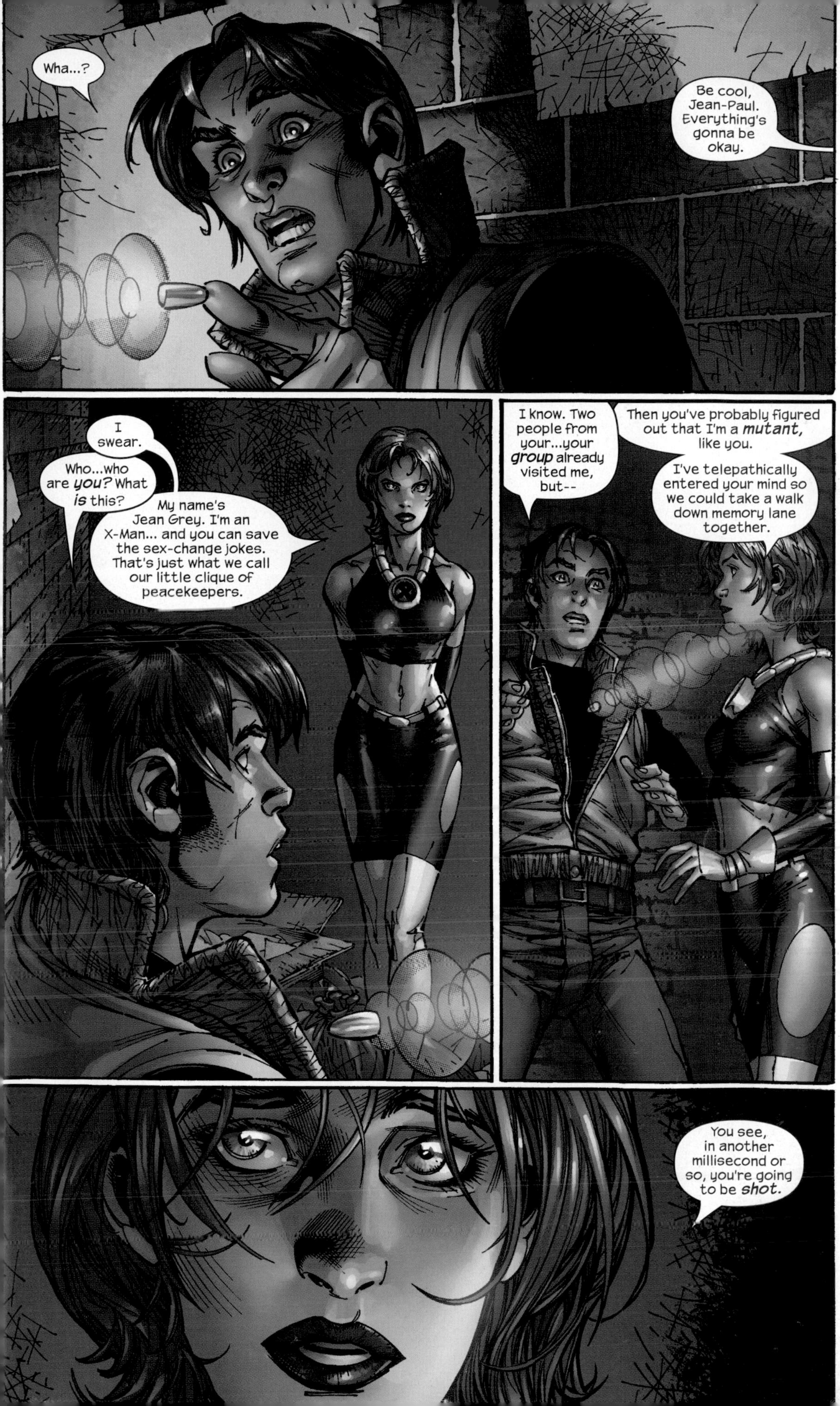
Wha...?
Be cool, Jean-Paul. Everything's gonna be okay.
I swear.
Who...who are *you?* What *is* this?
My name's Jean Grey. I'm an X-Man... and you can save the sex-change jokes. That's just what we call our little clique of peacekeepers.
I know. Two people from your...your *group* already visited me, but--
Then you've probably figured out that I'm a *mutant,* like you.
I've telepathically entered your mind so we could take a walk down memory lane together.
You see, in another millisecond or so, you're going to be *shot.*

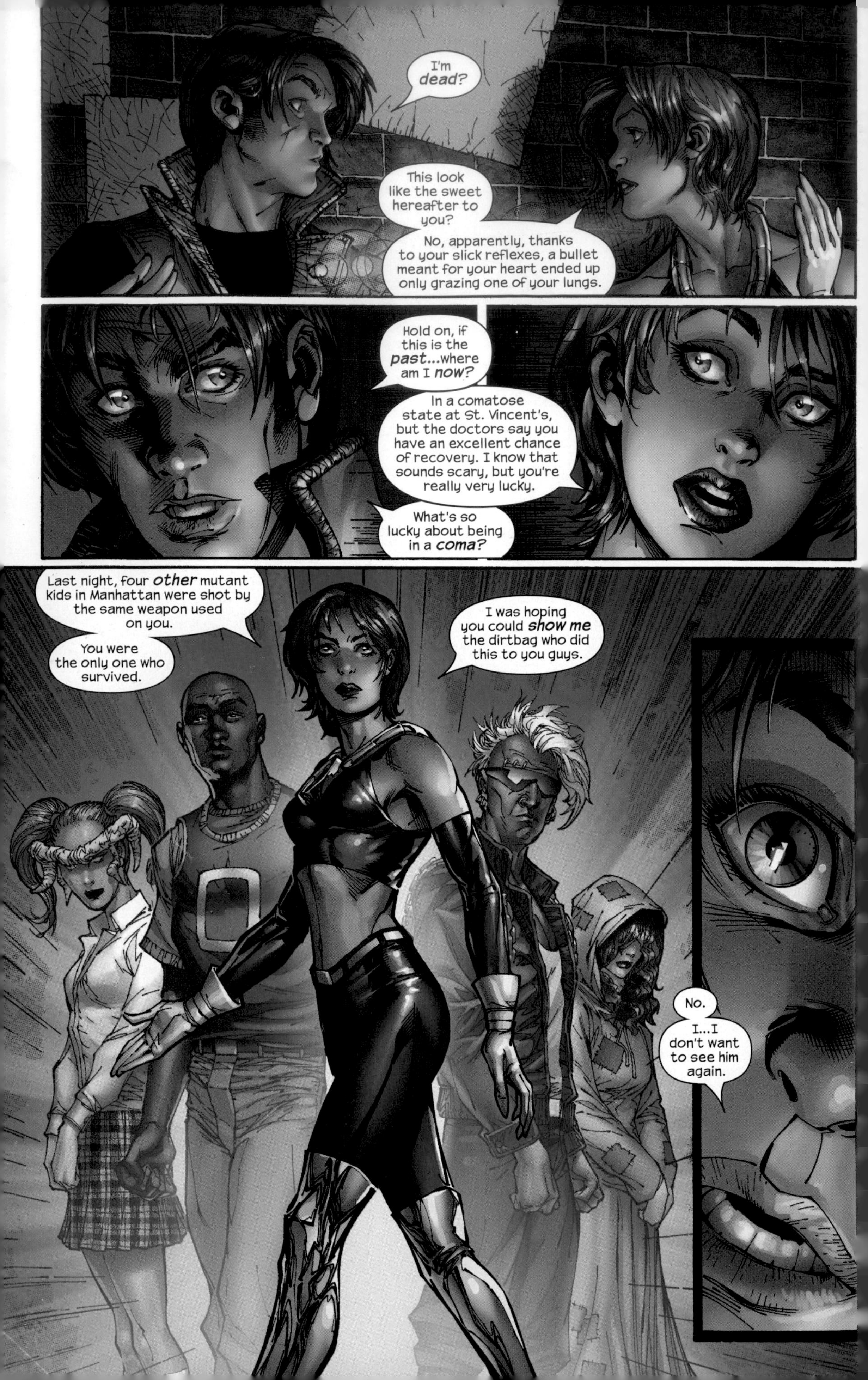
I'm dead?
This look like the sweet hereafter to you?
No, apparently, thanks to your slick reflexes, a bullet meant for your heart ended up only grazing one of your lungs.
Hold on, if this is the past...where am I now?
In a comatose state at St. Vincent's, but the doctors say you have an excellent chance of recovery. I know that sounds scary, but you're really very lucky.
What's so lucky about being in a coma?
Last night, four other mutant kids in Manhattan were shot by the same weapon used on you.
You were the only one who survived.
I was hoping you could show me the dirtbag who did this to you guys.
No.
I...I don't want to see him again.

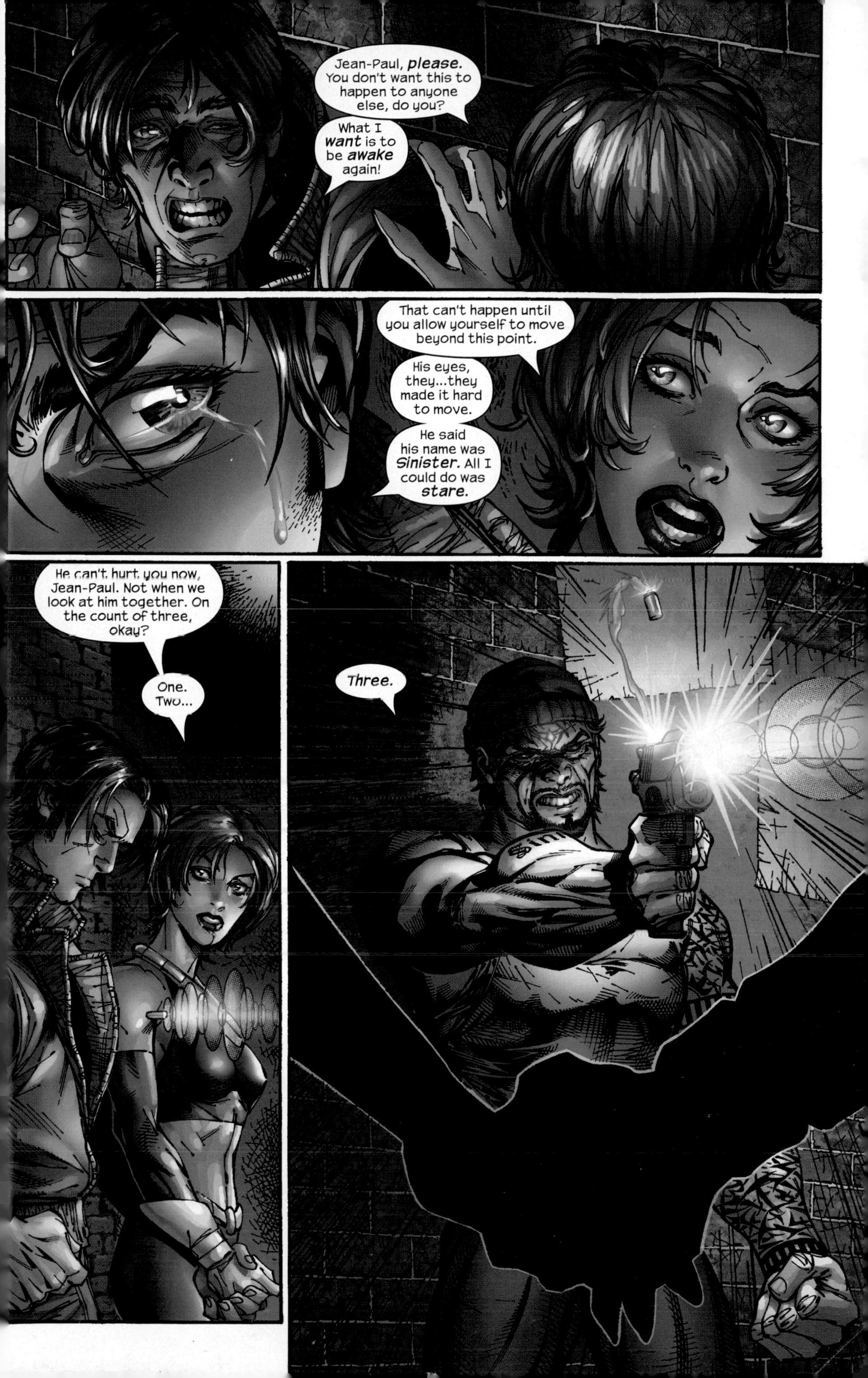
Jean-Paul, please. You don't want this to happen to anyone else, do you?
What I want is to be awake again!
That can't happen until you allow yourself to move beyond this point.
His eyes, they...they made it hard to move.
He said his name was Sinister. All I could do was stare.
He can't hurt you now, Jean-Paul. Not when we look at him together. On the count of three, okay?
One. Two...
Three.

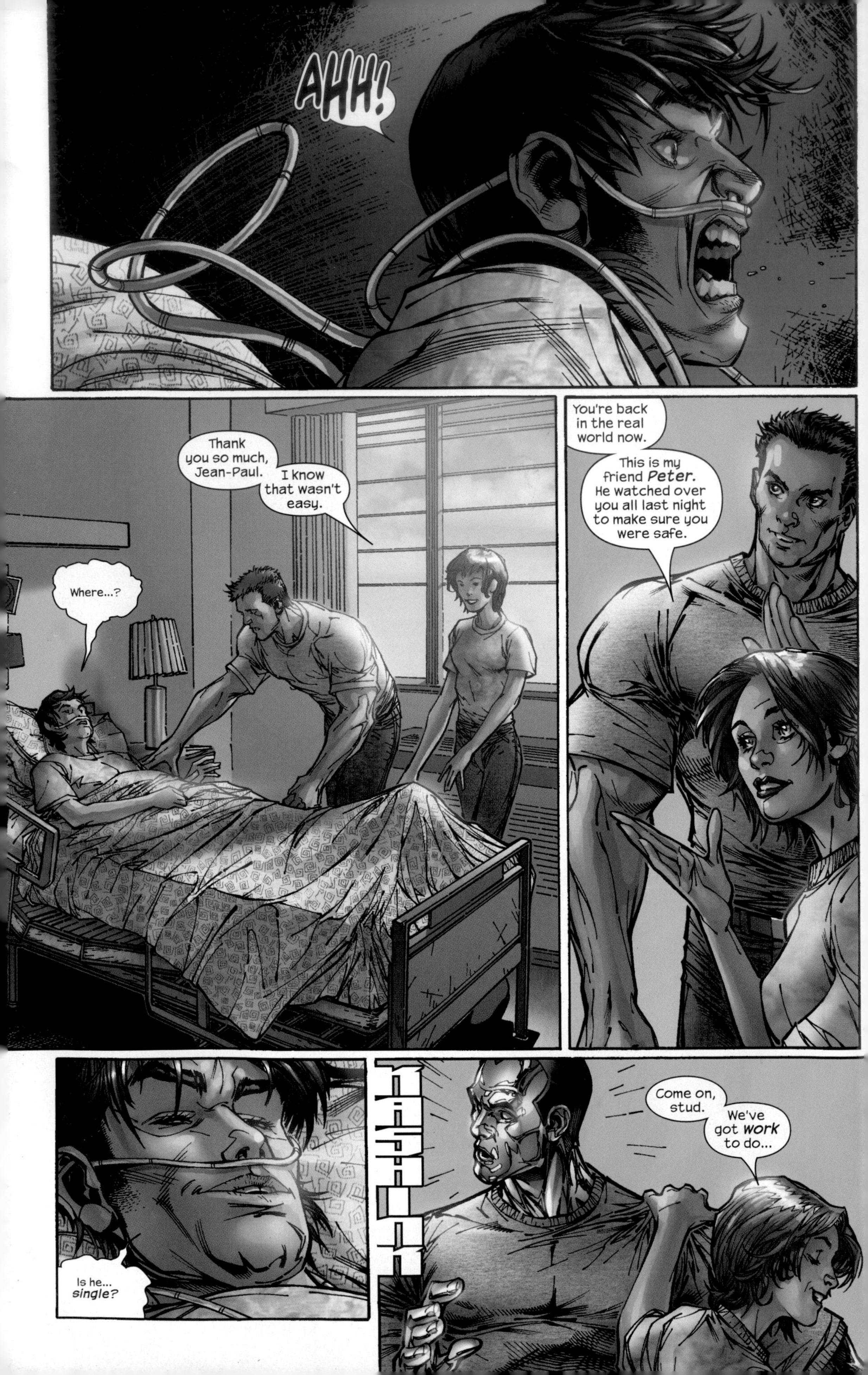

AHH!
Thank you so much, Jean-Paul.
I know that wasn't easy.
Where...?
You're back in the real world now.
This is my friend *Peter.* He watched over you all last night to make sure you were safe.
Is he... *single?*
Come on, stud.
We've got *work* to do...

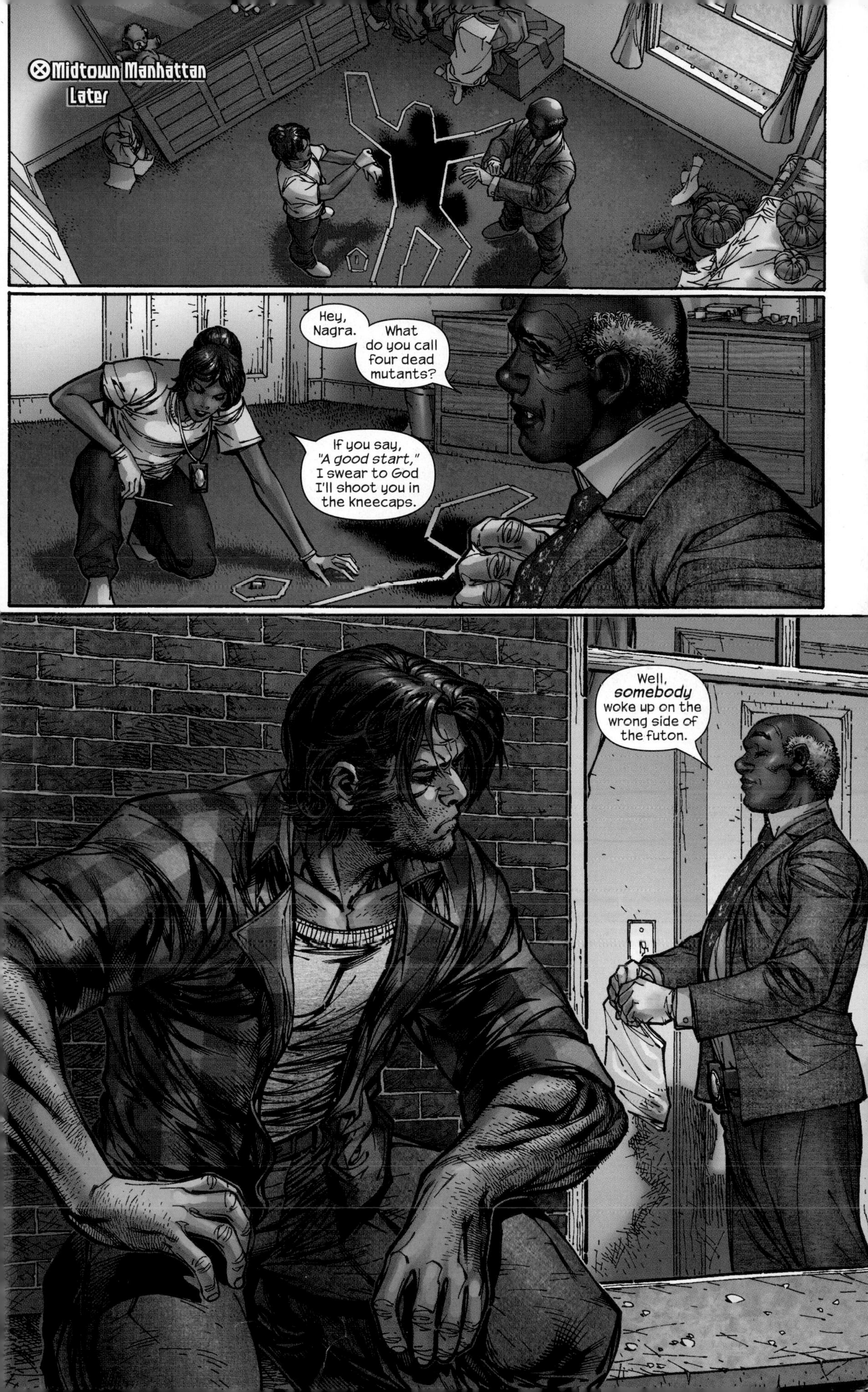
Midtown Manhattan
Later
Hey, Nagra.
What do you call four dead mutants?
If you say, "A good start," I swear to God I'll shoot you in the kneecaps.
Well, somebody woke up on the wrong side of the futon.

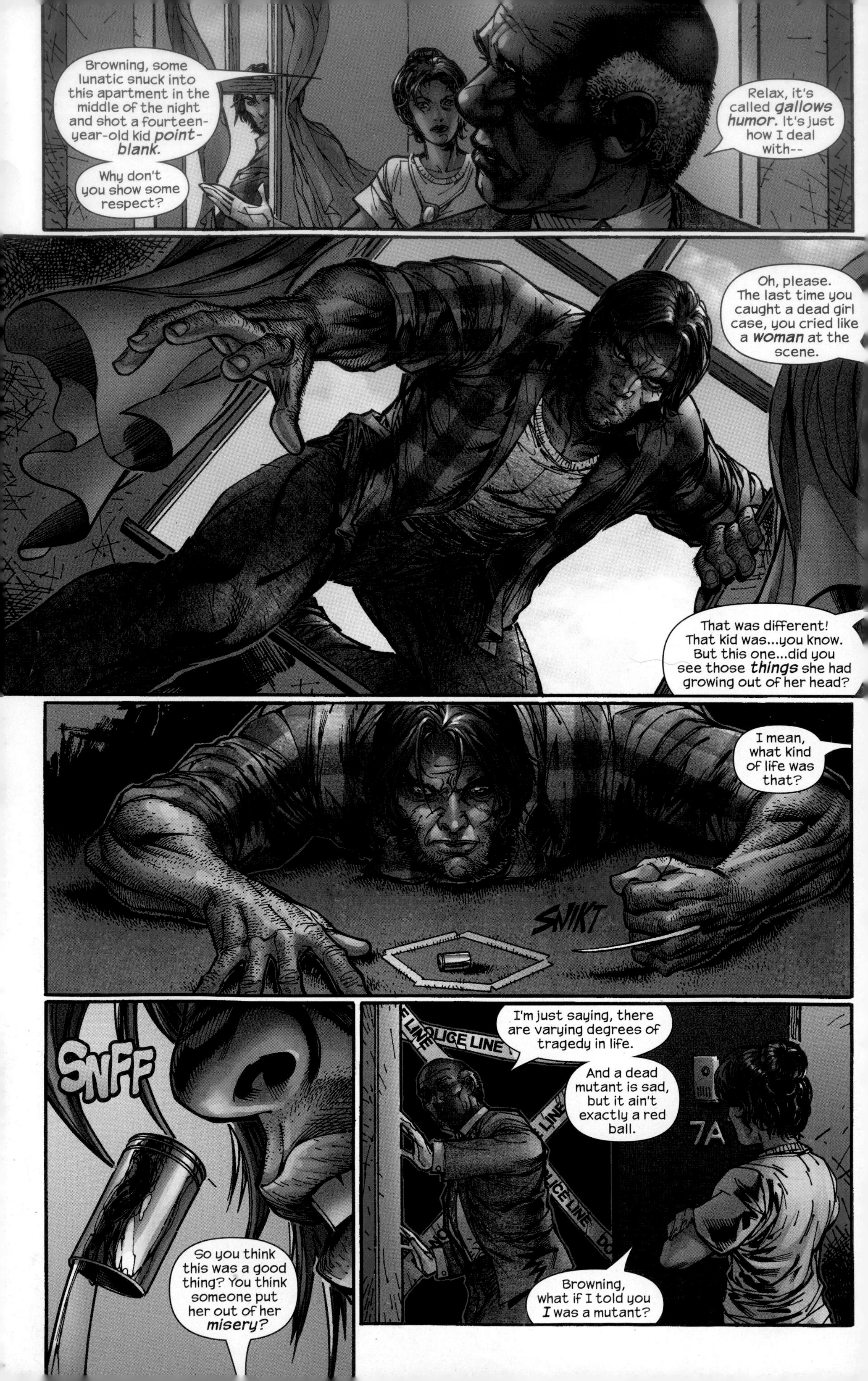
Browning, some lunatic snuck into this apartment in the middle of the night and shot a fourteen-year-old kid point-blank.
Why don't you show some respect?
Relax, it's called gallows humor. It's just how I deal with--
Oh, please. The last time you caught a dead girl case, you cried like a woman at the scene.
That was different! That kid was...you know. But this one...did you see those things she had growing out of her head?
I mean, what kind of life was that?
SNIKT
SNFF
So you think this was a good thing? You think someone put her out of her misery?
I'm just saying, there are varying degrees of tragedy in life.
And a dead mutant is sad, but it ain't exactly a red ball.
Browning, what if I told you I was a mutant?
POLICE LINE
7A

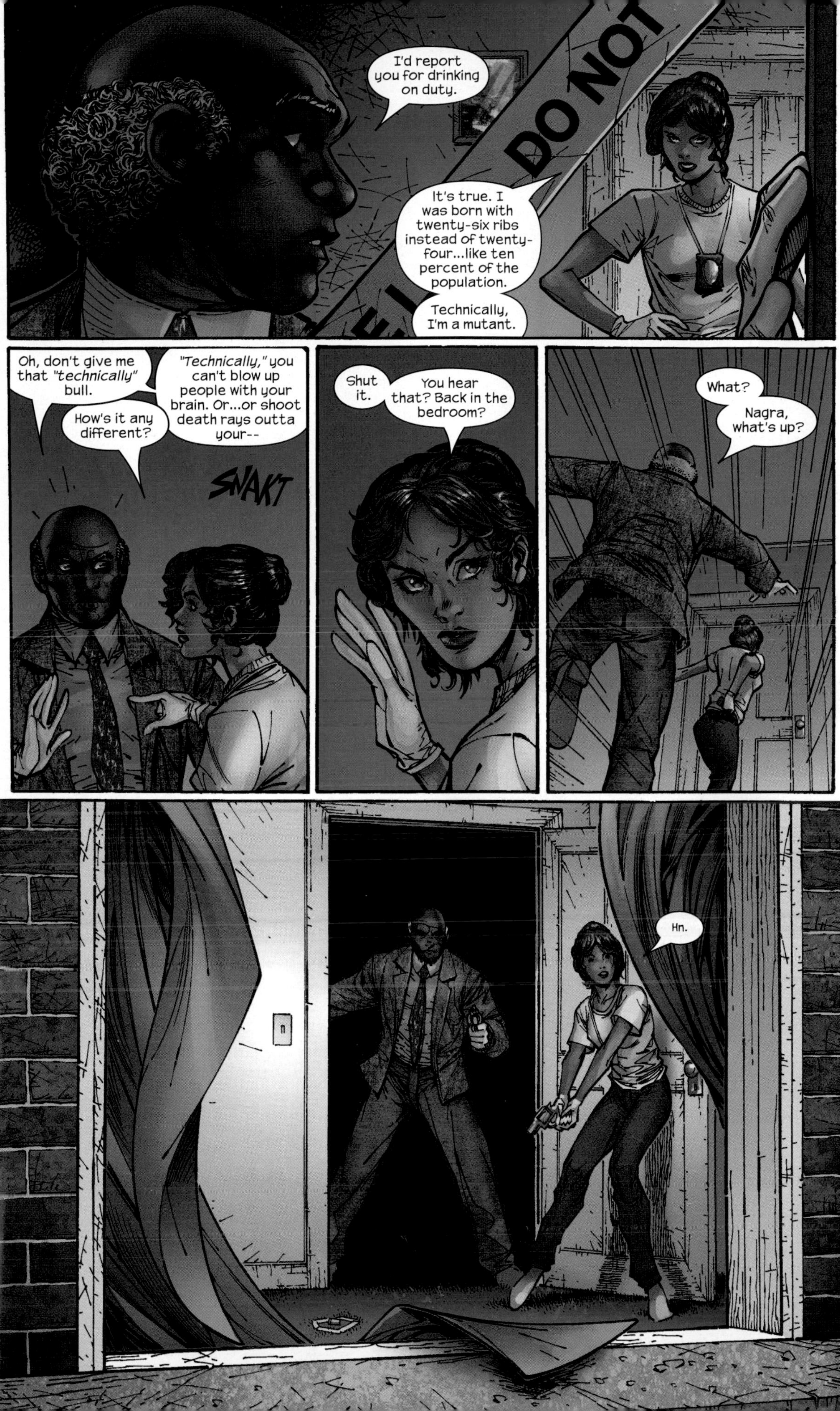
I'd report you for drinking on duty.
DO NOT
It's true. I was born with twenty-six ribs instead of twenty-four...like ten percent of the population.
Technically, I'm a mutant.
Oh, don't give me that "technically" bull.
How's it any different?
"Technically," you can't blow up people with your brain. Or...or shoot death rays outta your--
SNAKT
Shut it.
You hear that? Back in the bedroom?
What?
Nagra, what's up?
Hn.

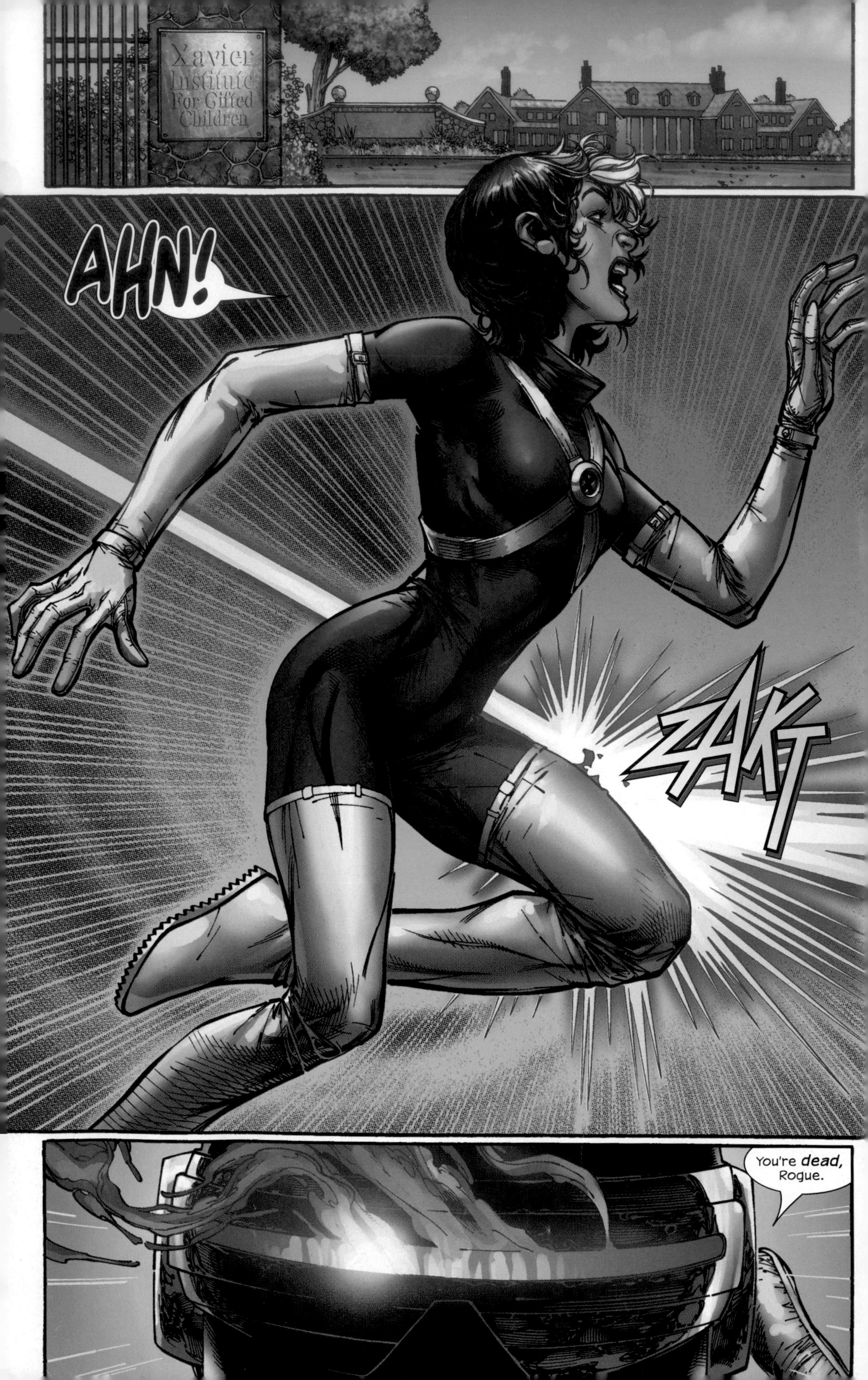
Xavier Institute For Gifted Children
AHN!
ZAKT
You're *dead,* Rogue.

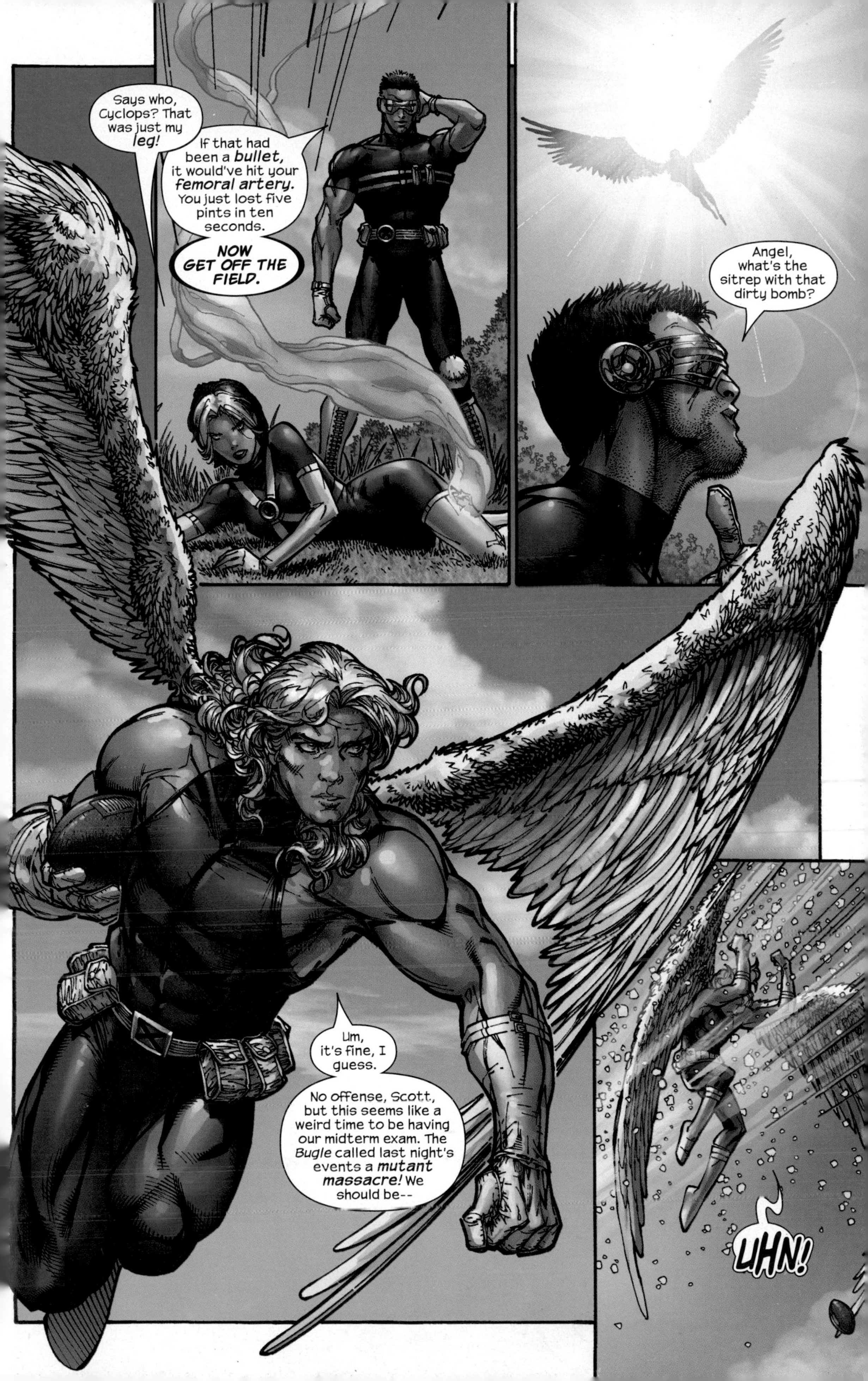
Says who, Cyclops? That was just my leg!
If that had been a bullet, it would've hit your femoral artery. You just lost five pints in ten seconds.
NOW GET OFF THE FIELD.
Angel, what's the sitrep with that dirty bomb?
Um, it's fine, I guess.
No offense, Scott, but this seems like a weird time to be having our midterm exam. The Bugle called last night's events a mutant massacre! We should be--
UHN!

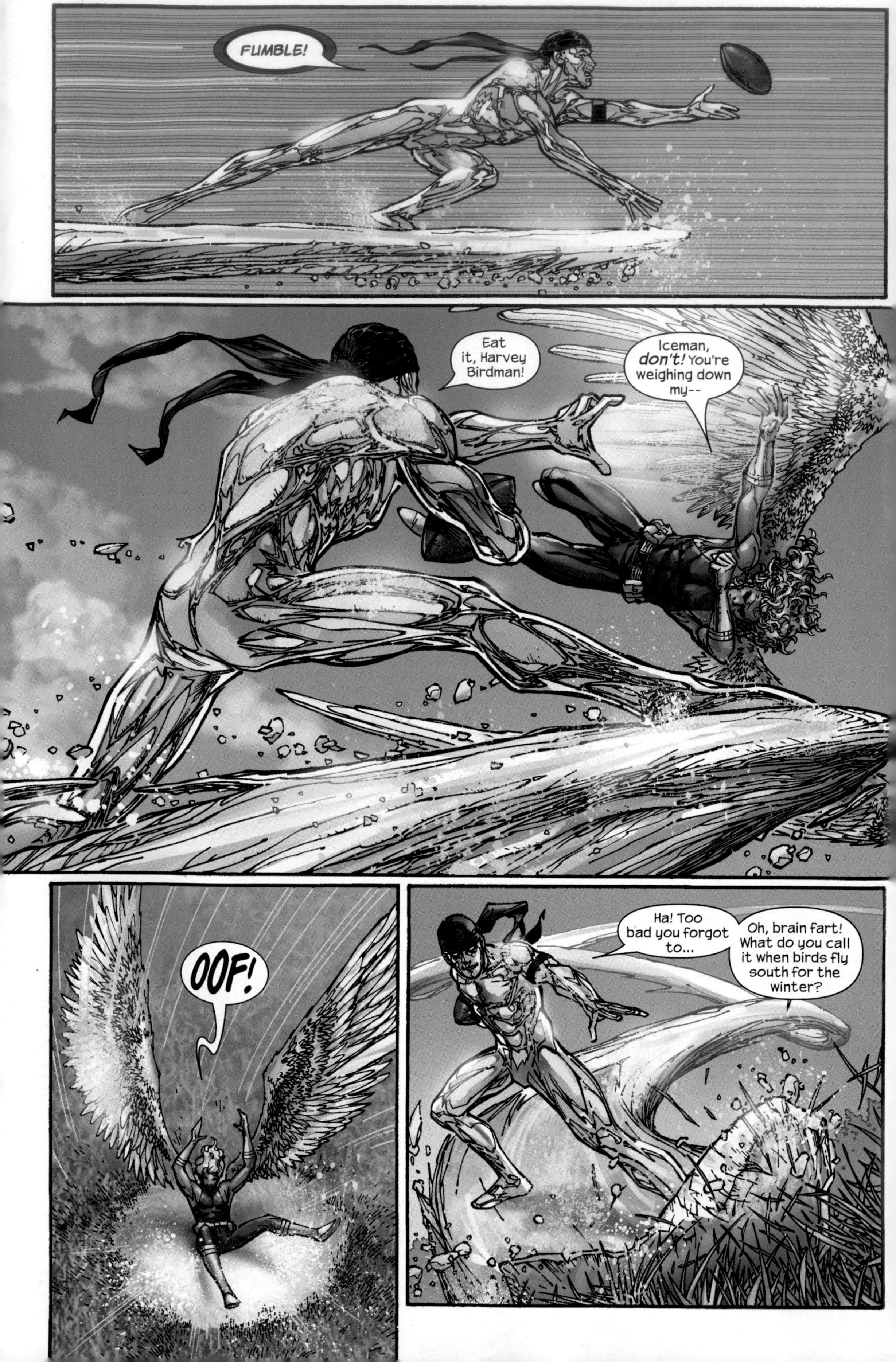
FUMBLE!
Eat it, Harvey Birdman!
Iceman, don't! You're weighing down my--
OOF!
Ha! Too bad you forgot to...
Oh, brain fart! What do you call it when birds fly south for the winter?

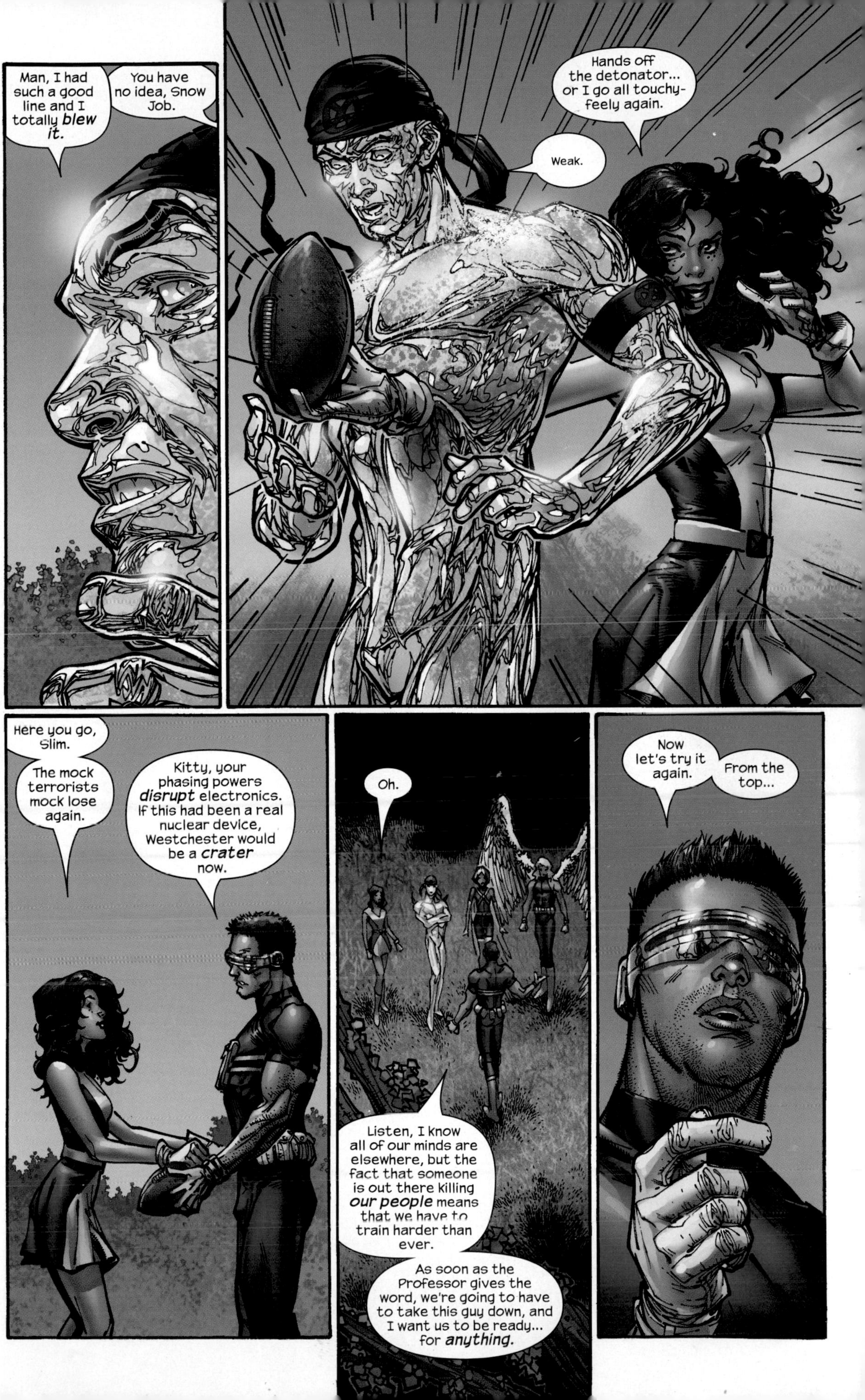
Man, I had such a good line and I totally blew it.
You have no idea, Snow Job.
Hands off the detonator... or I go all touchy-feely again.
Weak.
Here you go, Slim.
The mock terrorists mock lose again.
Kitty, your phasing powers disrupt electronics. If this had been a real nuclear device, Westchester would be a crater now.
Oh.
Listen, I know all of our minds are elsewhere, but the fact that someone is out there killing our people means that we have to train harder than ever.
As soon as the Professor gives the word, we're going to have to take this guy down, and I want us to be ready... for anything.
Now let's try it again.
From the top...

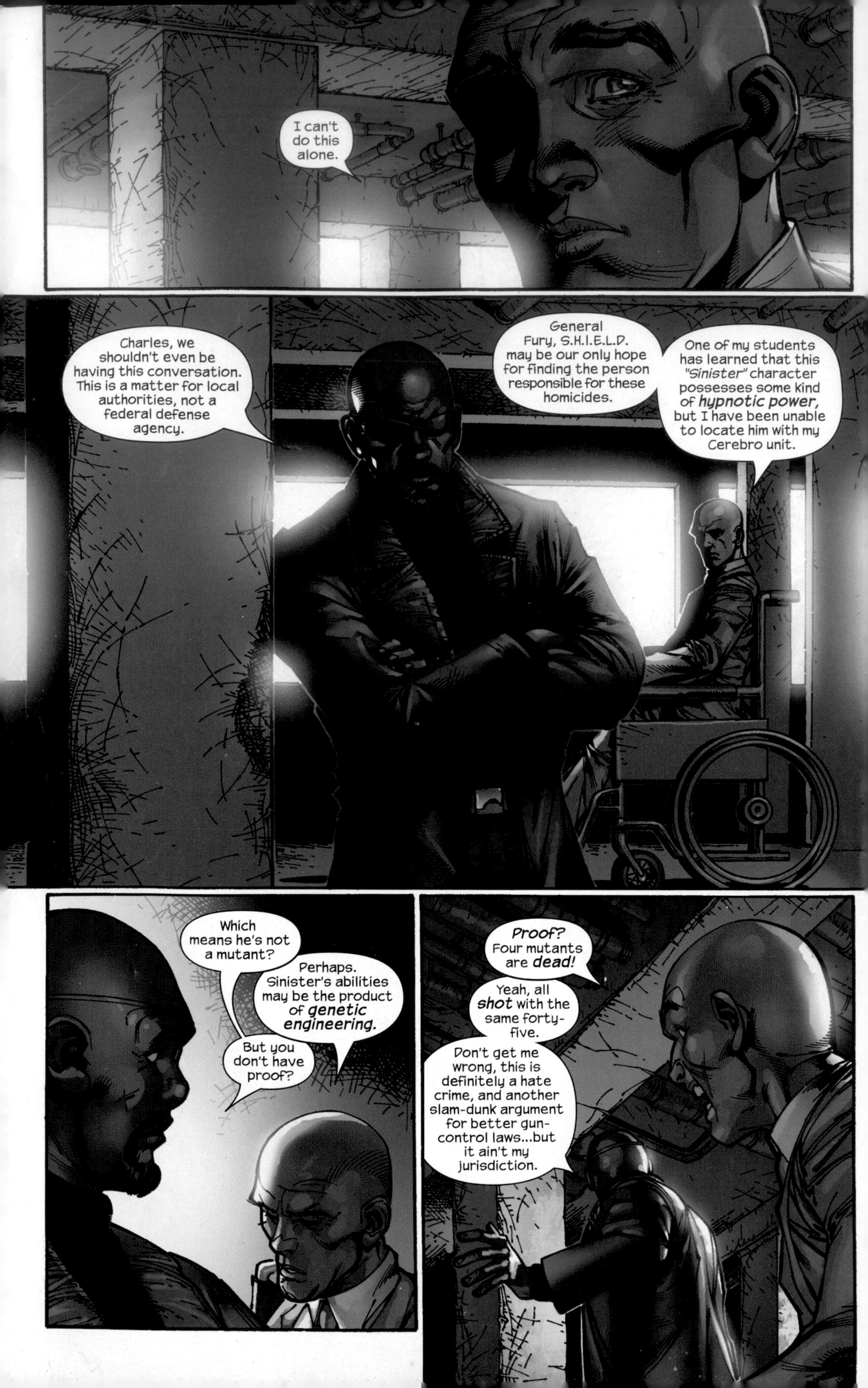
I can't do this alone.
Charles, we shouldn't even be having this conversation. This is a matter for local authorities, not a federal defense agency.
General Fury, S.H.I.E.L.D. may be our only hope for finding the person responsible for these homicides.
One of my students has learned that this "Sinister" character possesses some kind of hypnotic power, but I have been unable to locate him with my Cerebro unit.
Which means he's not a mutant?
Perhaps. Sinister's abilities may be the product of genetic engineering.
But you don't have proof?
Proof? Four mutants are dead!
Yeah, all shot with the same forty-five.
Don't get me wrong, this is definitely a hate crime, and another slam-dunk argument for better gun-control laws...but it ain't my jurisdiction.

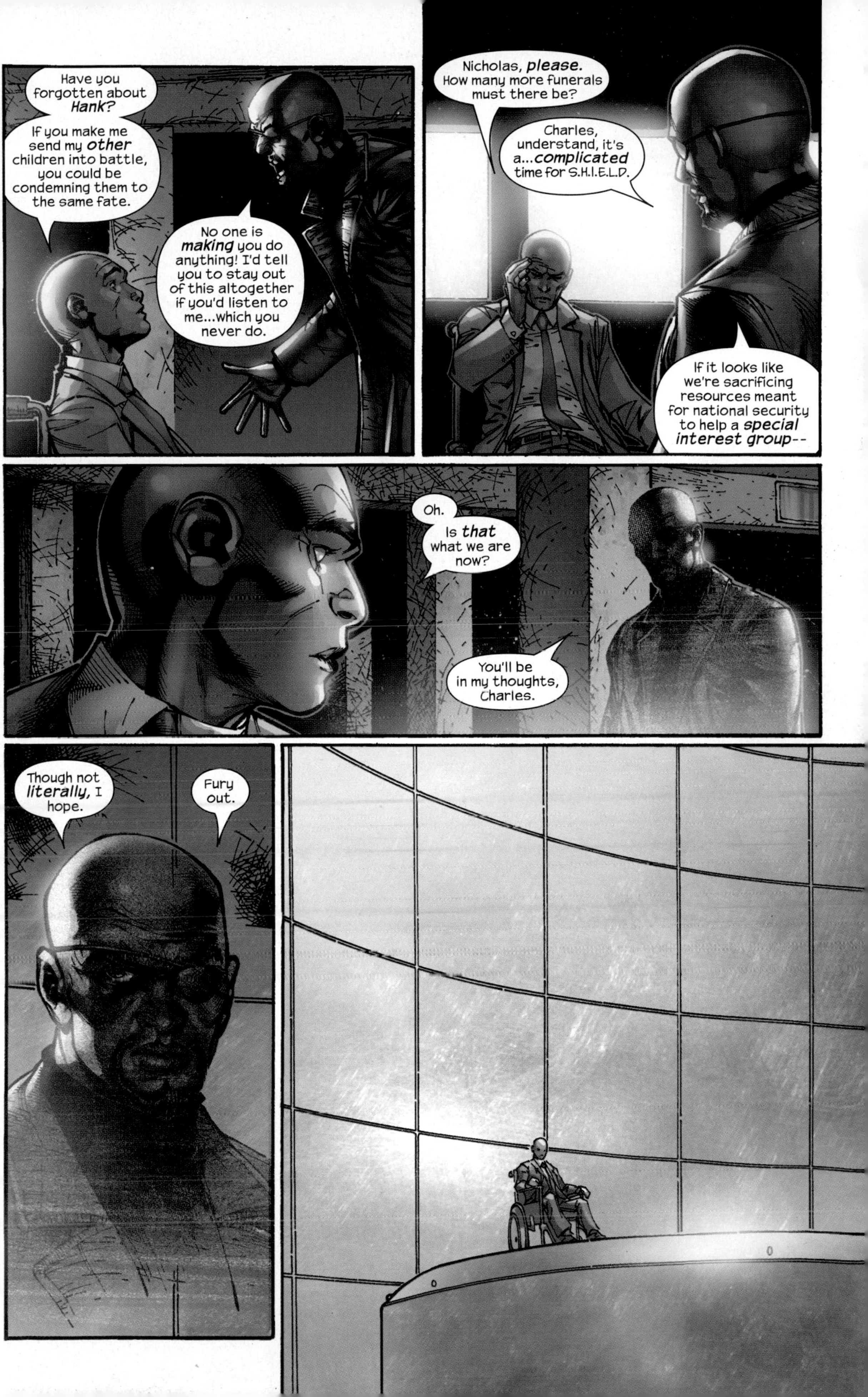
Have you forgotten about *Hank?*
If you make me send my *other* children into battle, you could be condemning them to the same fate.
No one is *making* you do anything! I'd tell you to stay out of this altogether if you'd listen to me...which you never do.
Nicholas, ***please.*** How many more funerals must there be?
Charles, understand, it's a...*complicated* time for S.H.I.E.L.D.
If it looks like we're sacrificing resources meant for national security to help a *special interest group*--
Oh.
Is *that* what we are now?
You'll be in my thoughts, Charles.
Though not *literally,* I hope.
Fury out.

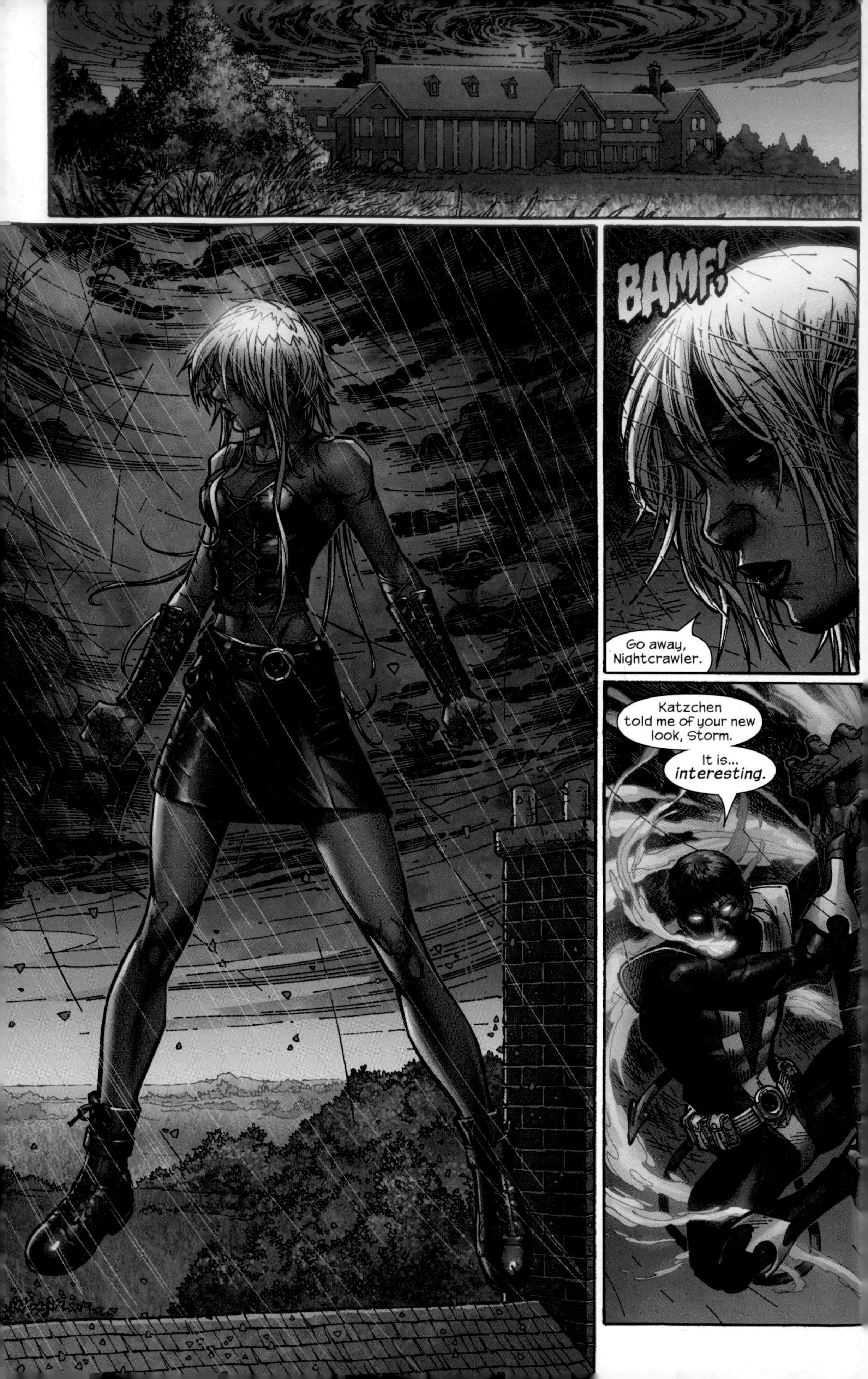
BAMF!
Go away, Nightcrawler.
Katzchen told me of your new look, Storm.
It is... *interesting.*

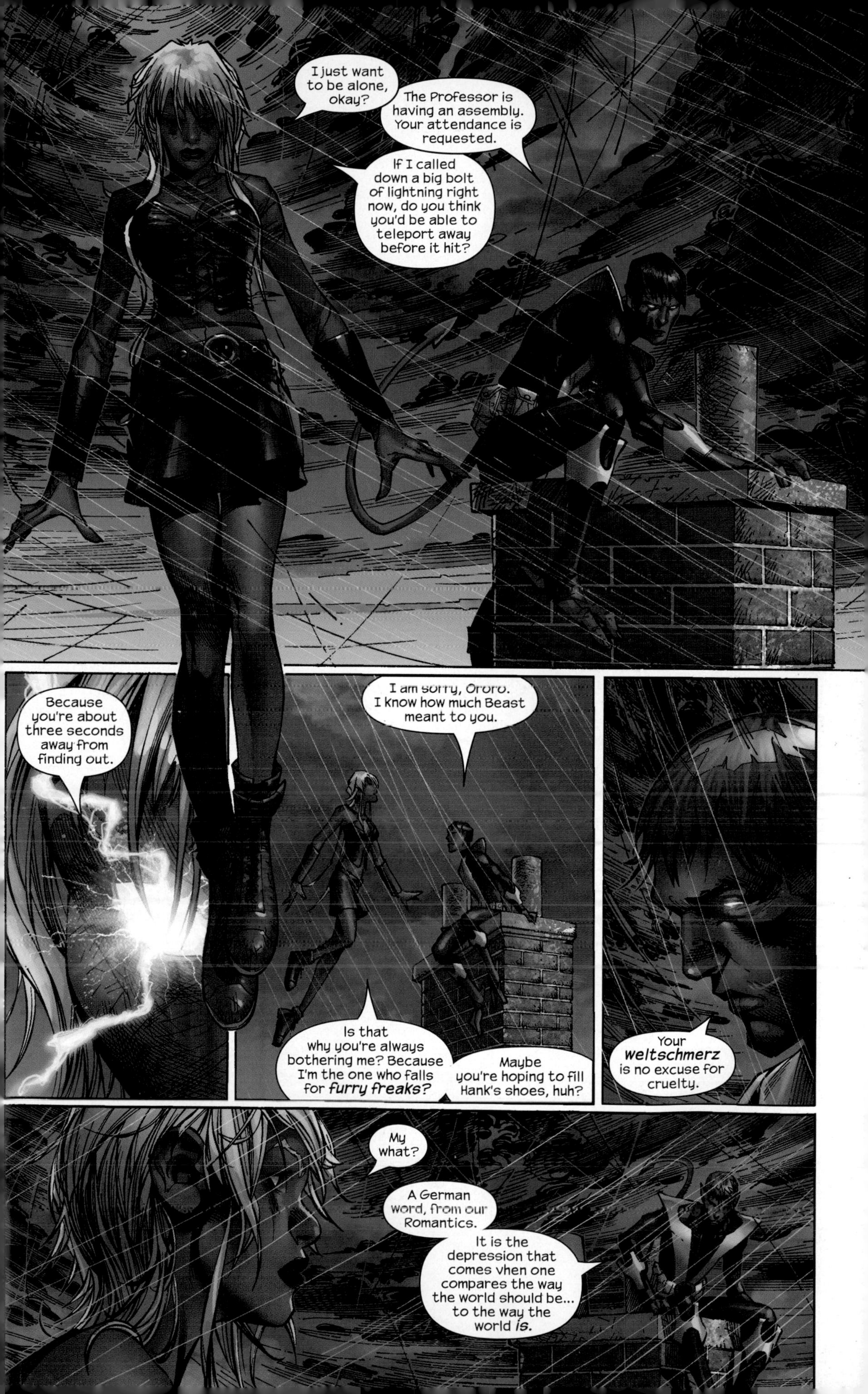
I just want to be alone, okay?
The Professor is having an assembly. Your attendance is requested.
If I called down a big bolt of lightning right now, do you think you'd be able to teleport away before it hit?
Because you're about three seconds away from finding out.
I am sorry, Ororo. I know how much Beast meant to you.
Is that why you're always bothering me? Because I'm the one who falls for *furry freaks?*
Maybe you're hoping to fill Hank's shoes, huh?
Your ***weltschmerz*** is no excuse for cruelty.
My what?
A German word, from our Romantics.
It is the depression that comes vhen one compares the way the world should be... to the way the world ***is.***

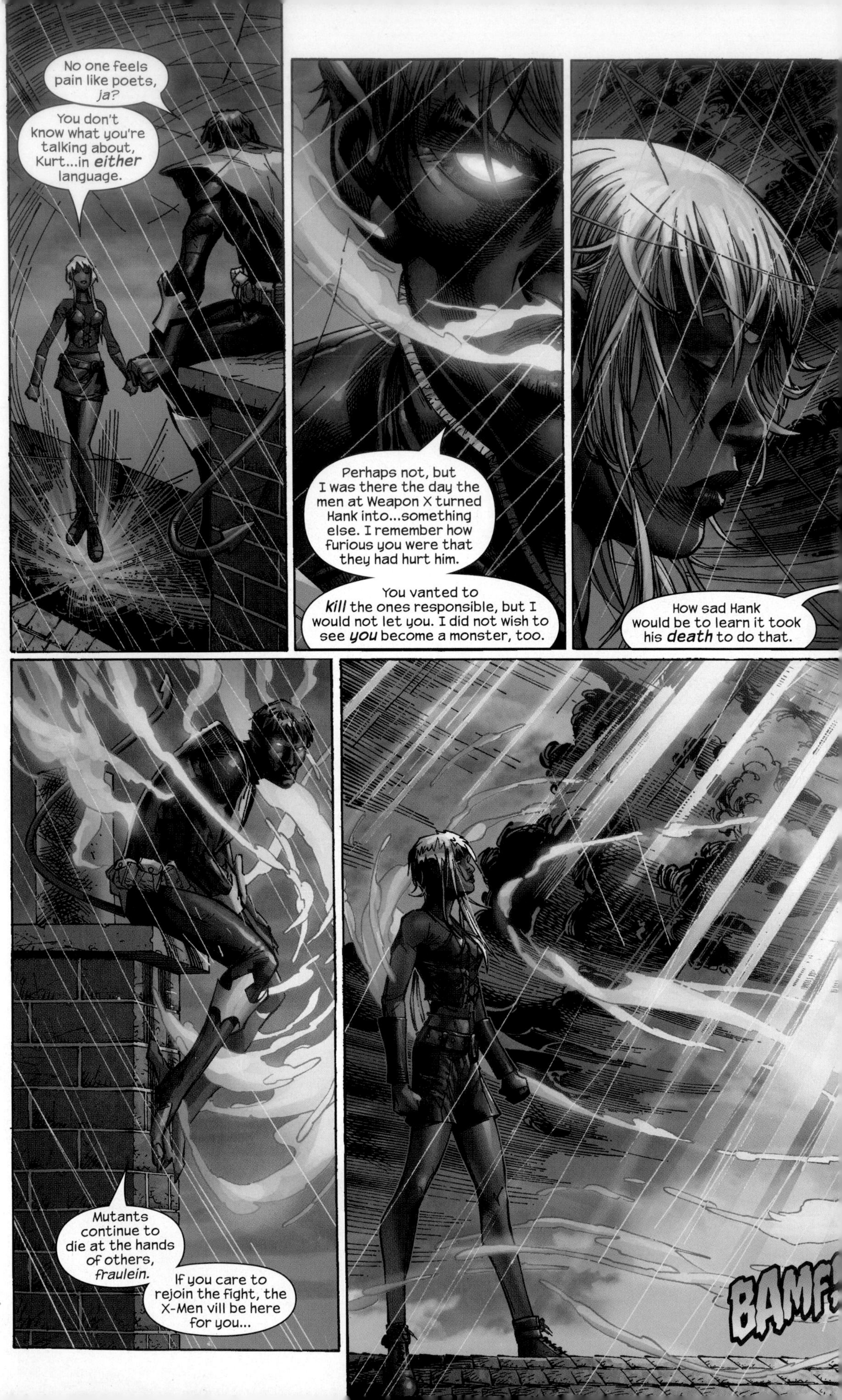
No one feels pain like poets, *ja?*
You don't know what you're talking about, Kurt...in **either** language.
Perhaps not, but I was there the day the men at Weapon X turned Hank into...something else. I remember how furious you were that they had hurt him.
You vanted to **kill** the ones responsible, but I would not let you. I did not wish to see **you** become a monster, too.
How sad Hank would be to learn it took his **death** to do that.
Mutants continue to die at the hands of others, *fraulein.*
If you care to rejoin the fight, the X-Men vill be here for you...
BAMF

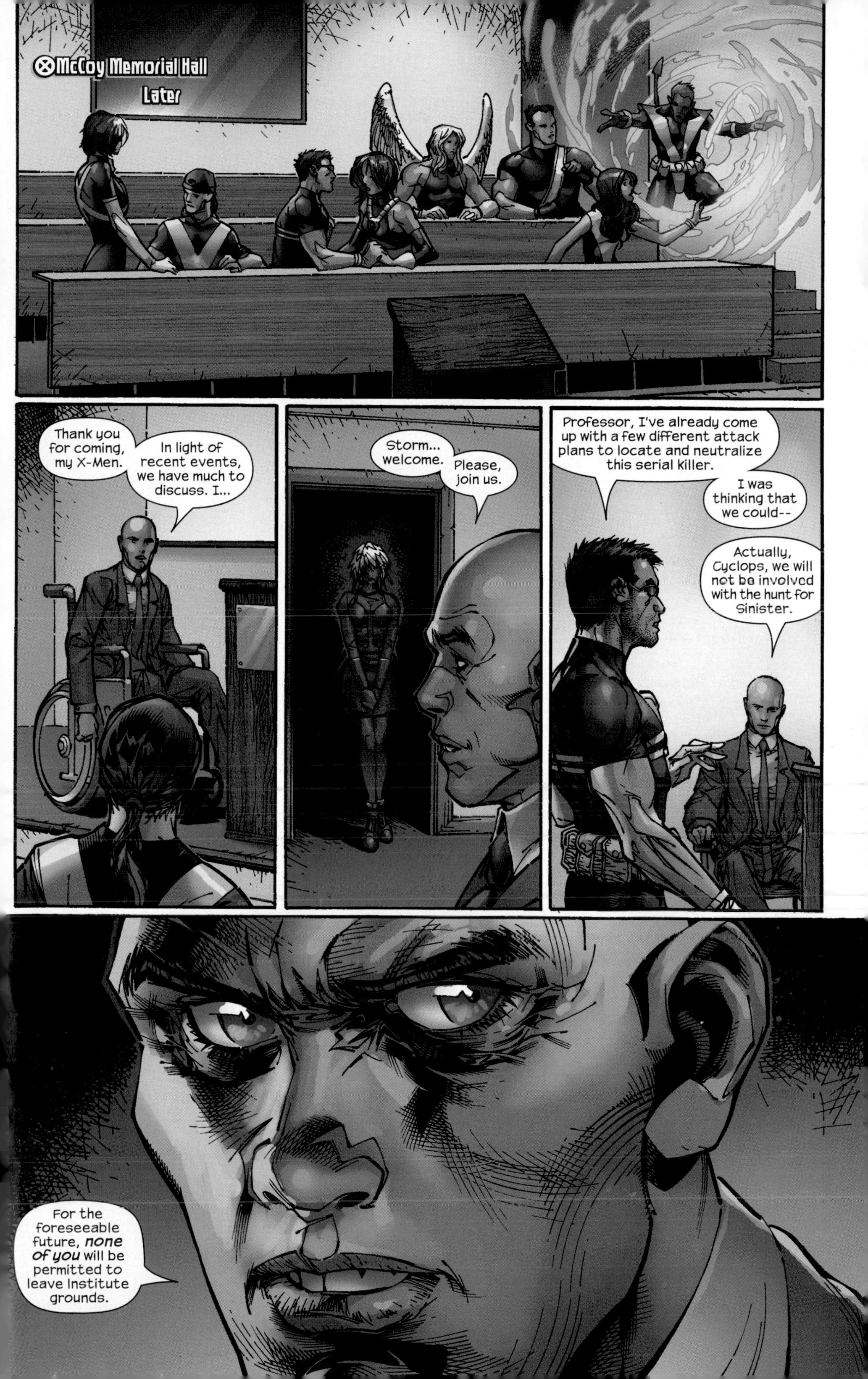
McCoy Memorial Hall
Later
Thank you for coming, my X-Men.
In light of recent events, we have much to discuss. I...
Storm... welcome.
Please, join us.
Professor, I've already come up with a few different attack plans to locate and neutralize this serial killer.
I was thinking that we could--
Actually, Cyclops, we will not be involved with the hunt for Sinister.
For the foreseeable future, *none of you* will be permitted to leave Institute grounds.

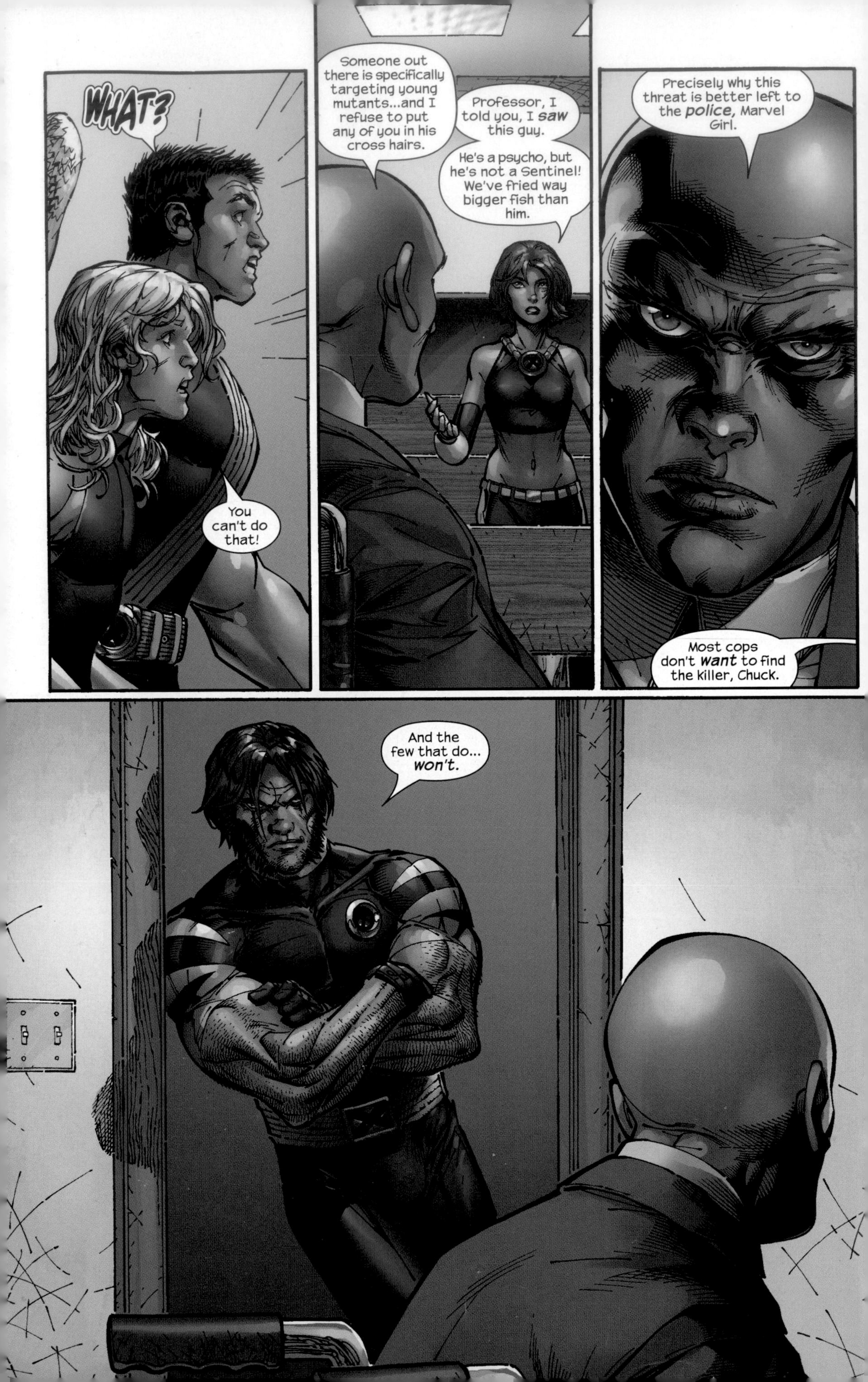
WHAT?
You can't do that!
Someone out there is specifically targeting young mutants...and I refuse to put any of you in his cross hairs.
Professor, I told you, I *saw* this guy.
He's a psycho, but he's not a Sentinel! We've fried way bigger fish than him.
Precisely why this threat is better left to the *police,* Marvel Girl.
Most cops don't *want* to find the killer, Chuck.
And the few that do... *won't.*

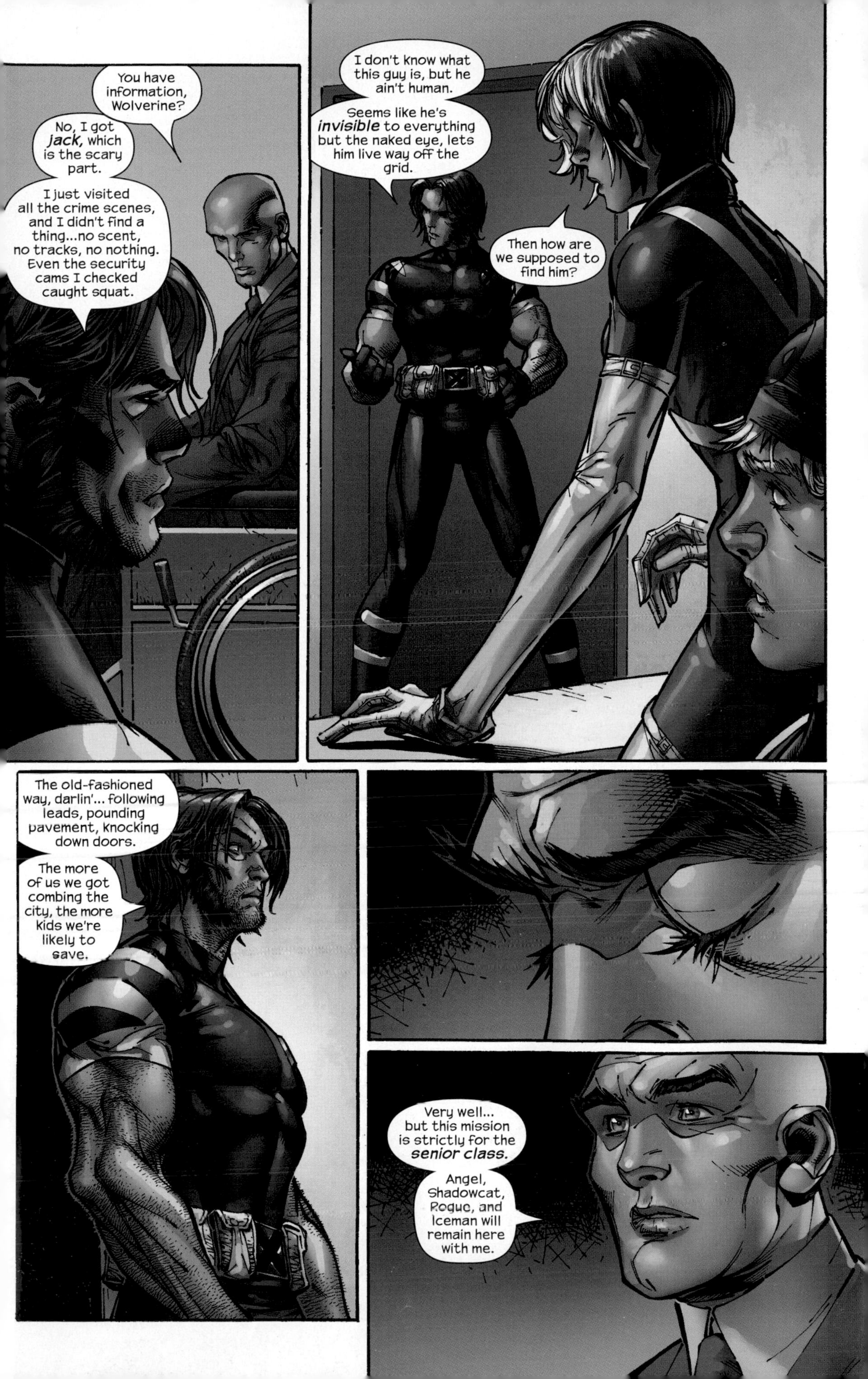
You have information, Wolverine?
No, I got *jack,* which is the scary part.
I just visited all the crime scenes, and I didn't find a thing...no scent, no tracks, no nothing. Even the security cams I checked caught squat.
I don't know what this guy is, but he ain't human.
Seems like he's *invisible* to everything but the naked eye, lets him live way off the grid.
Then how are we supposed to find him?
The old-fashioned way, darlin'... following leads, pounding pavement, knocking down doors.
The more of us we got combing the city, the more kids we're likely to save.
Very well... but this mission is strictly for the *senior class.*
Angel, Shadowcat, Rogue, and Iceman will remain here with me.

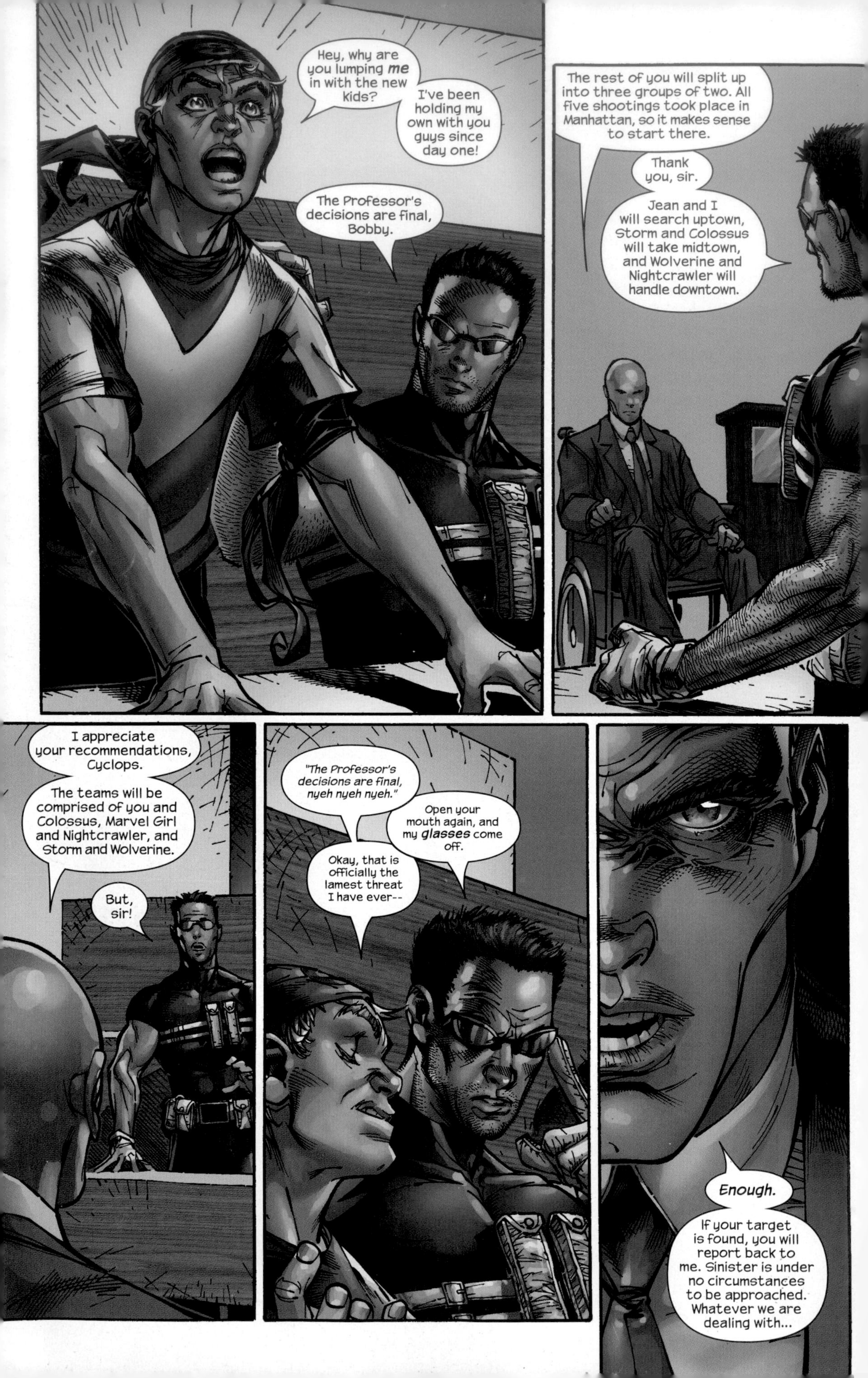
Hey, why are you lumping *me* in with the new kids?
I've been holding my own with you guys since day one!
The Professor's decisions are final, Bobby.
The rest of you will split up into three groups of two. All five shootings took place in Manhattan, so it makes sense to start there.
Thank you, sir.
Jean and I will search uptown, Storm and Colossus will take midtown, and Wolverine and Nightcrawler will handle downtown.
I appreciate your recommendations, Cyclops.
The teams will be comprised of you and Colossus, Marvel Girl and Nightcrawler, and Storm and Wolverine.
But, sir!
"The Professor's decisions are final, nyeh nyeh nyeh."
Open your mouth again, and my *glasses* come off.
Okay, that is officially the lamest threat I have ever--
Enough.
If your target is found, you will report back to me. Sinister is under no circumstances to be approached. Whatever we are dealing with...

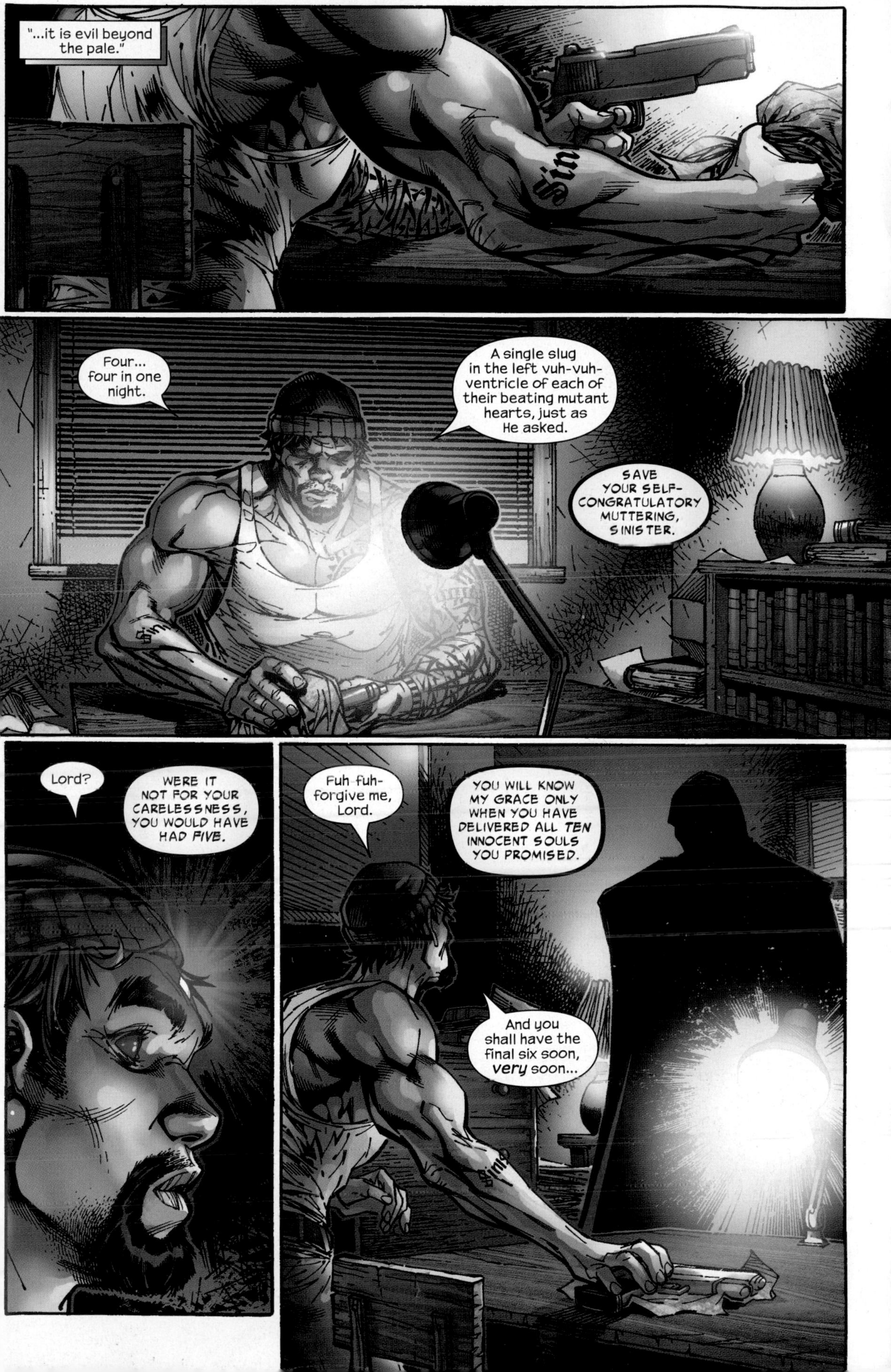
"...it is evil beyond the pale."
Sin
Four... four in one night.
A single slug in the left vuh-vuh-ventricle of each of their beating mutant hearts, just as He asked.
SAVE YOUR SELF-CONGRATULATORY MUTTERING, SINISTER.
Lord?
WERE IT NOT FOR YOUR CARELESSNESS, YOU WOULD HAVE HAD FIVE.
Fuh fuh-forgive me, Lord.
YOU WILL KNOW MY GRACE ONLY WHEN YOU HAVE DELIVERED ALL TEN INNOCENT SOULS YOU PROMISED.
And you shall have the final six soon, very soon...

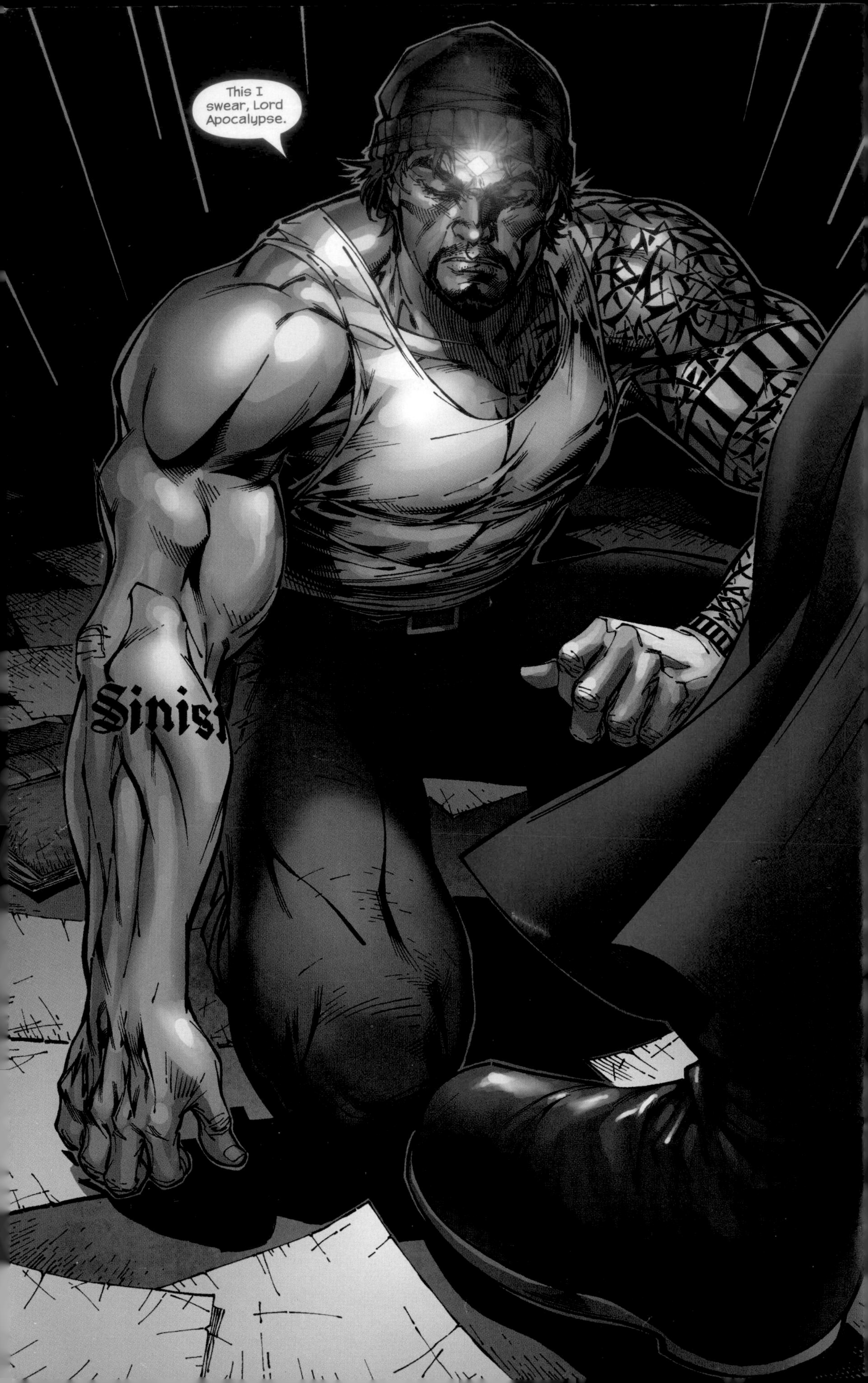
This I
swear, Lord
Apocalypse.

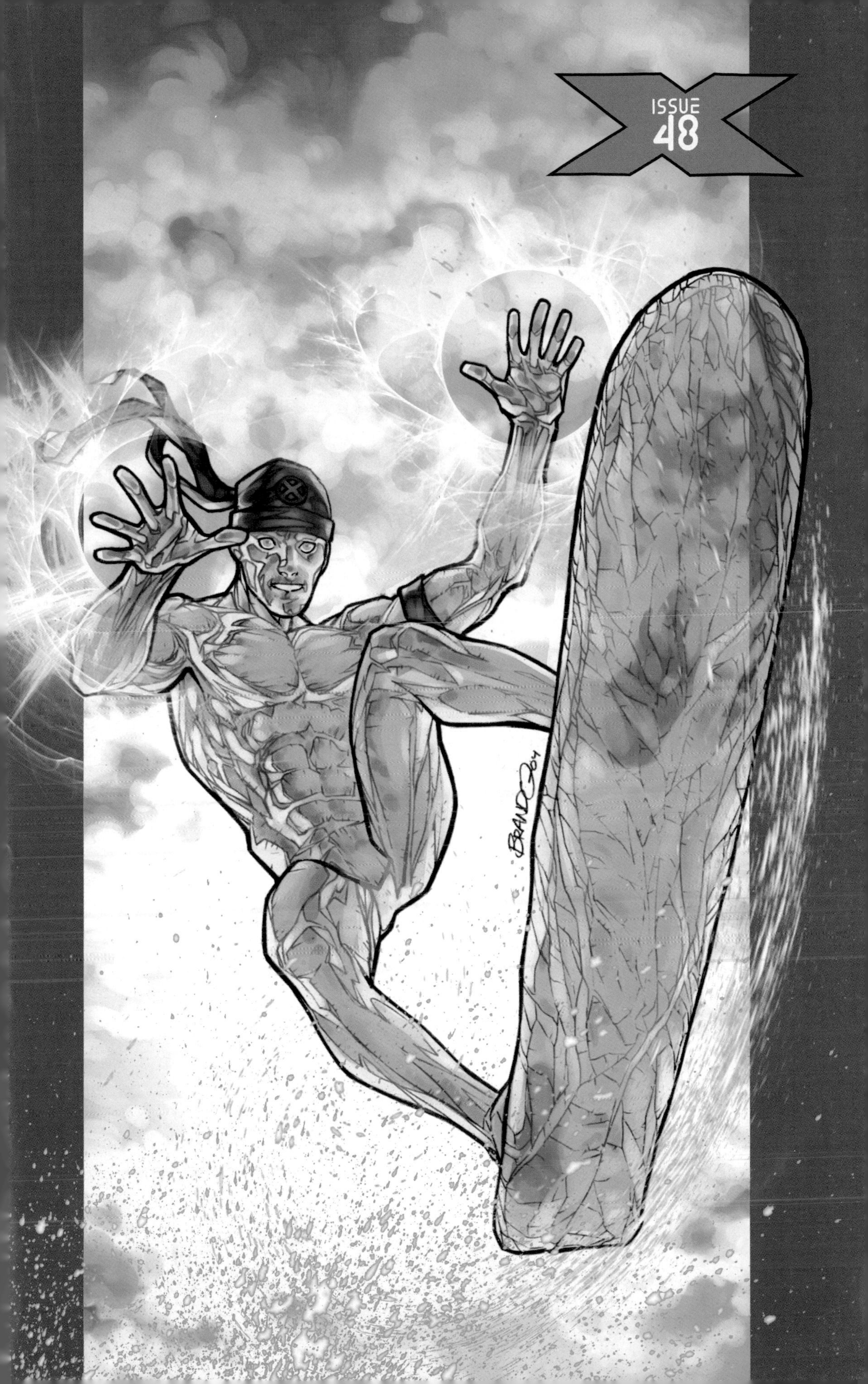
ISSUE
48
BRANDO '04

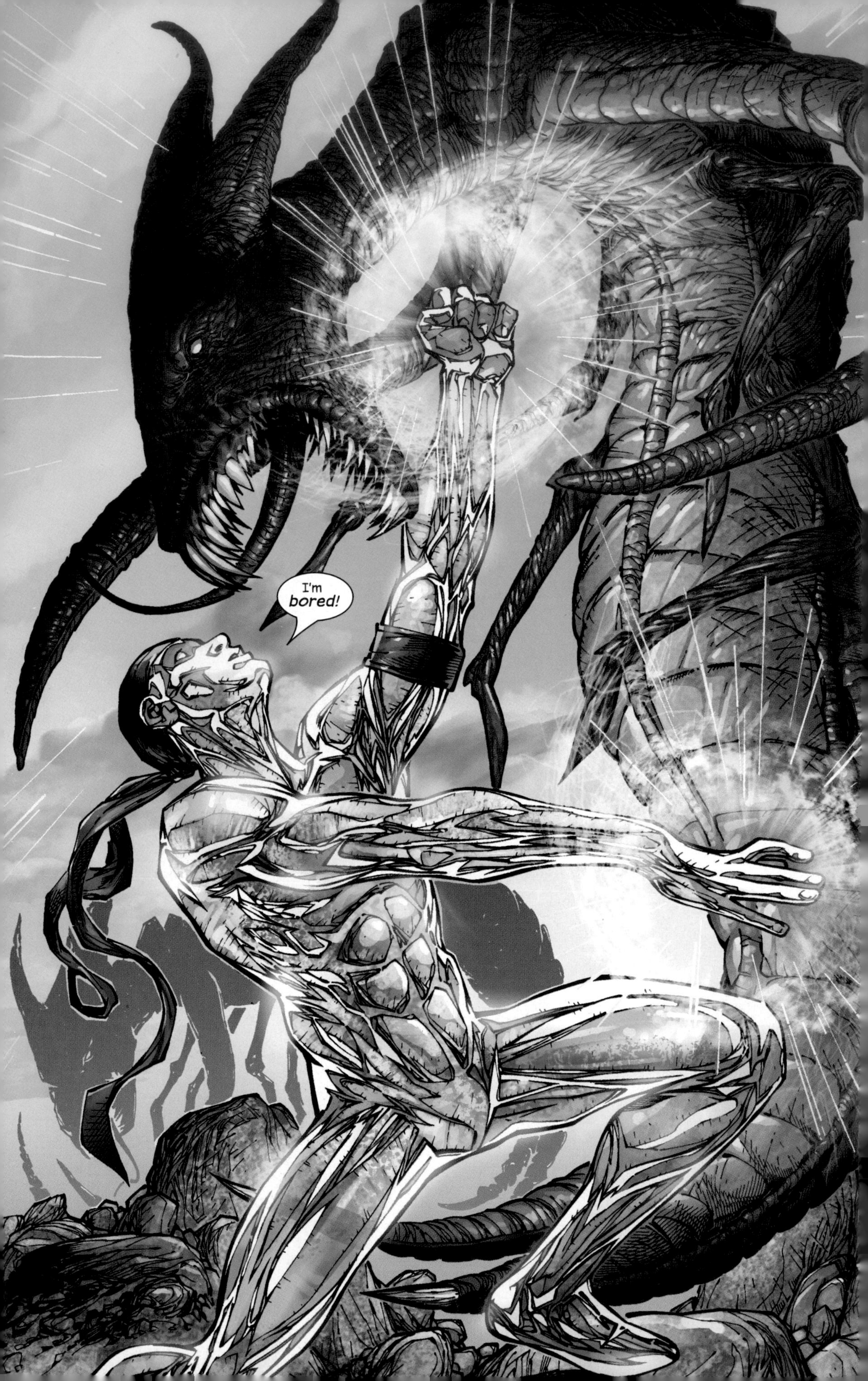
I'm bored!

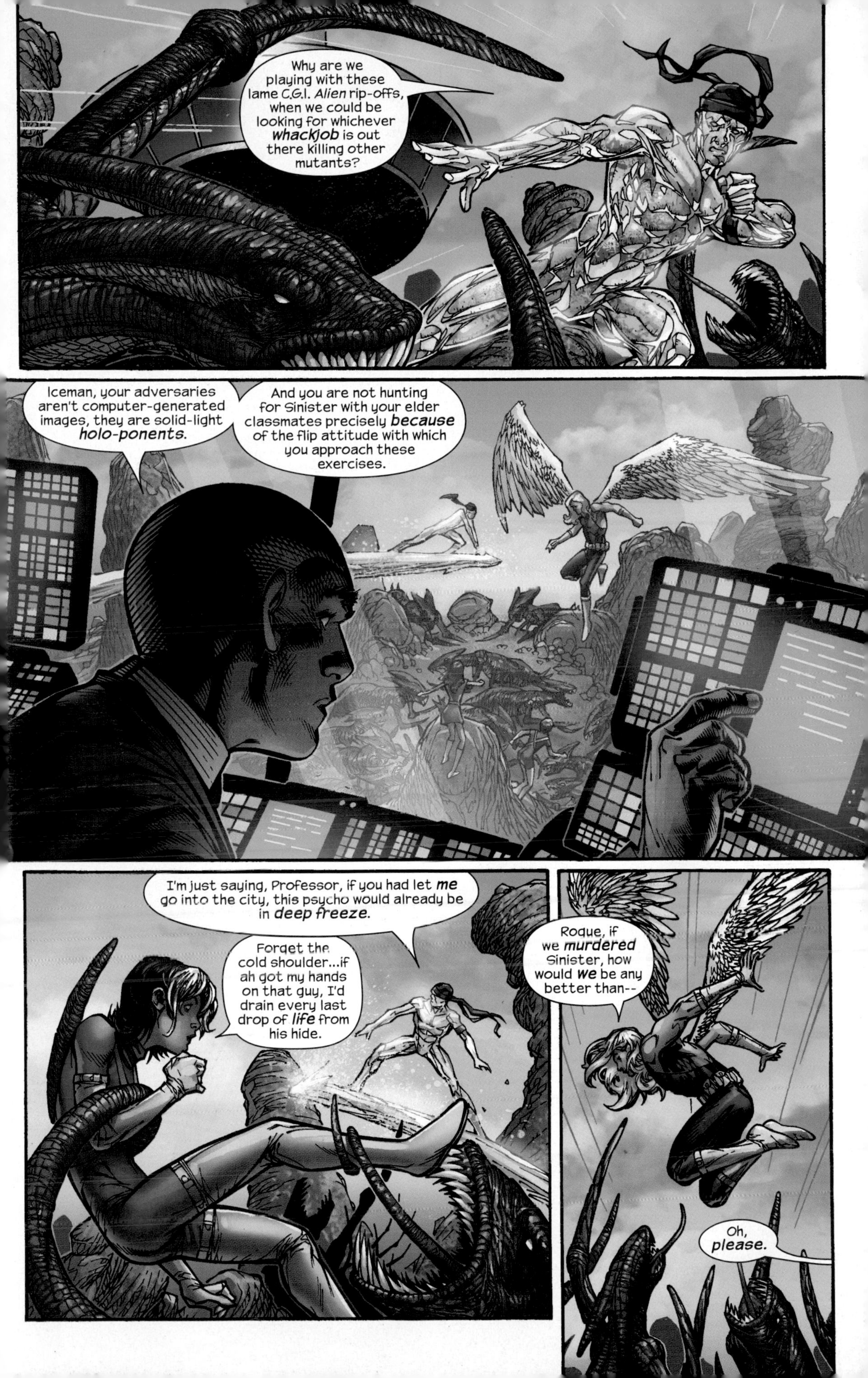
Why are we playing with these lame C.G.I. *Alien* rip-offs, when we could be looking for whichever **whackjob** is out there killing other mutants?
Iceman, your adversaries aren't computer-generated images, they are solid-light ***holo-ponents***.
And you are not hunting for Sinister with your elder classmates precisely ***because*** of the flip attitude with which you approach these exercises.
I'm just saying, Professor, if you had let ***me*** go into the city, this psycho would already be in ***deep freeze***.
Forget the cold shoulder...if ah got my hands on that guy, I'd drain every last drop of ***life*** from his hide.
Rogue, if we ***murdered*** Sinister, how would ***we*** be any better than--
Oh, ***please***.

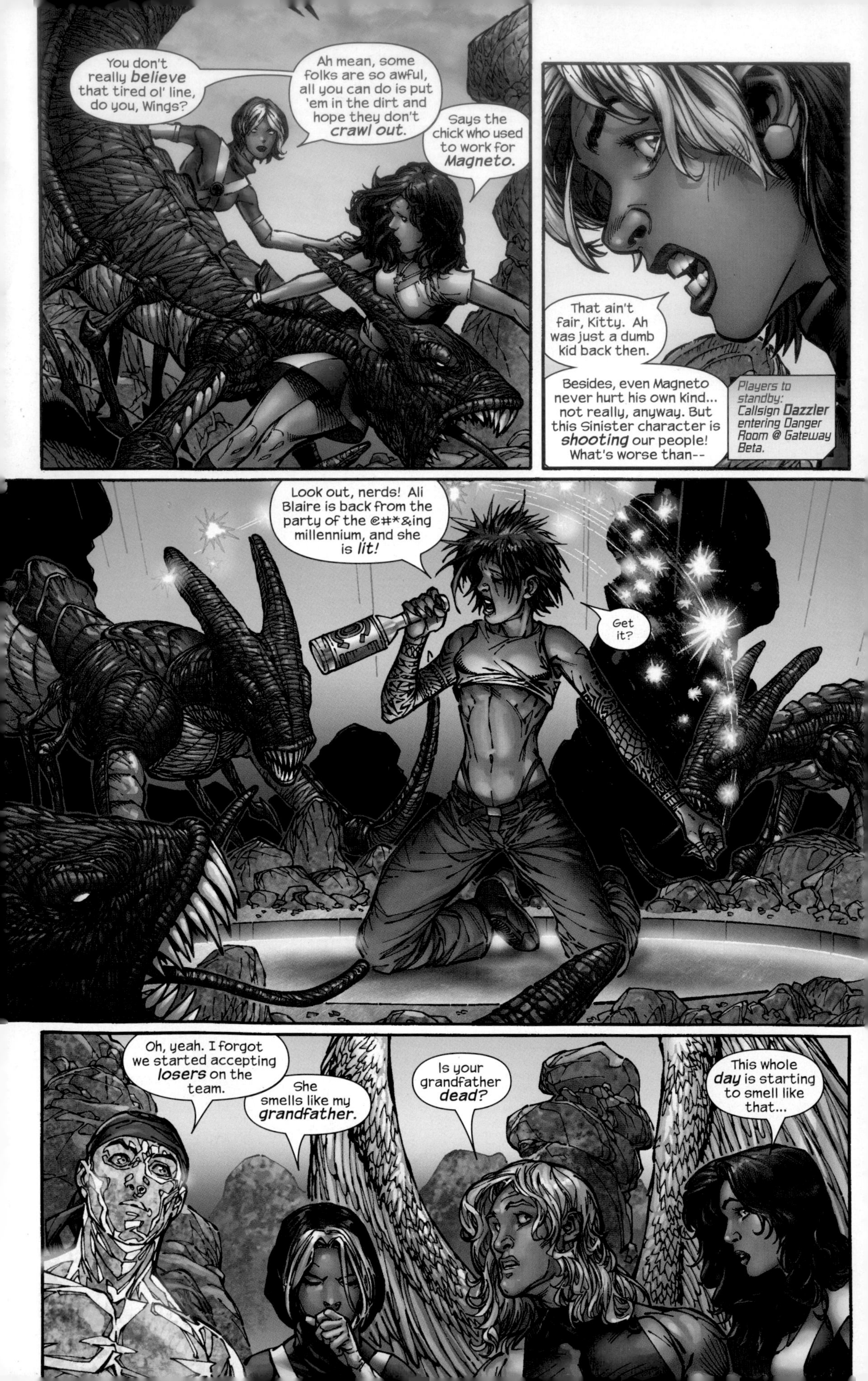
You don't really believe that tired ol' line, do you, Wings?
Ah mean, some folks are so awful, all you can do is put 'em in the dirt and hope they don't crawl out.
Says the chick who used to work for Magneto.
That ain't fair, Kitty. Ah was just a dumb kid back then.
Besides, even Magneto never hurt his own kind... not really, anyway. But this Sinister character is shooting our people! What's worse than--
Players to standby: Callsign Dazzler entering Danger Room @ Gateway Beta.
Look out, nerds! Ali Blaire is back from the party of the @#*&ing millennium, and she is lit!
Get it?
Oh, yeah. I forgot we started accepting losers on the team.
She smells like my grandfather.
Is your grandfather dead?
This whole day is starting to smell like that...

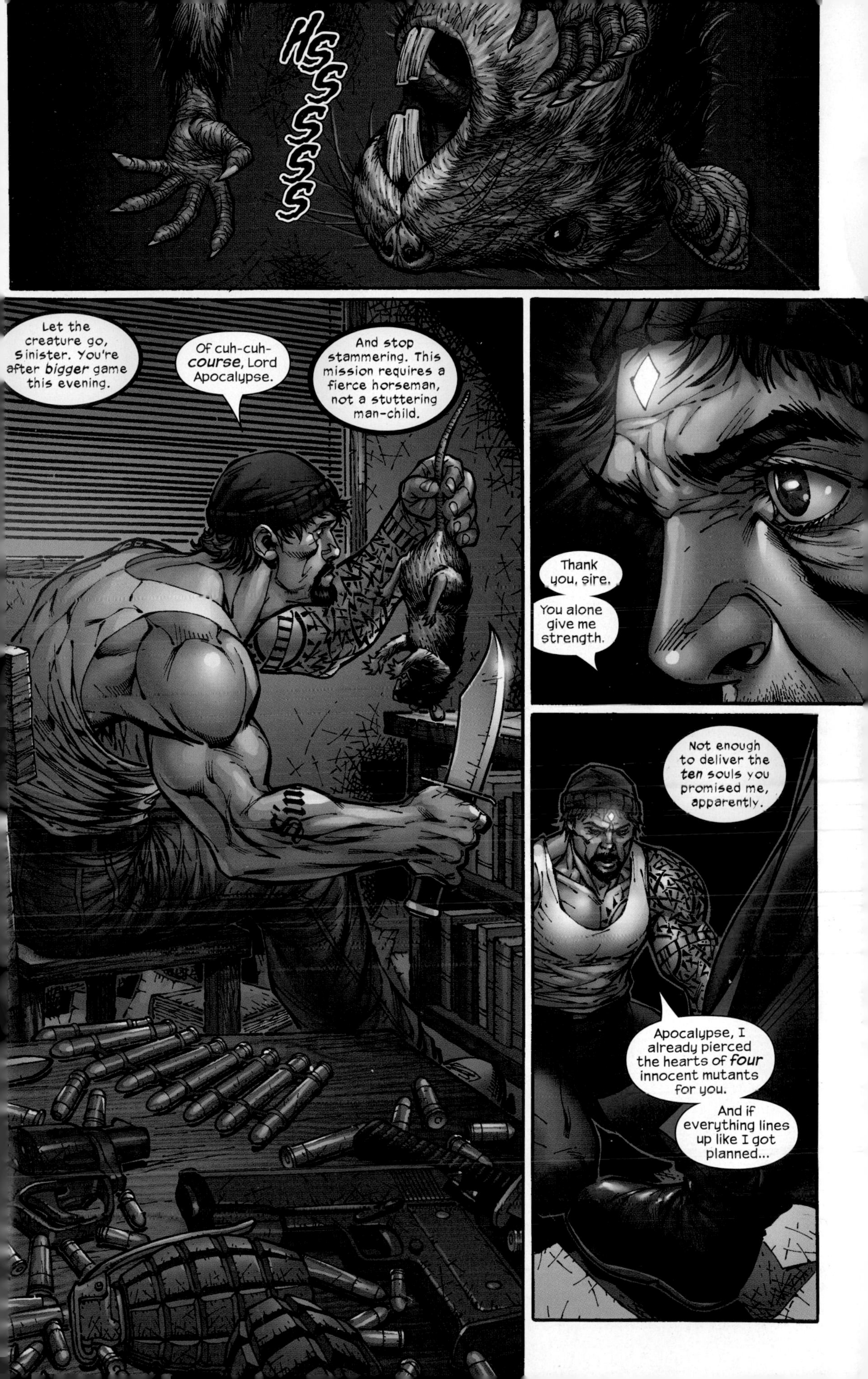
HSSSSSS
Let the creature go, Sinister. You're after *bigger* game this evening.
Of cuh-cuh-*course*, Lord Apocalypse.
And stop stammering. This mission requires a fierce horseman, not a stuttering man-child.
Thank you, sire.
You alone give me strength.
Not enough to deliver the *ten* souls you promised me, apparently.
Apocalypse, I already pierced the hearts of *four* innocent mutants for you.
And if everything lines up like I got planned...

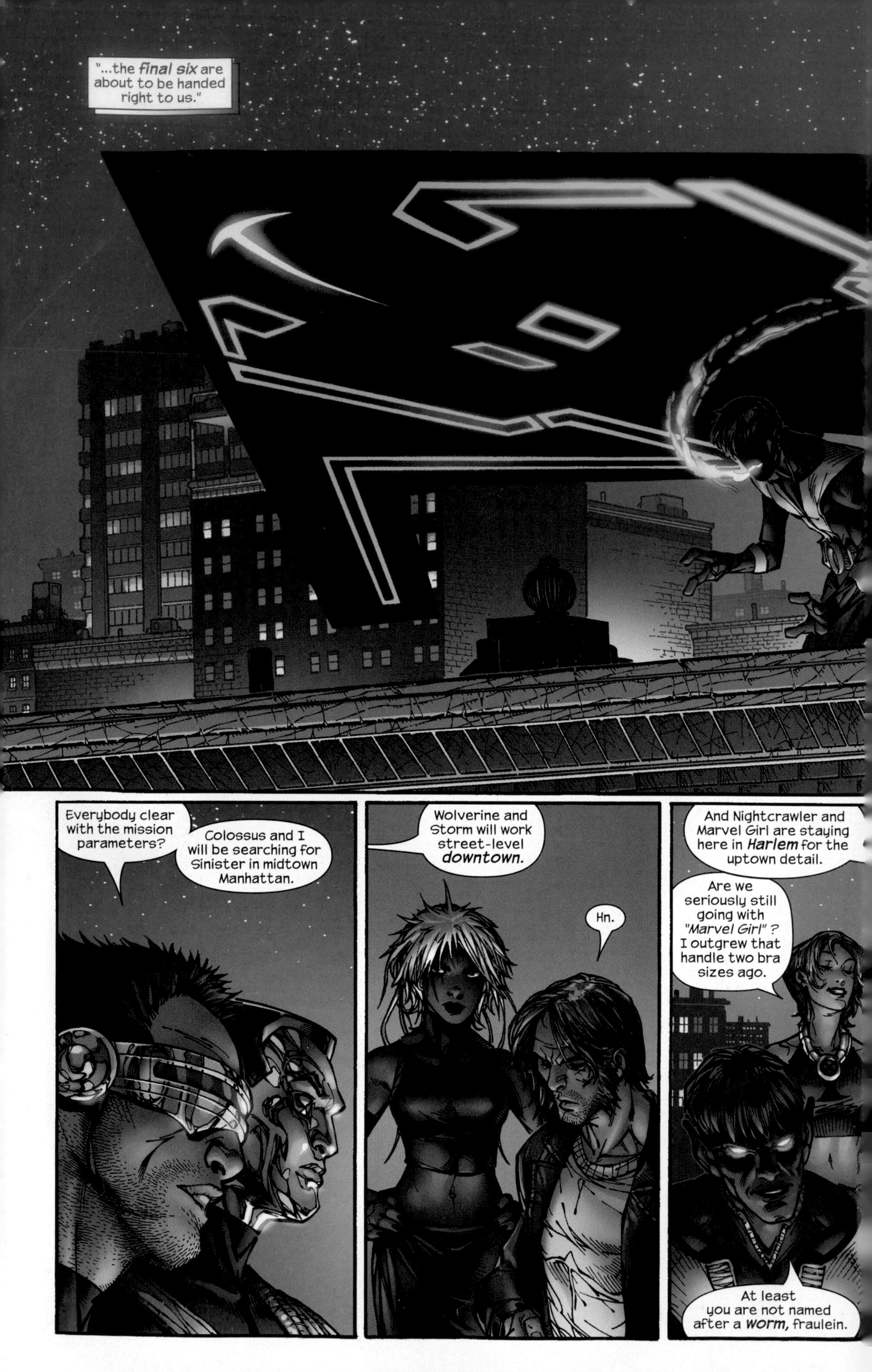
"...the *final six* are about to be handed right to us."
Everybody clear with the mission parameters?
Colossus and I will be searching for Sinister in midtown Manhattan.
Wolverine and Storm will work street-level ***downtown.***
Hn.
And Nightcrawler and Marvel Girl are staying here in ***Harlem*** for the uptown detail.
Are we seriously still going with *"Marvel Girl"* ? I outgrew that handle two bra sizes ago.
At least you are not named after a ***worm,*** fraulein.

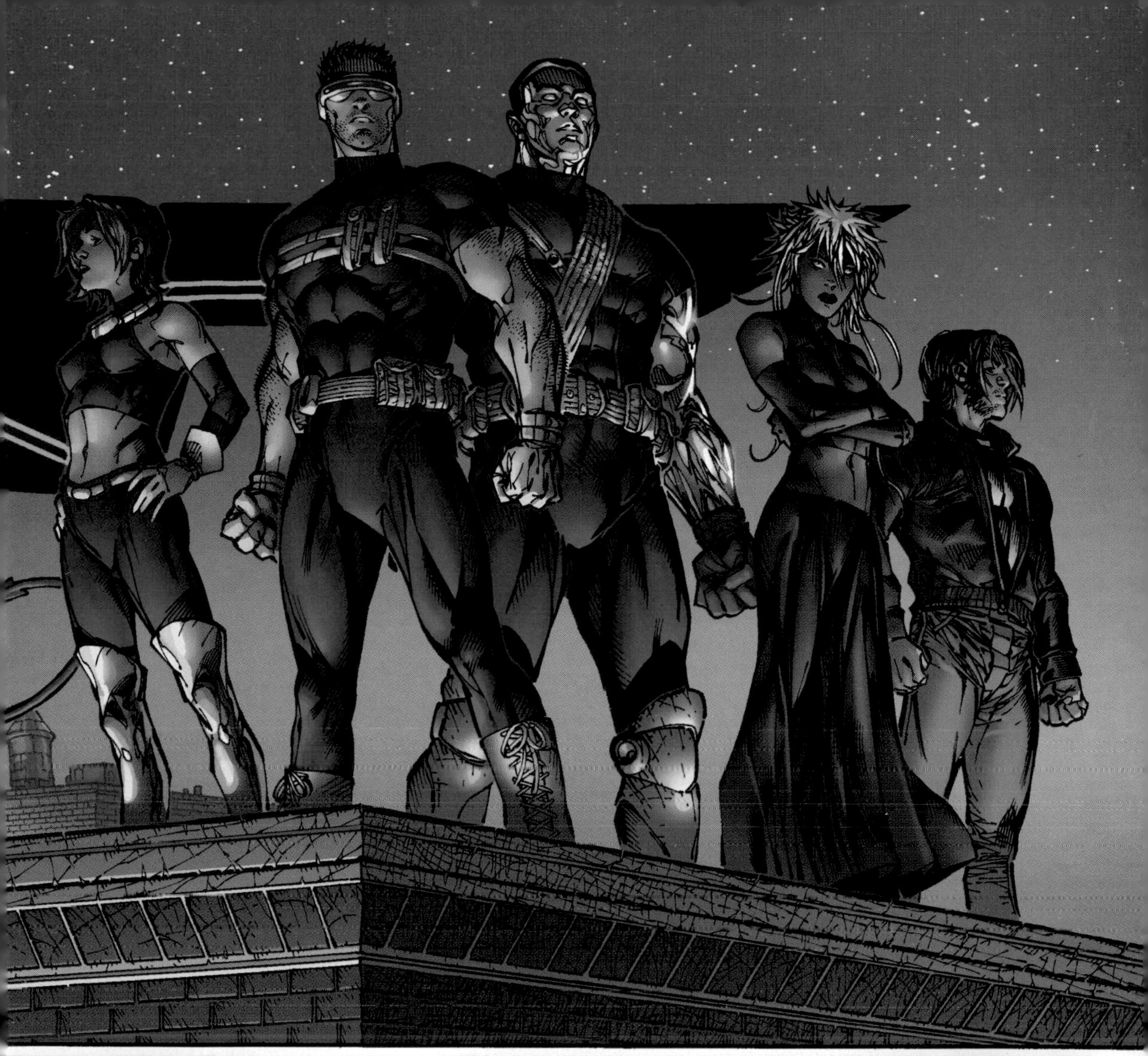

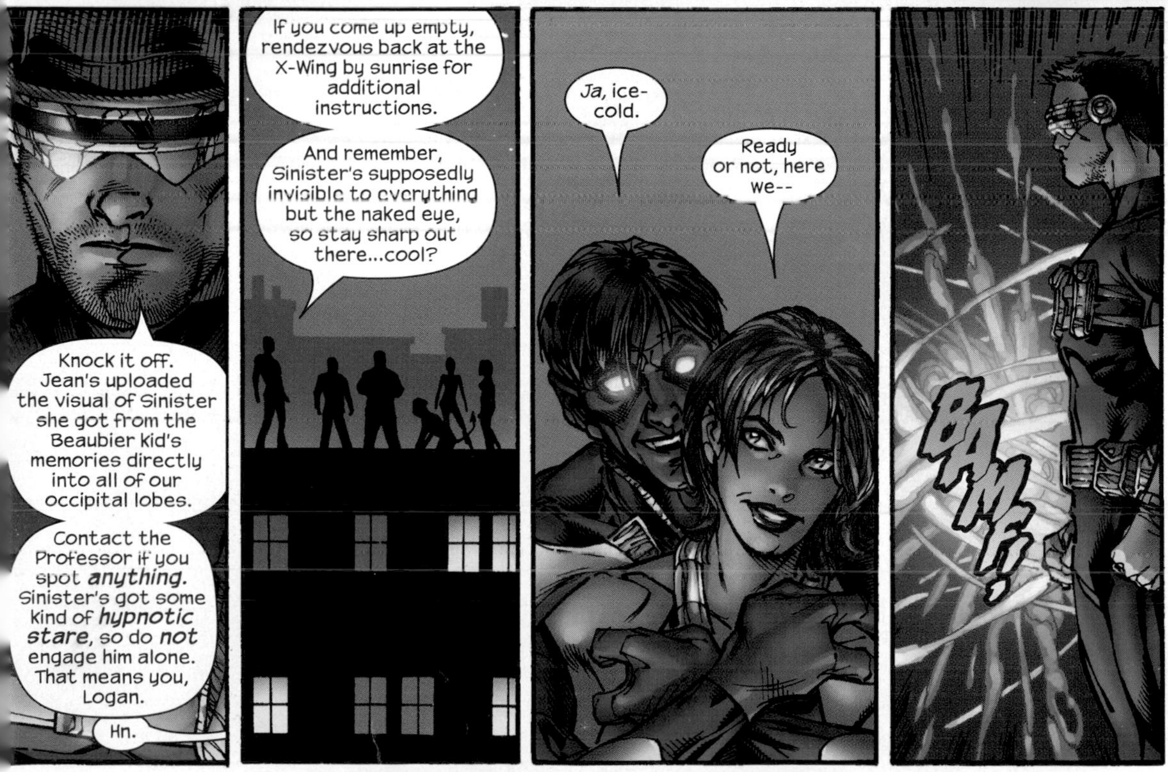
Knock it off. Jean's uploaded the visual of Sinister she got from the Beaubier kid's memories directly into all of our occipital lobes.
Contact the Professor if you spot *anything*. Sinister's got some kind of *hypnotic stare*, so do *not* engage him alone. That means you, Logan.
Hn.
If you come up empty, rendezvous back at the X-Wing by sunrise for additional instructions.
And remember, Sinister's supposedly invisible to everything but the naked eye, so stay sharp out there...cool?
Ja, ice-cold.
Ready or not, here we--
BAMF!

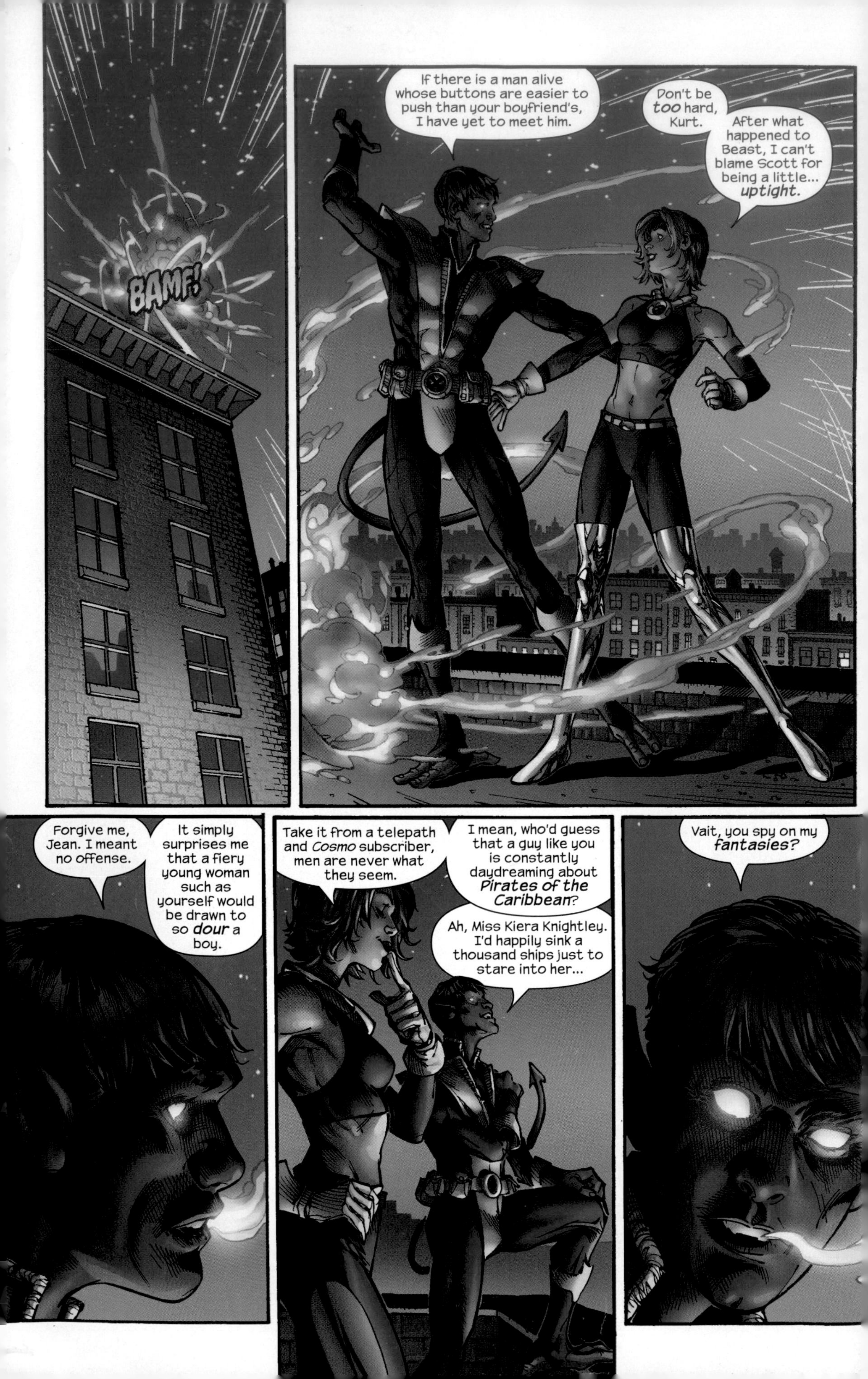
BAMF!
If there is a man alive whose buttons are easier to push than your boyfriend's, I have yet to meet him.
Don't be *too* hard, Kurt.
After what happened to Beast, I can't blame Scott for being a little... ***uptight.***
Forgive me, Jean. I meant no offense.
It simply surprises me that a fiery young woman such as yourself would be drawn to so ***dour*** a boy.
Take it from a telepath and *Cosmo* subscriber, men are never what they seem.
I mean, who'd guess that a guy like you is constantly daydreaming about ***Pirates of the Caribbean?***
Ah, Miss Kiera Knightley. I'd happily sink a thousand ships just to stare into her...
Vait, you spy on my ***fantasies?***

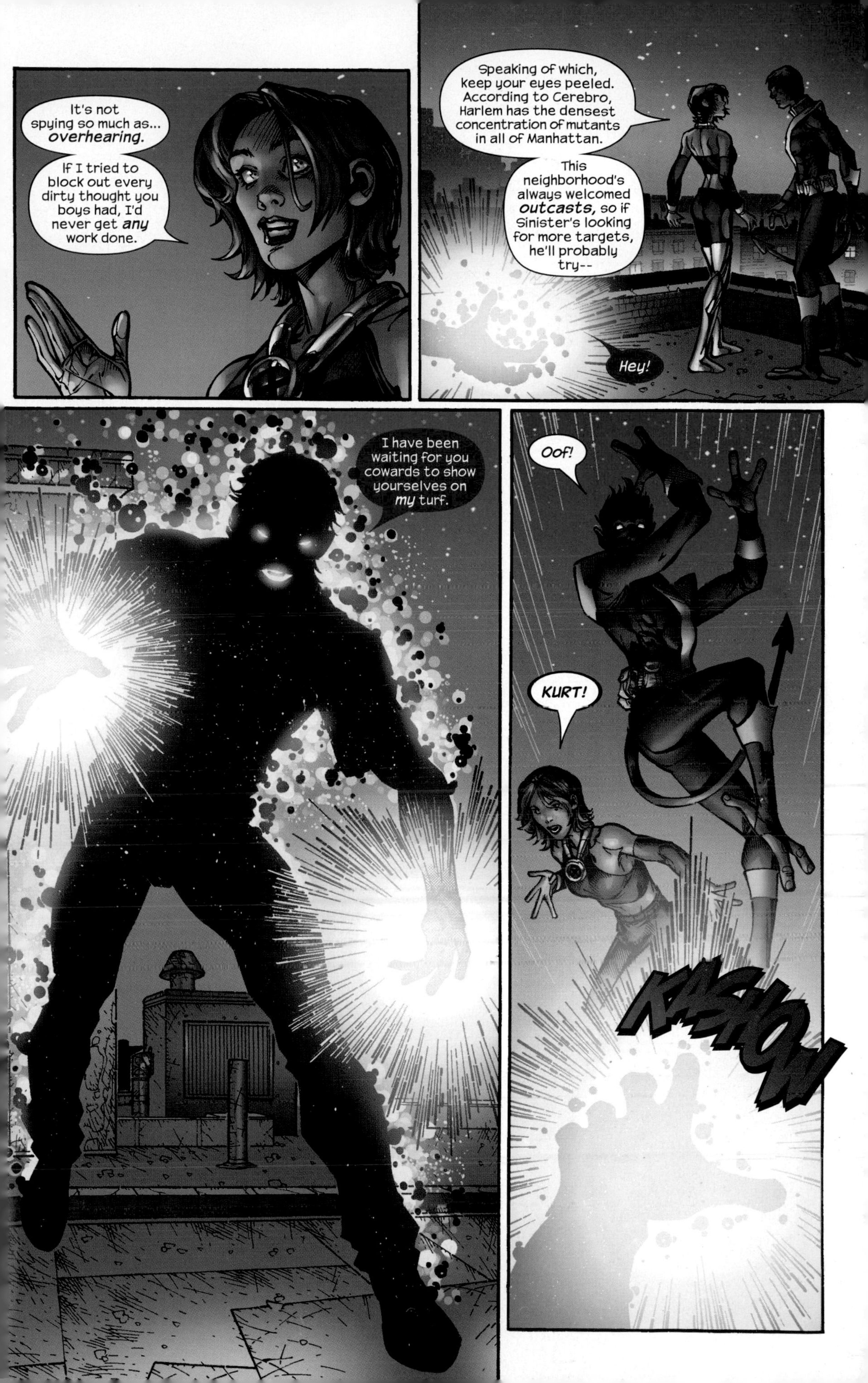
It's not spying so much as... overhearing.
If I tried to block out every dirty thought you boys had, I'd never get any work done.
Speaking of which, keep your eyes peeled. According to Cerebro, Harlem has the densest concentration of mutants in all of Manhattan.
This neighborhood's always welcomed outcasts, so if Sinister's looking for more targets, he'll probably try--
Hey!
I have been waiting for you cowards to show yourselves on my turf.
Oof!
KURT!
KASHOW

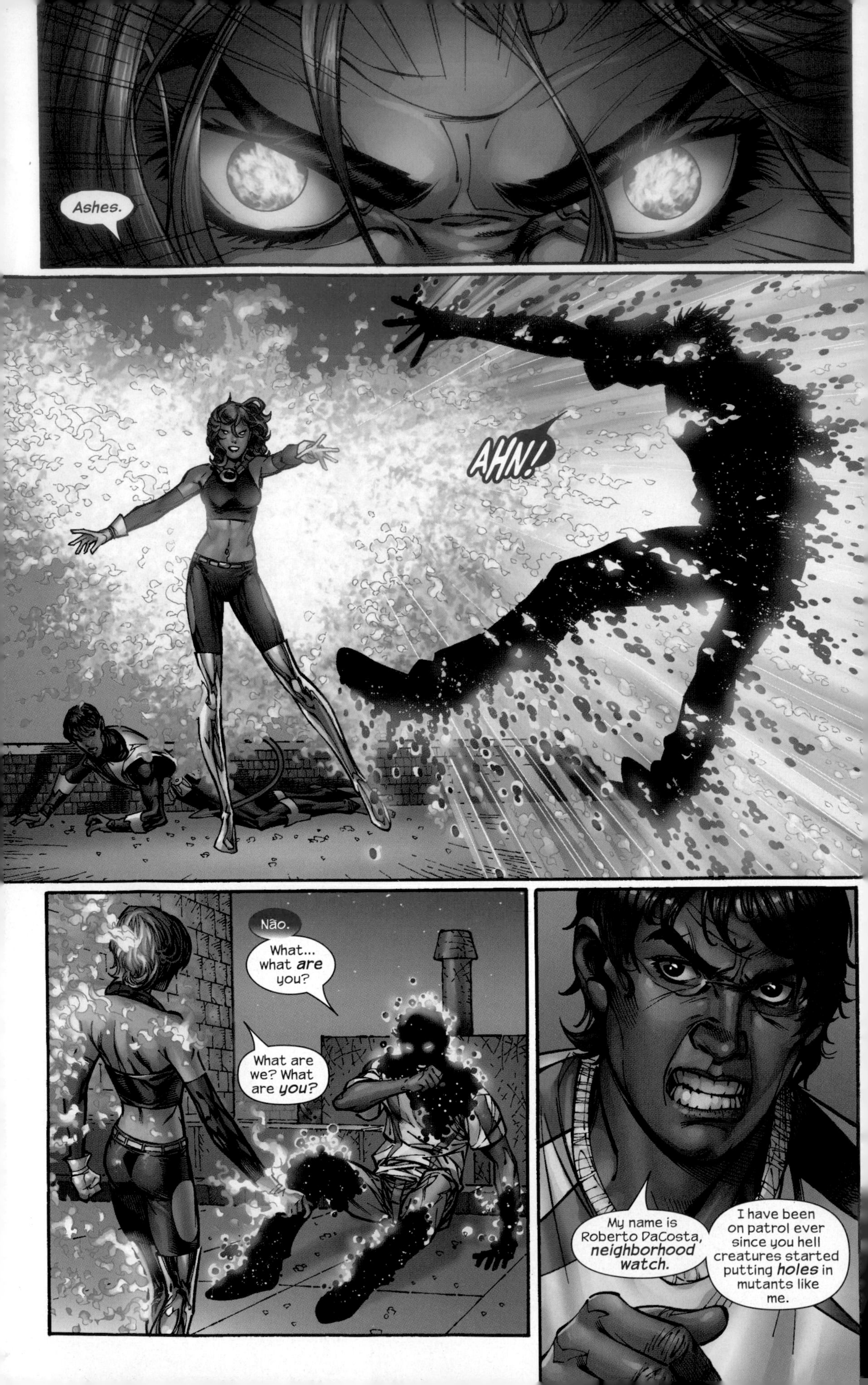
Ashes.
AHN!
Não.
What... what are you?
What are we? What are you?
My name is Roberto DaCosta, neighborhood watch.
I have been on patrol ever since you hell creatures started putting holes in mutants like me.

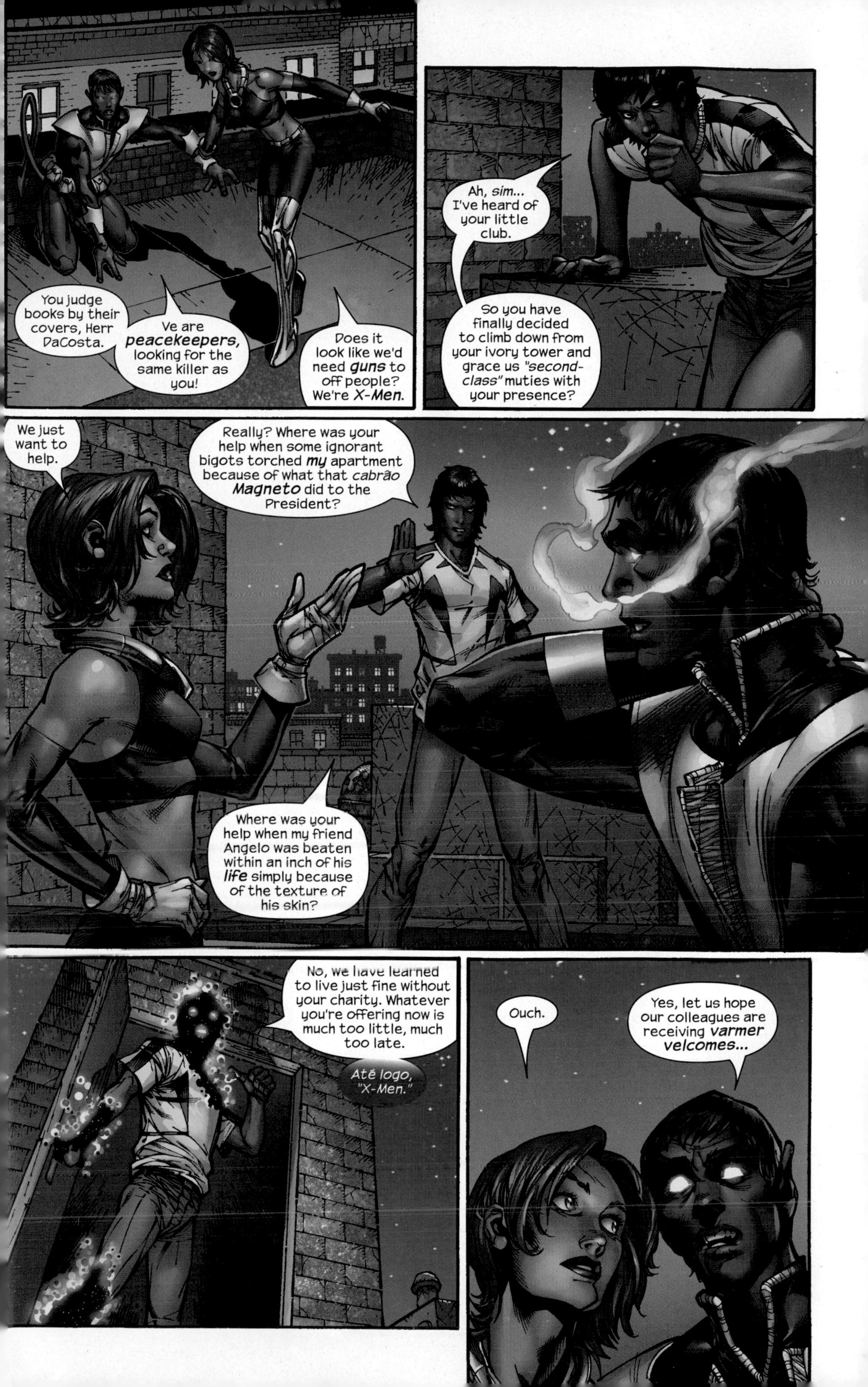

You judge books by their covers, Herr DaCosta.
Ve are *peacekeepers,* looking for the same killer as you!
Does it look like we'd need *guns* to off people? We're *X-Men.*
Ah, *sim...* I've heard of your little club.
So you have finally decided to climb down from your ivory tower and grace us *"second-class"* muties with your presence?
We just want to help.
Really? Where was your help when some ignorant bigots torched *my* apartment because of what that *cabrão* *Magneto* did to the President?
Where was your help when my friend Angelo was beaten within an inch of his *life* simply because of the texture of his skin?
No, we have learned to live just fine without your charity. Whatever you're offering now is much too little, much too late.
Até logo, "X-Men."
Ouch.
Yes, let us hope our colleagues are receiving *varmer velcomes...*

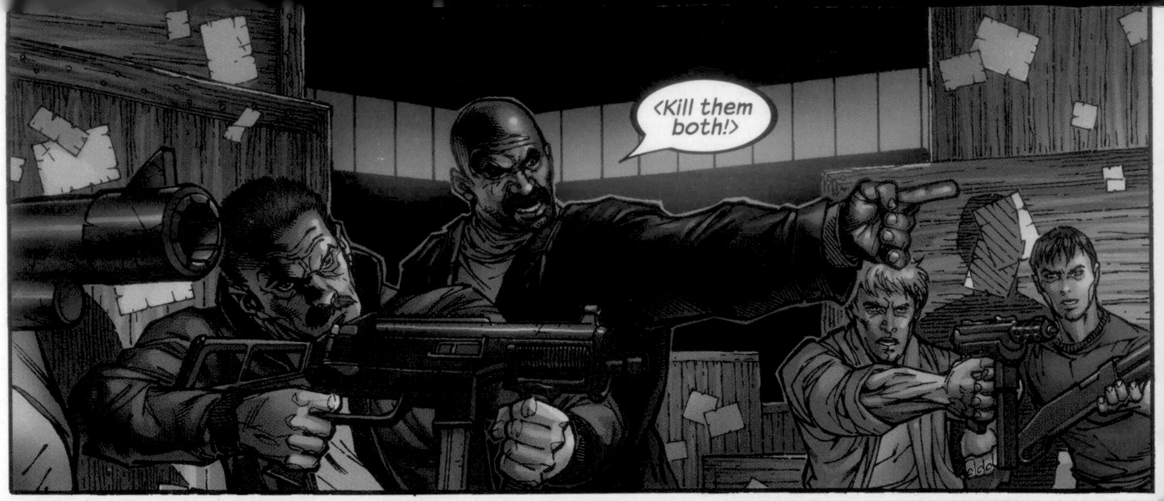
<Kill them both!>

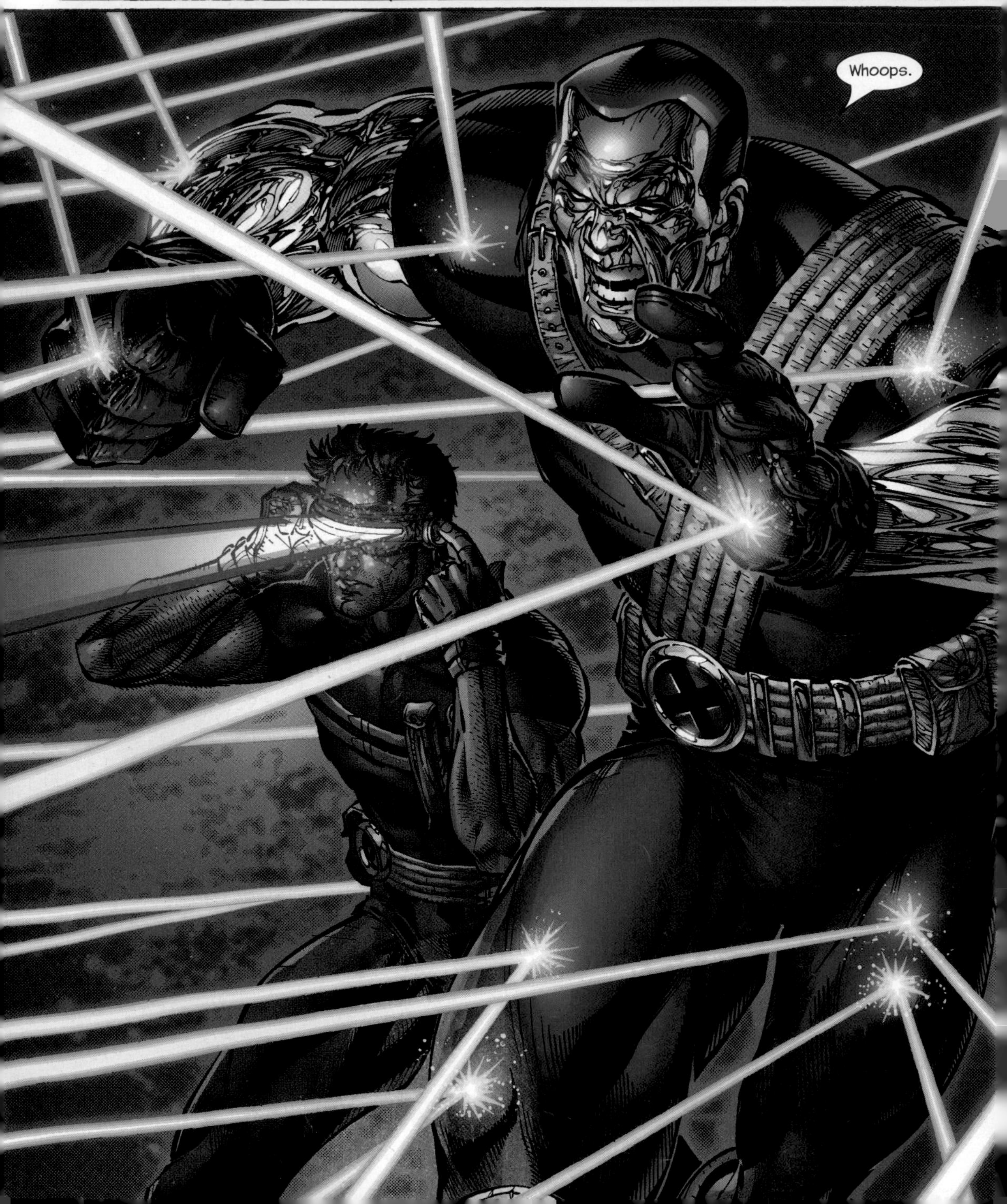
Whoops.

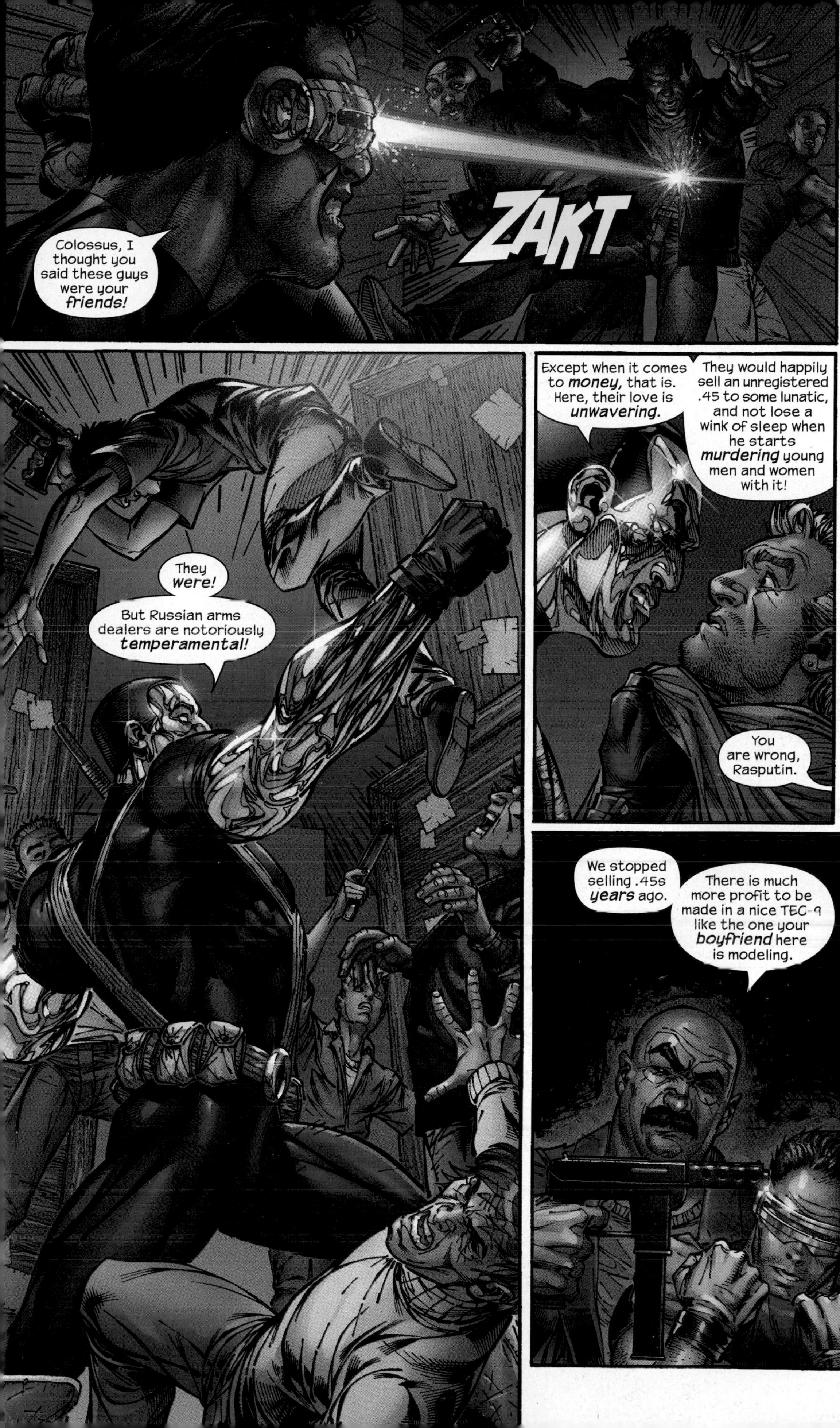

Colossus, I thought you said these guys were your friends!
ZAKT
They were!
But Russian arms dealers are notoriously temperamental!
Except when it comes to money, that is. Here, their love is unwavering.
They would happily sell an unregistered .45 to some lunatic, and not lose a wink of sleep when he starts murdering young men and women with it!
You are wrong, Rasputin.
We stopped selling .45s years ago.
There is much more profit to be made in a nice TEC-9 like the one your boyfriend here is modeling.

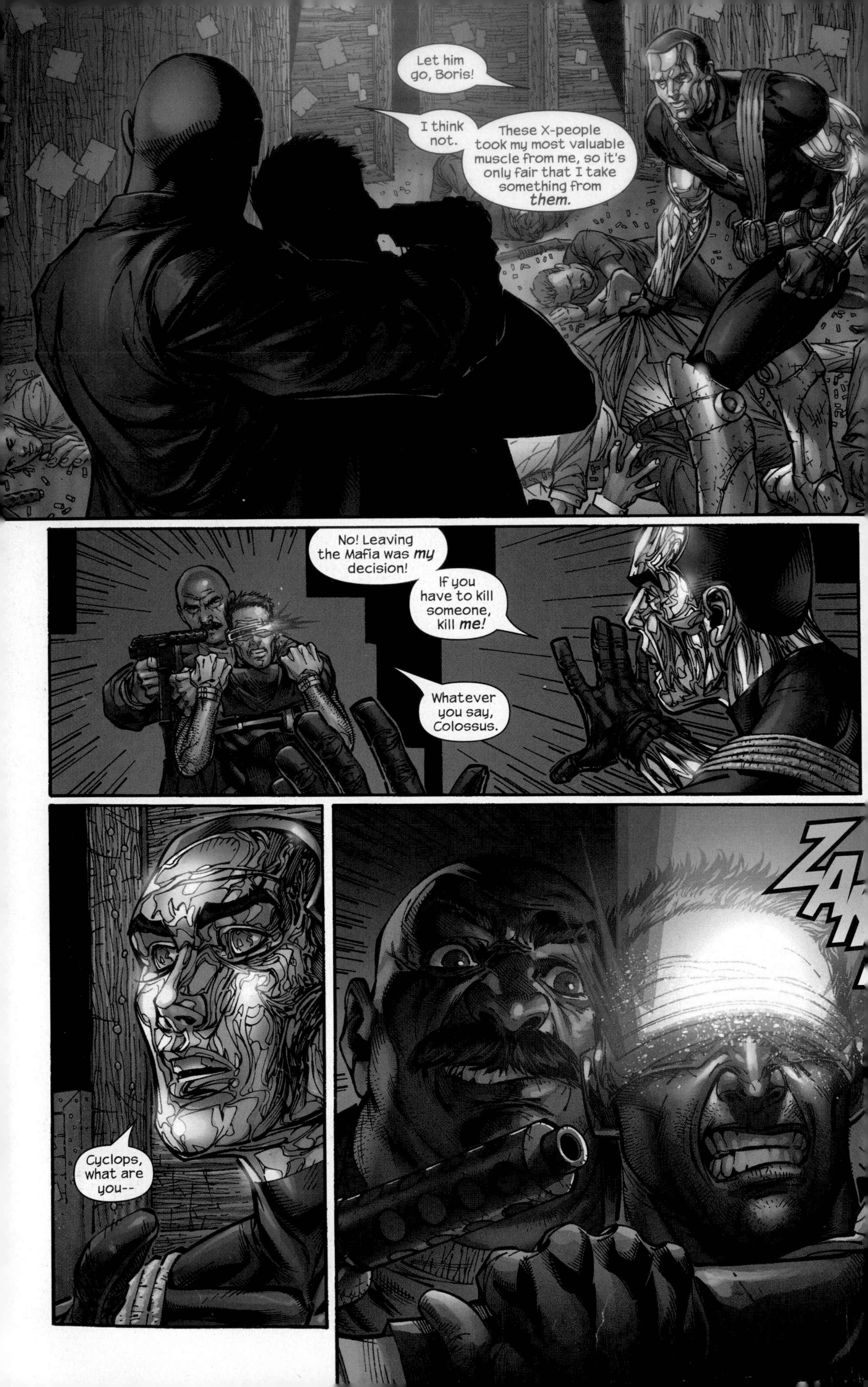
Let him go, Boris!
I think not.
These X-people took my most valuable muscle from me, so it's only fair that I take something from *them*.
No! Leaving the Mafia was *my* decision!
If you have to kill someone, kill *me!*
Whatever you say, Colossus.
Cyclops, what are you--

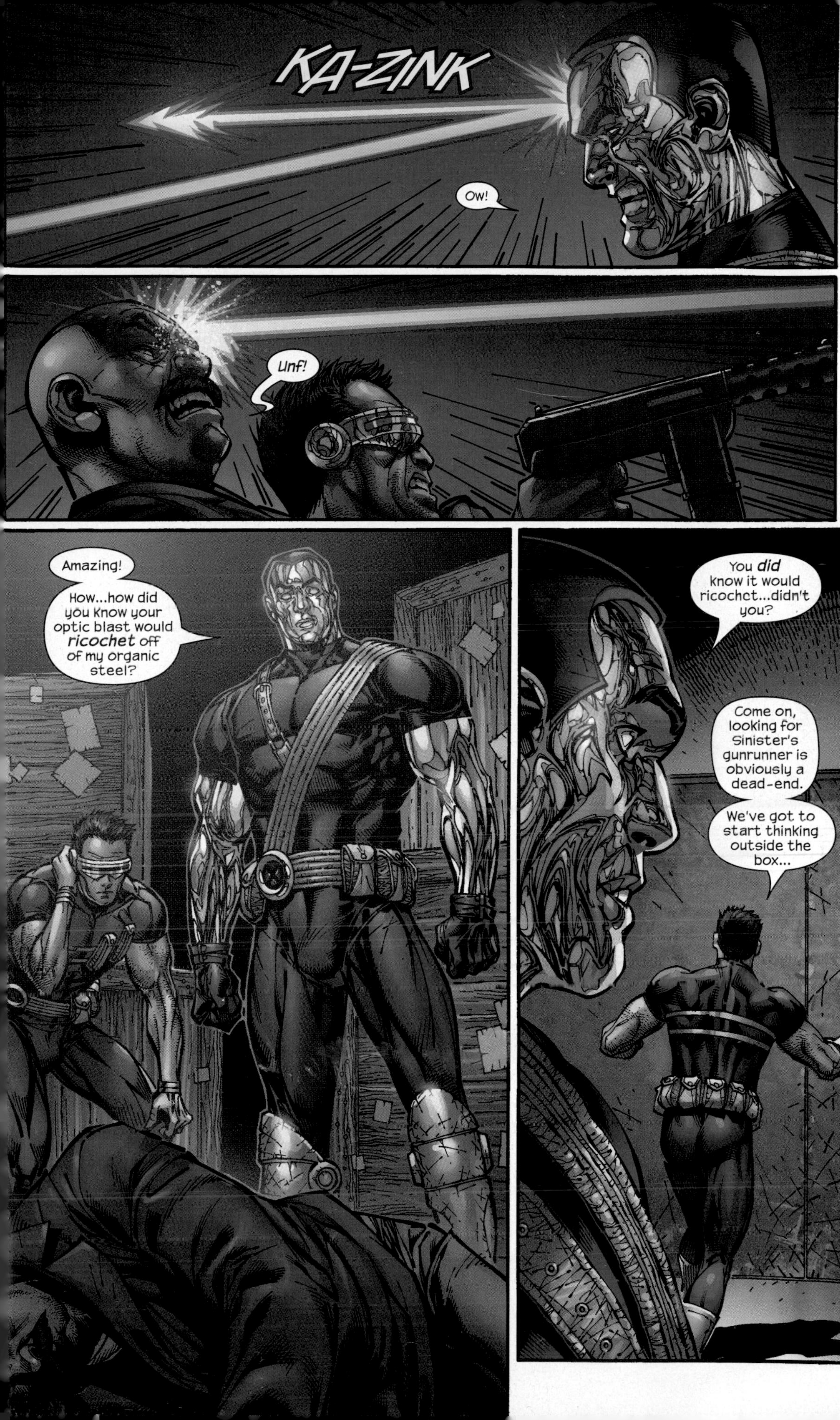
KA-ZINK
Ow!
Unf!
Amazing!
How...how did you know your optic blast would *ricochet* off of my organic steel?
You *did* know it would ricochet...didn't you?
Come on, looking for Sinister's gunrunner is obviously a dead-end.
We've got to start thinking outside the box...

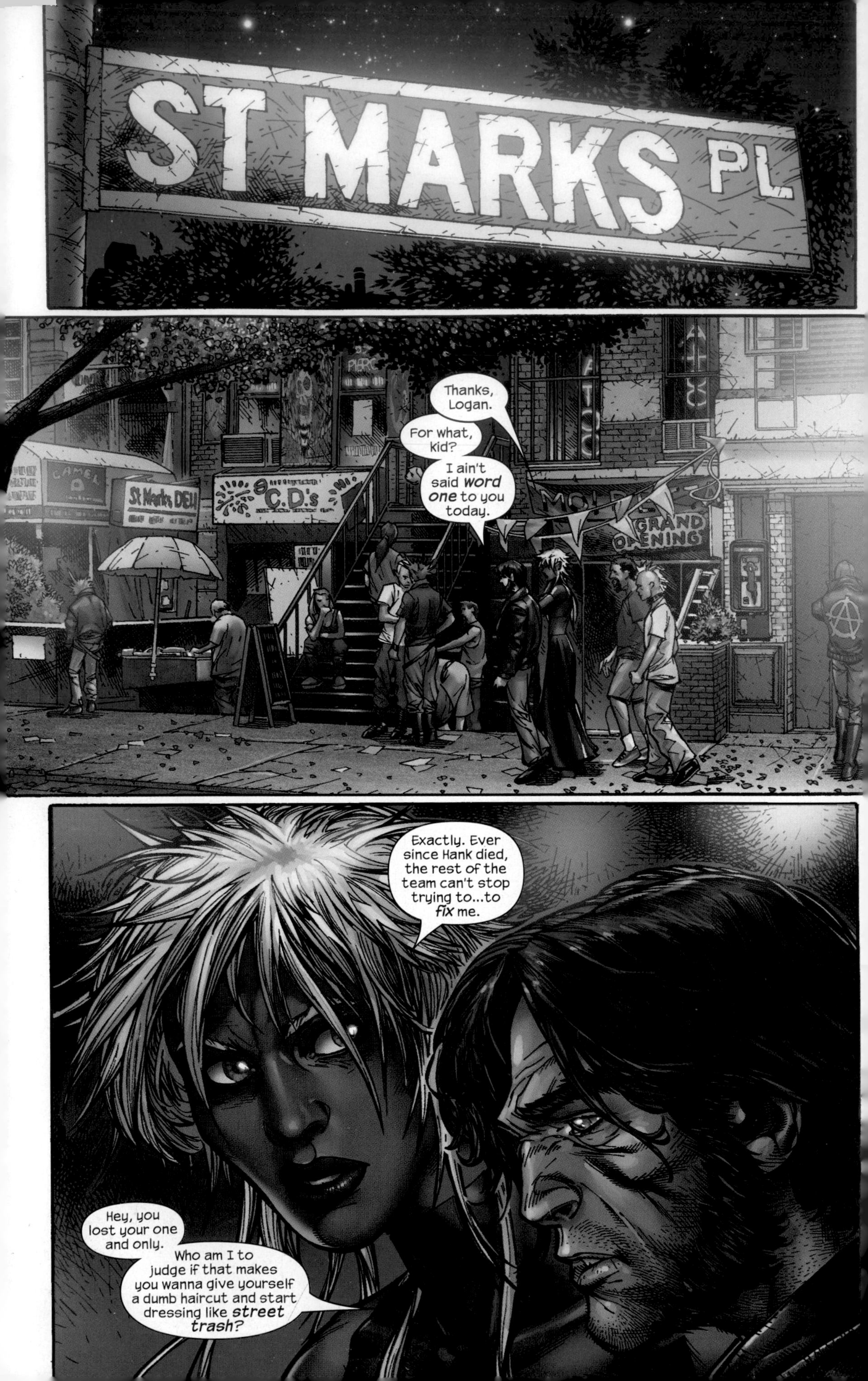
ST MARKS PL
St Marks DELI
C.D.'s
GRAND OPENING
Thanks, Logan.
For what, kid?
I ain't said *word one* to you today.
Exactly. Ever since Hank died, the rest of the team can't stop trying to...to *fix* me.
Hey, you lost your one and only.
Who am I to judge if that makes you wanna give yourself a dumb haircut and start dressing like *street trash*?

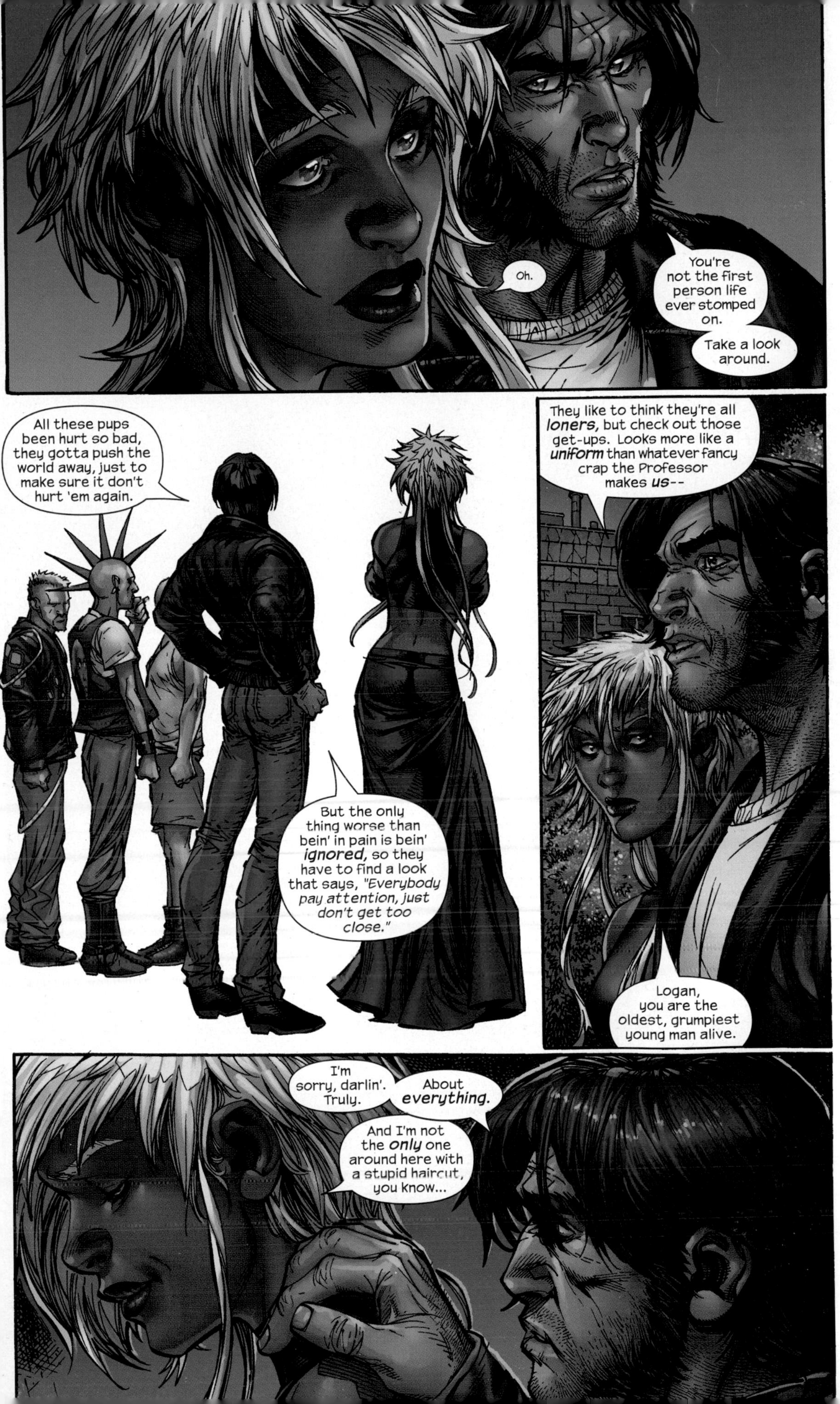
Oh.
You're not the first person life ever stomped on.
Take a look around.
All these pups been hurt so bad, they gotta push the world away, just to make sure it don't hurt 'em again.
But the only thing worse than bein' in pain is bein' *ignored,* so they have to find a look that says, *"Everybody pay attention, just don't get too close."*
They like to think they're all *loners,* but check out those get-ups. Looks more like a *uniform* than whatever fancy crap the Professor makes *us*--
Logan, you are the oldest, grumpiest young man alive.
I'm sorry, darlin'. Truly.
About *everything.*
And I'm not the *only* one around here with a stupid haircut, you know...

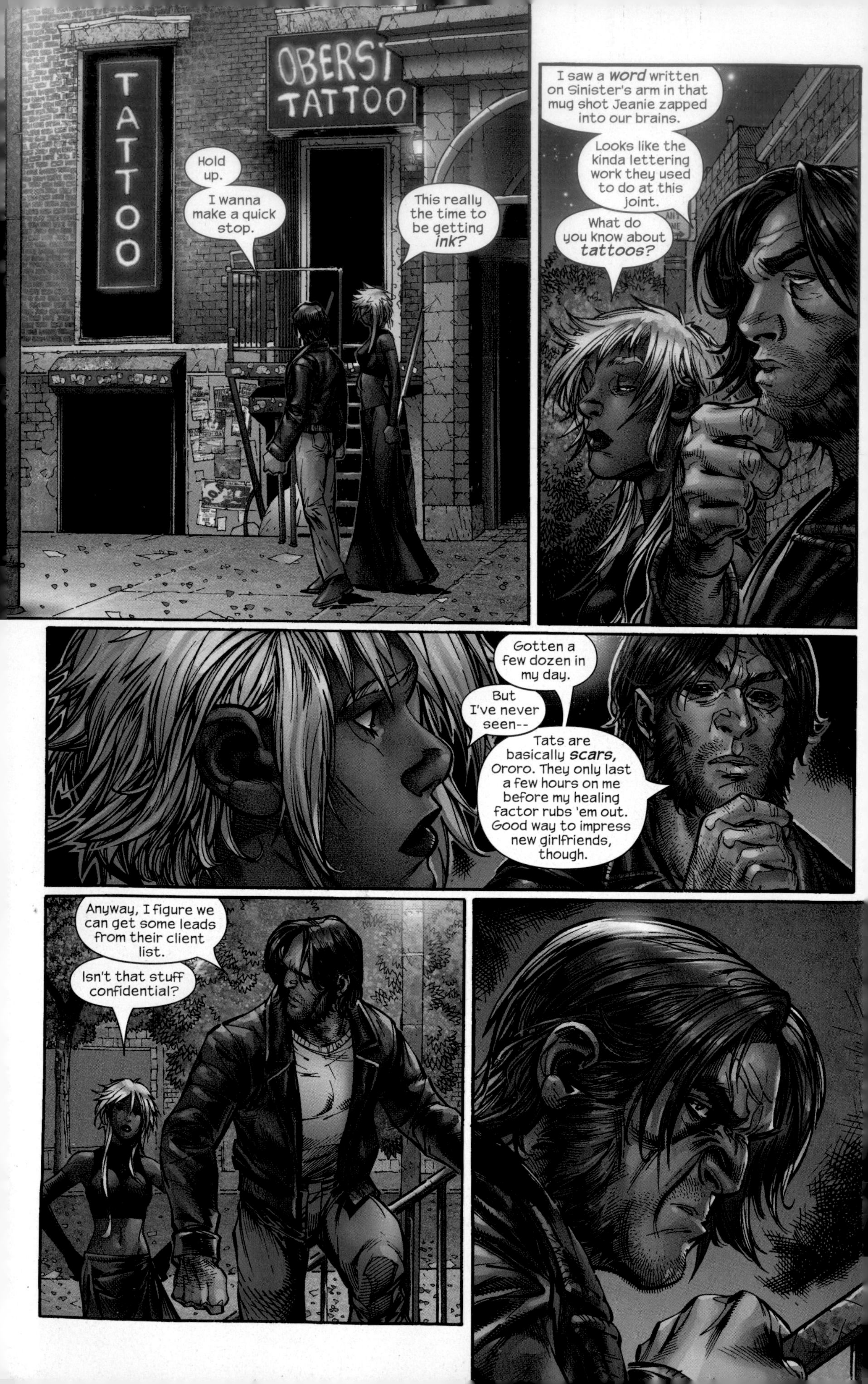

OBERST TATTOO
TATTOO
Hold up.
I wanna make a quick stop.
This really the time to be getting *ink?*
I saw a *word* written on Sinister's arm in that mug shot Jeanie zapped into our brains.
Looks like the kinda lettering work they used to do at this joint.
What do you know about *tattoos?*
Gotten a few dozen in my day.
But I've never seen--
Tats are basically *scars,* Ororo. They only last a few hours on me before my healing factor rubs 'em out. Good way to impress new girlfriends, though.
Anyway, I figure we can get some leads from their client list.
Isn't that stuff confidential?

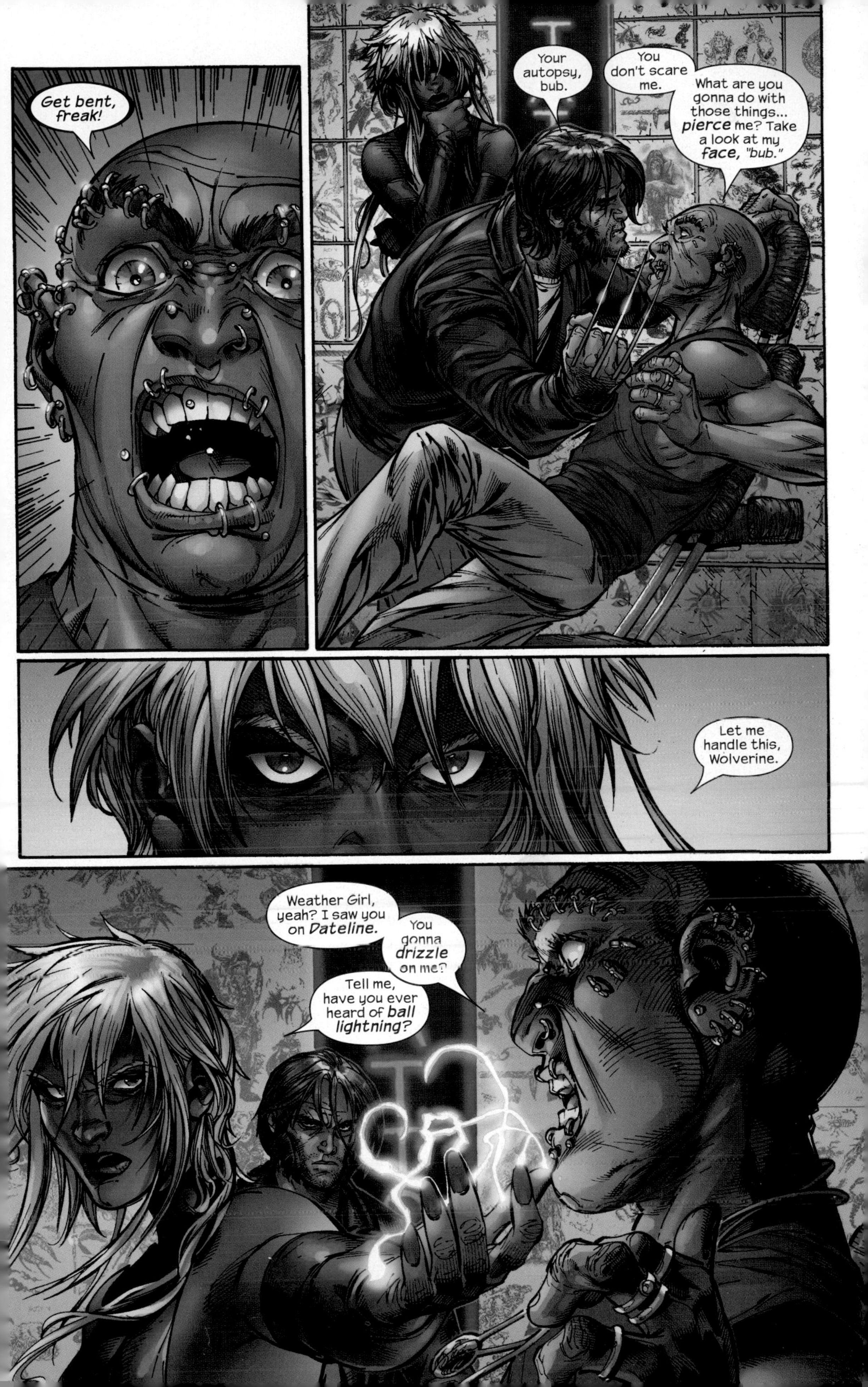
Get bent, freak!
Your autopsy, bub.
You don't scare me.
What are you gonna do with those things... *pierce* me? Take a look at my *face,* "bub."
Let me handle this, Wolverine.
Weather Girl, yeah? I saw you on *Dateline.*
You gonna *drizzle* on me?
Tell me, have you ever heard of *ball lightning*?

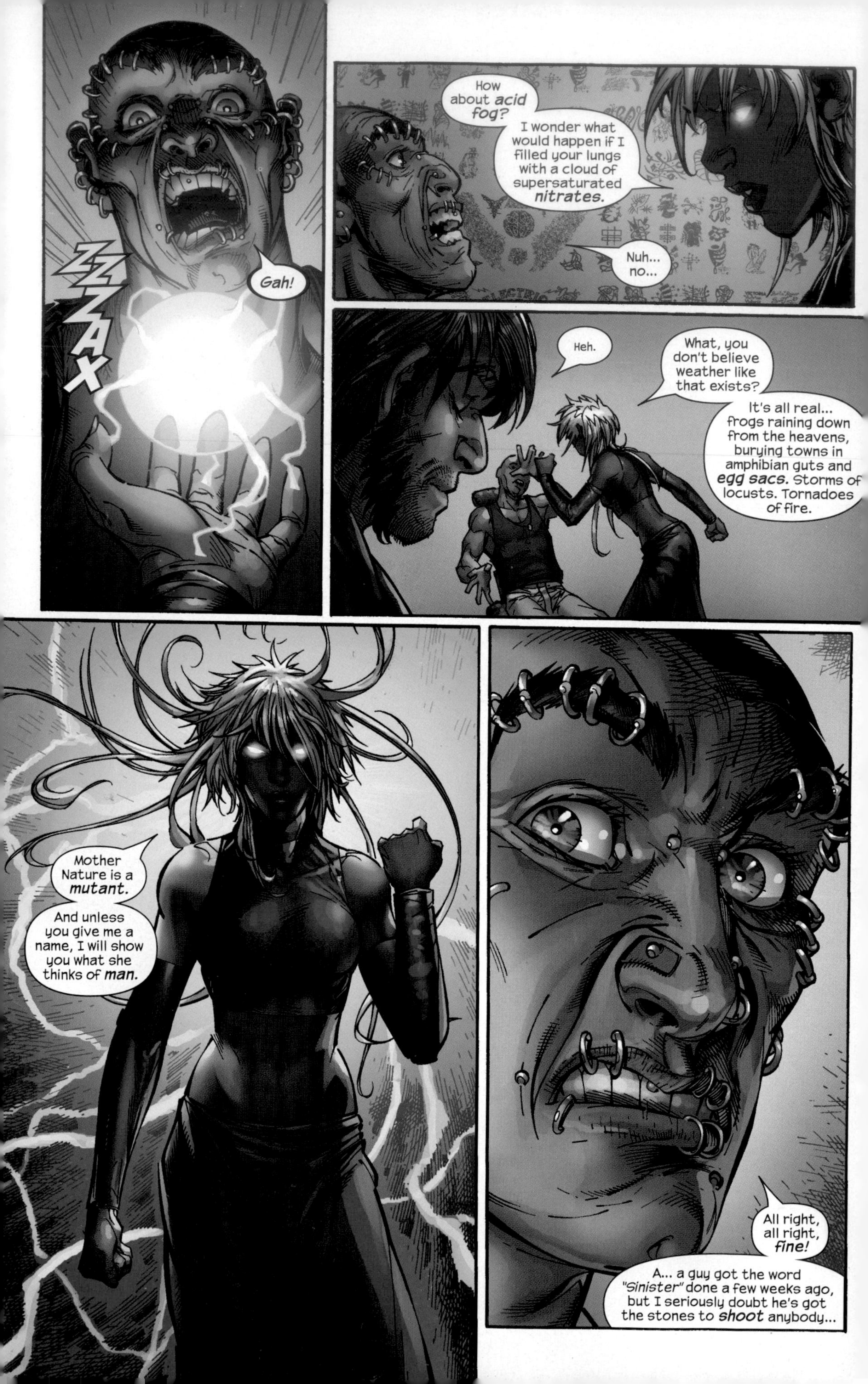
ZZZAX
Gah!
How about acid fog?
I wonder what would happen if I filled your lungs with a cloud of supersaturated nitrates.
Nuh... no...
Heh.
What, you don't believe weather like that exists?
It's all real... frogs raining down from the heavens, burying towns in amphibian guts and egg sacs. Storms of locusts. Tornadoes of fire.
Mother Nature is a mutant.
And unless you give me a name, I will show you what she thinks of man.
All right, all right, fine!
A... a guy got the word "Sinister" done a few weeks ago, but I seriously doubt he's got the stones to shoot anybody...

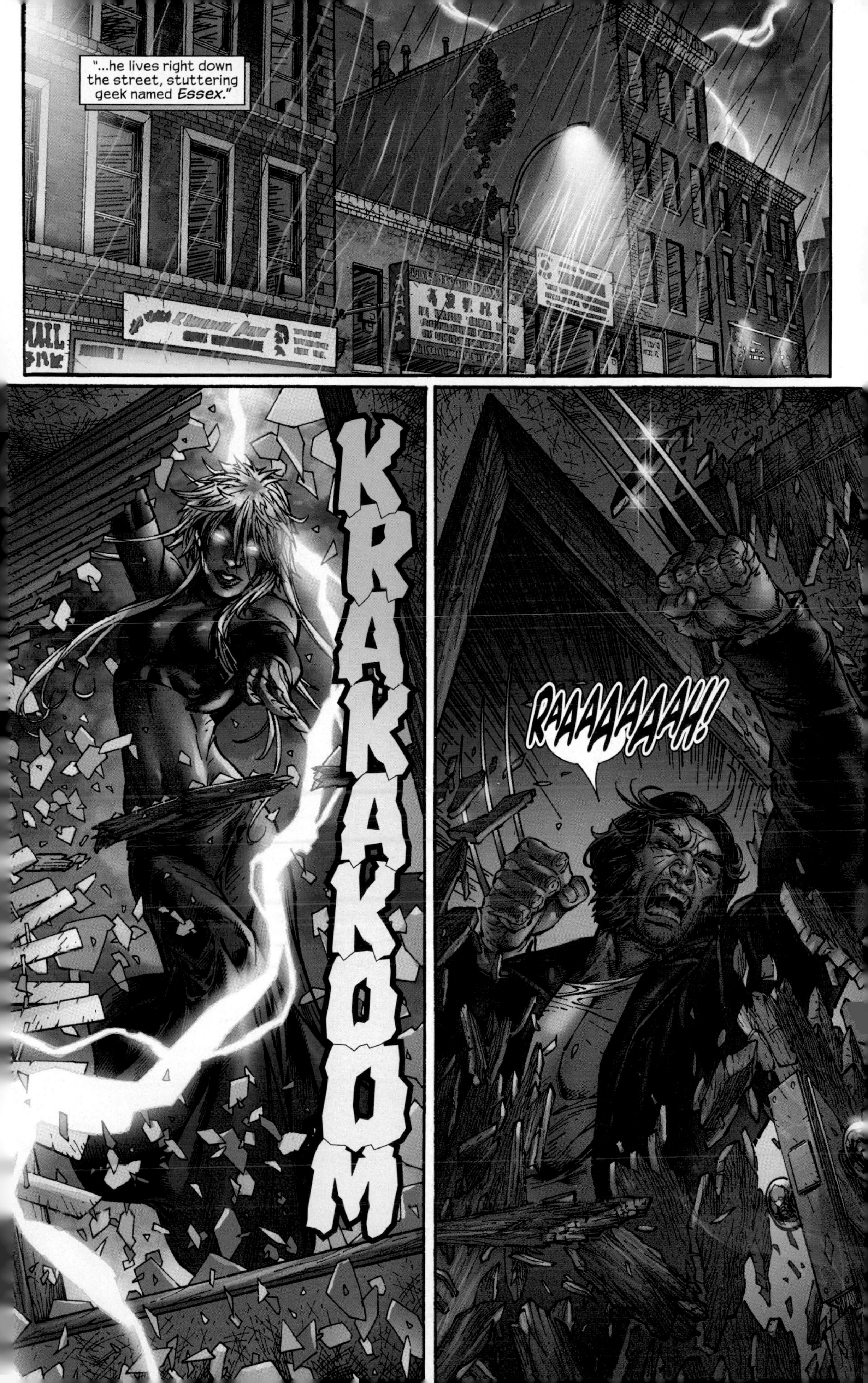
"...he lives right down the street, stuttering geek named *Essex.*"
KRAKOOM
RAAAAAAAAH!

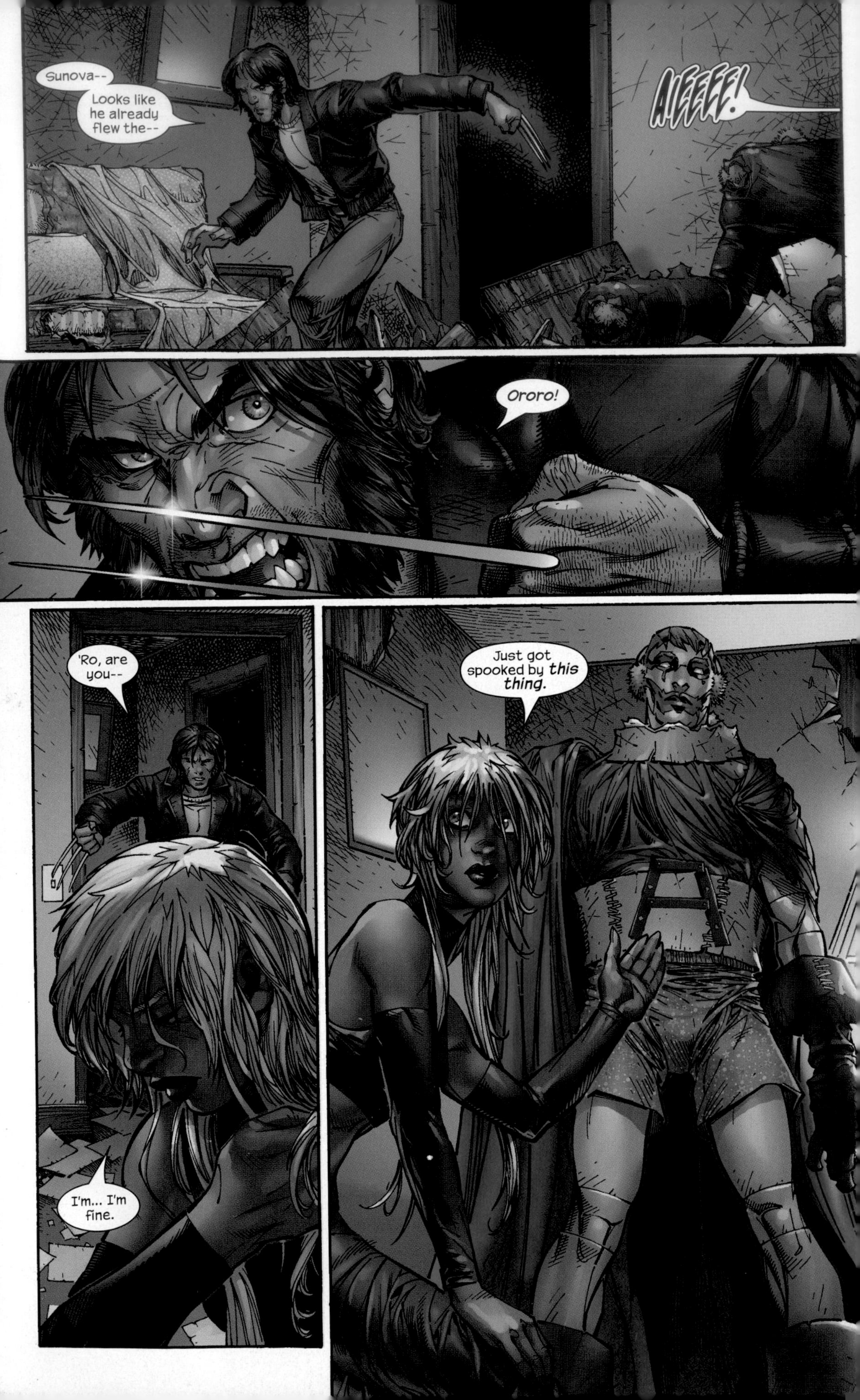
Sunova--
Looks like he already flew the--
AIEEEE!
Ororo!
'Ro, are you--
I'm... I'm fine.
Just got spooked by *this thing.*

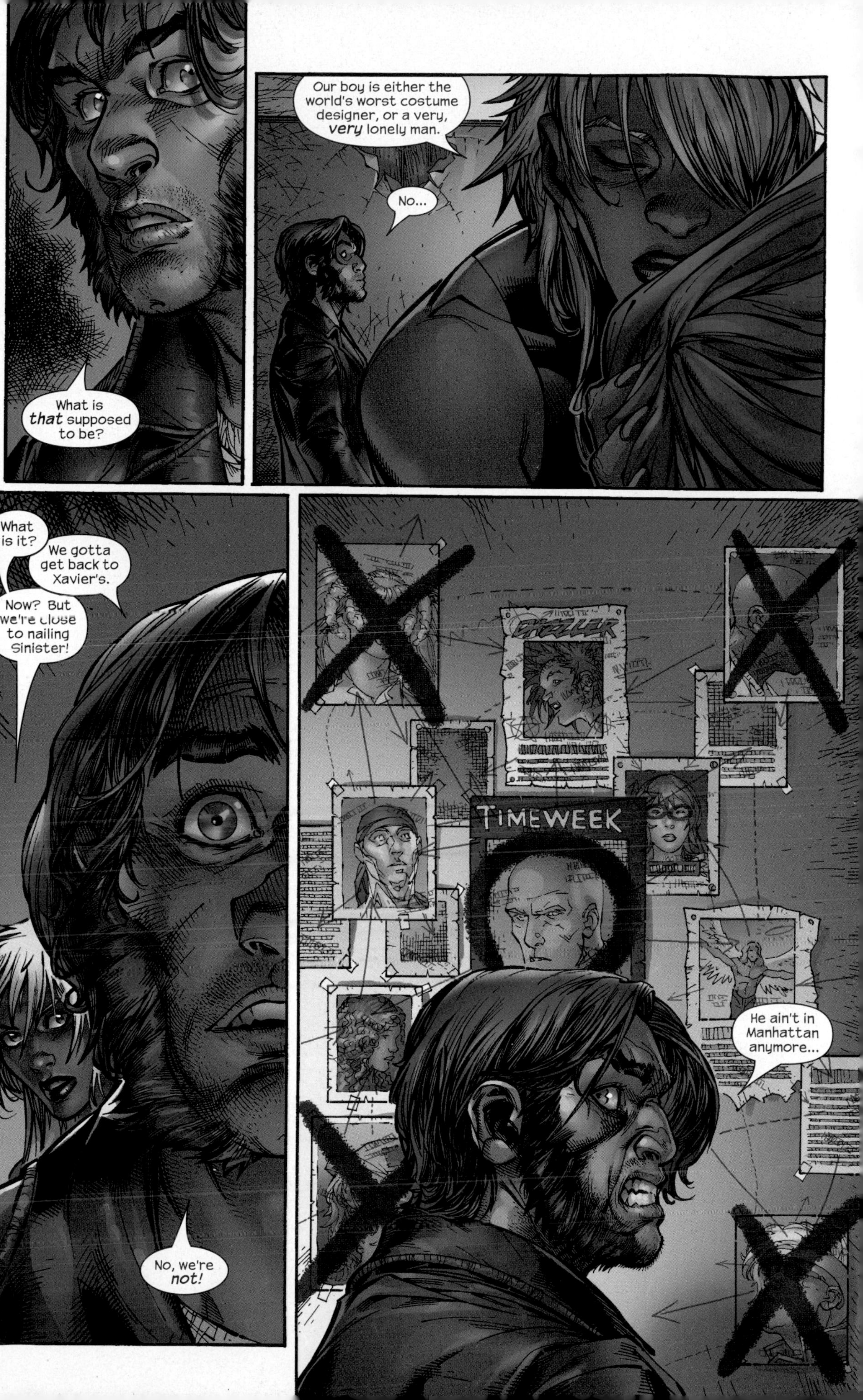
What is *that* supposed to be?
Our boy is either the world's worst costume designer, or a very, *very* lonely man.
No...
What is it?
We gotta get back to Xavier's.
Now? But we're close to nailing Sinister!
No, we're *not!*
TIMEWEEK
He ain't in Manhattan anymore...

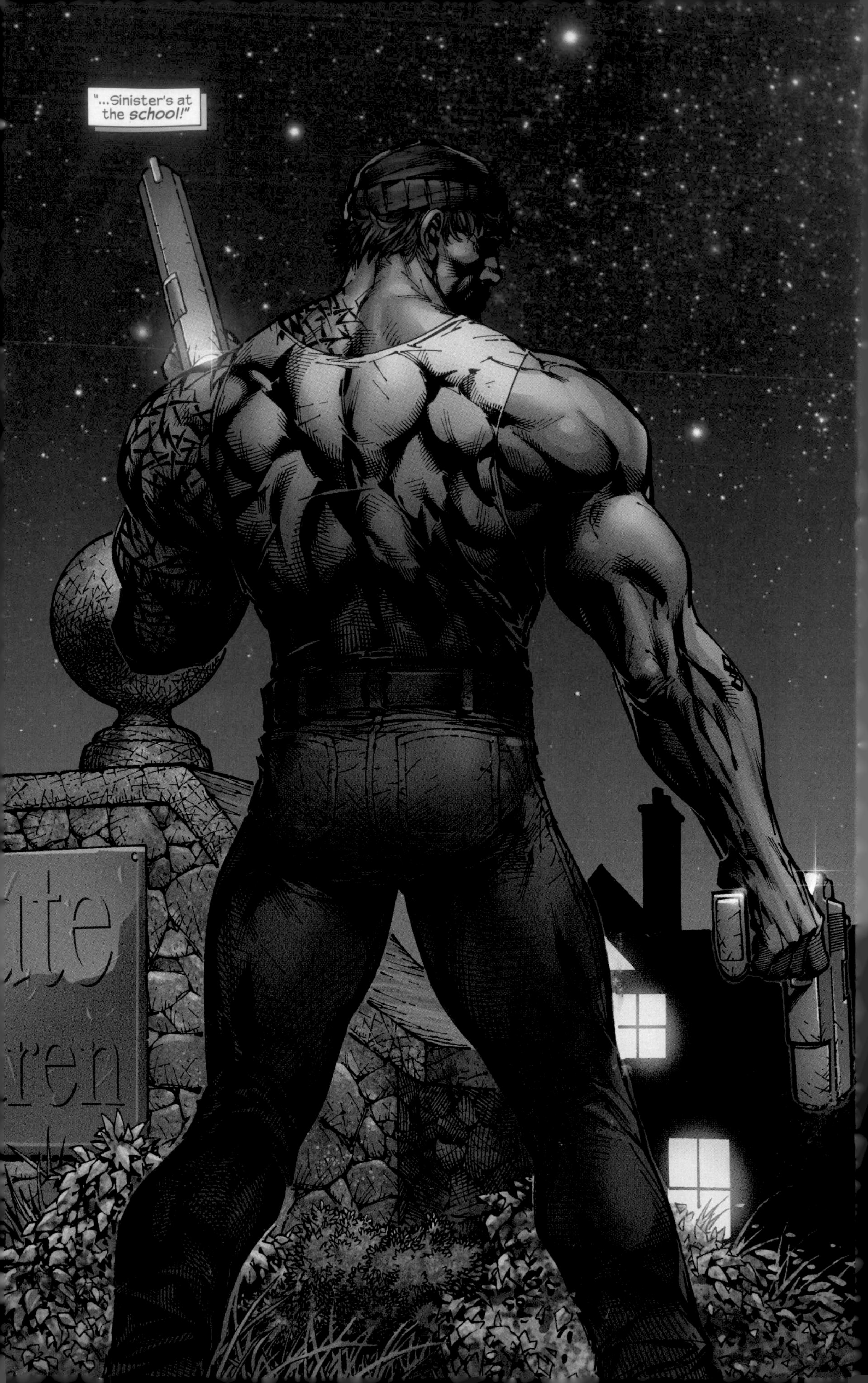
"...Sinister's at the school!"

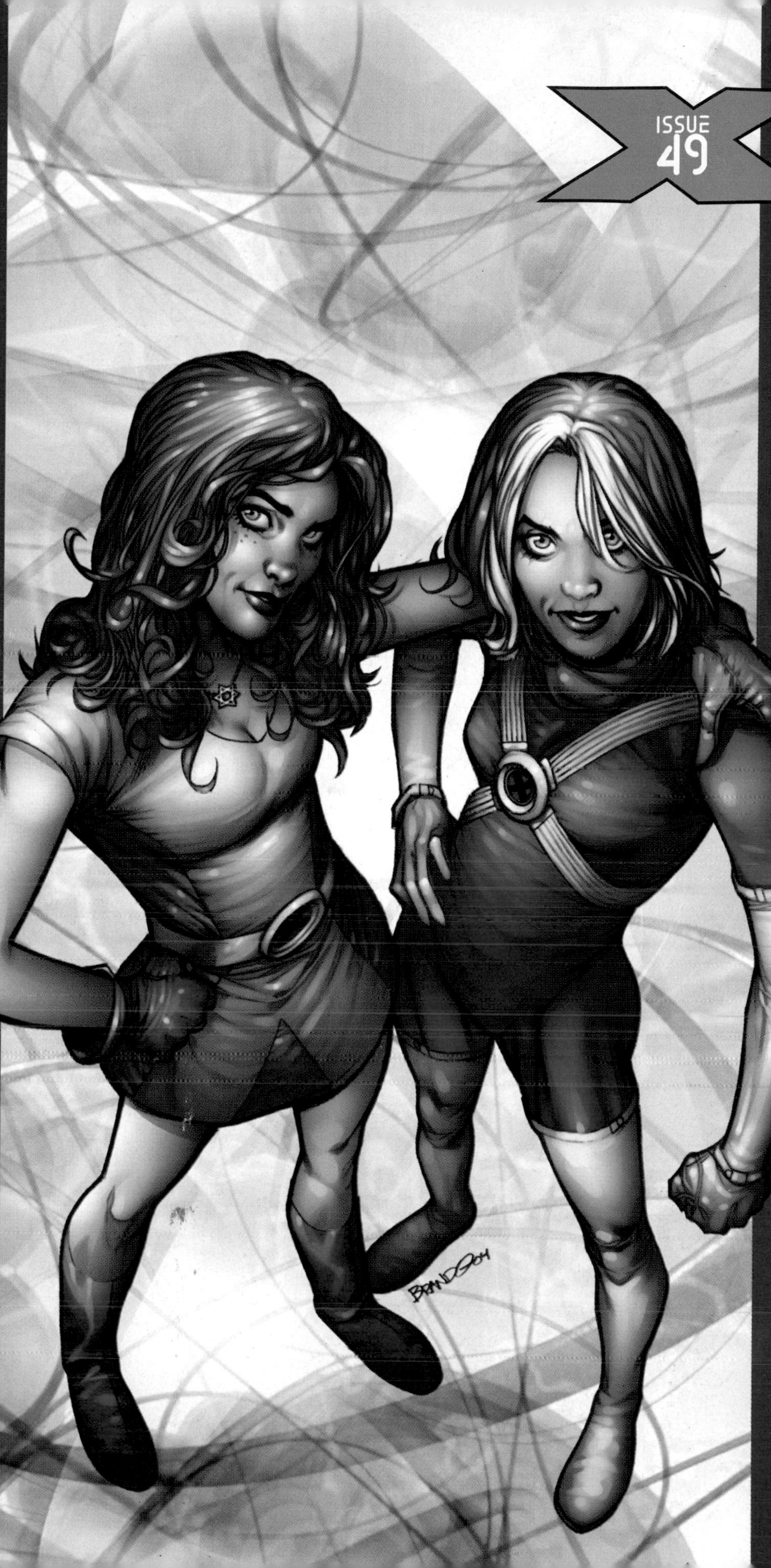
ISSUE
49

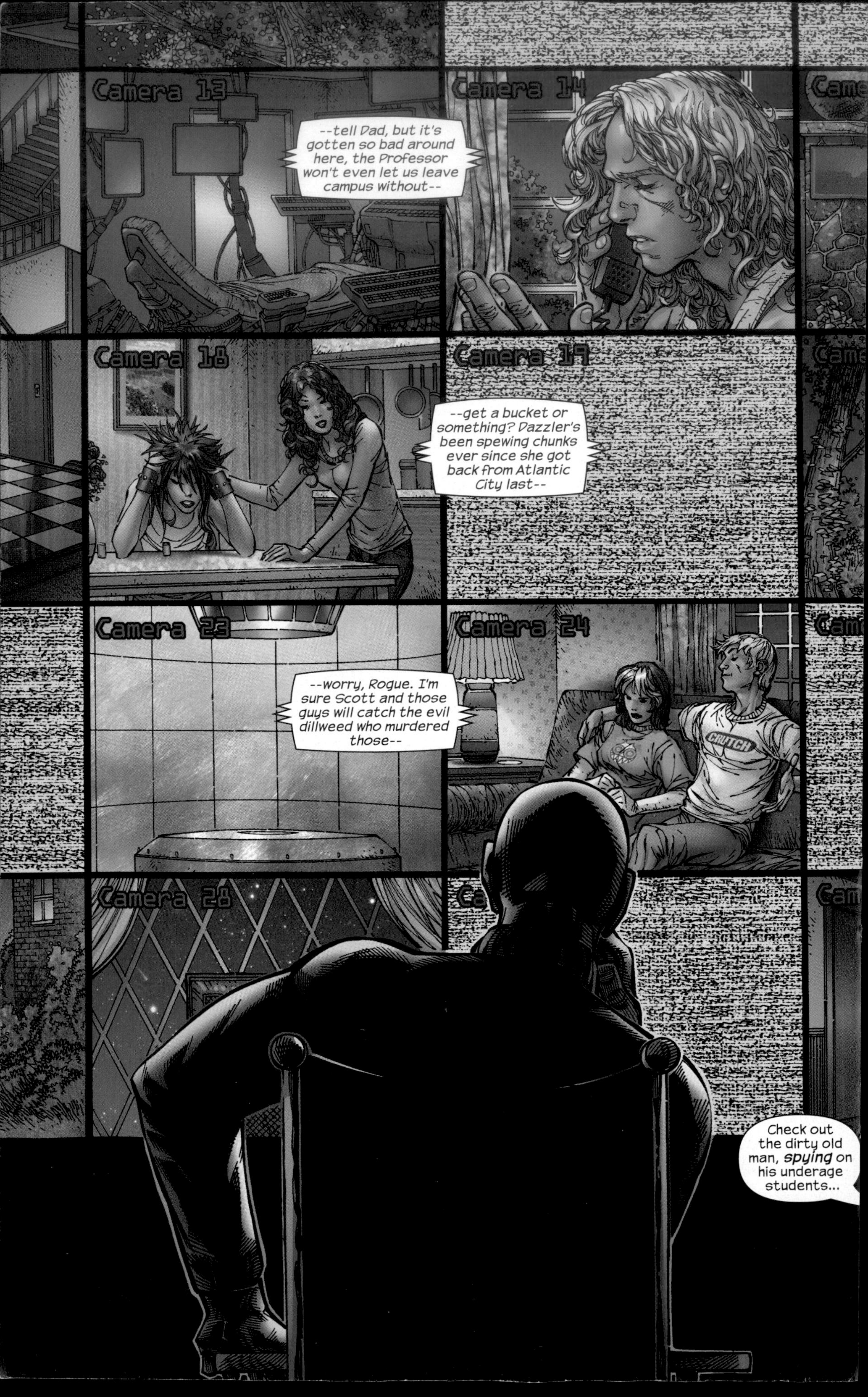
Camera 13
--tell Dad, but it's gotten so bad around here, the Professor won't even let us leave campus without--
Camera 14
Camera 18
Camera 19
--get a bucket or something? Dazzler's been spewing chunks ever since she got back from Atlantic City last--
Camera 23
--worry, Rogue. I'm sure Scott and those guys will catch the evil dillweed who murdered those--
Camera 24
CRUTCH
Camera 28
Check out the dirty old man, *spying* on his underage students...

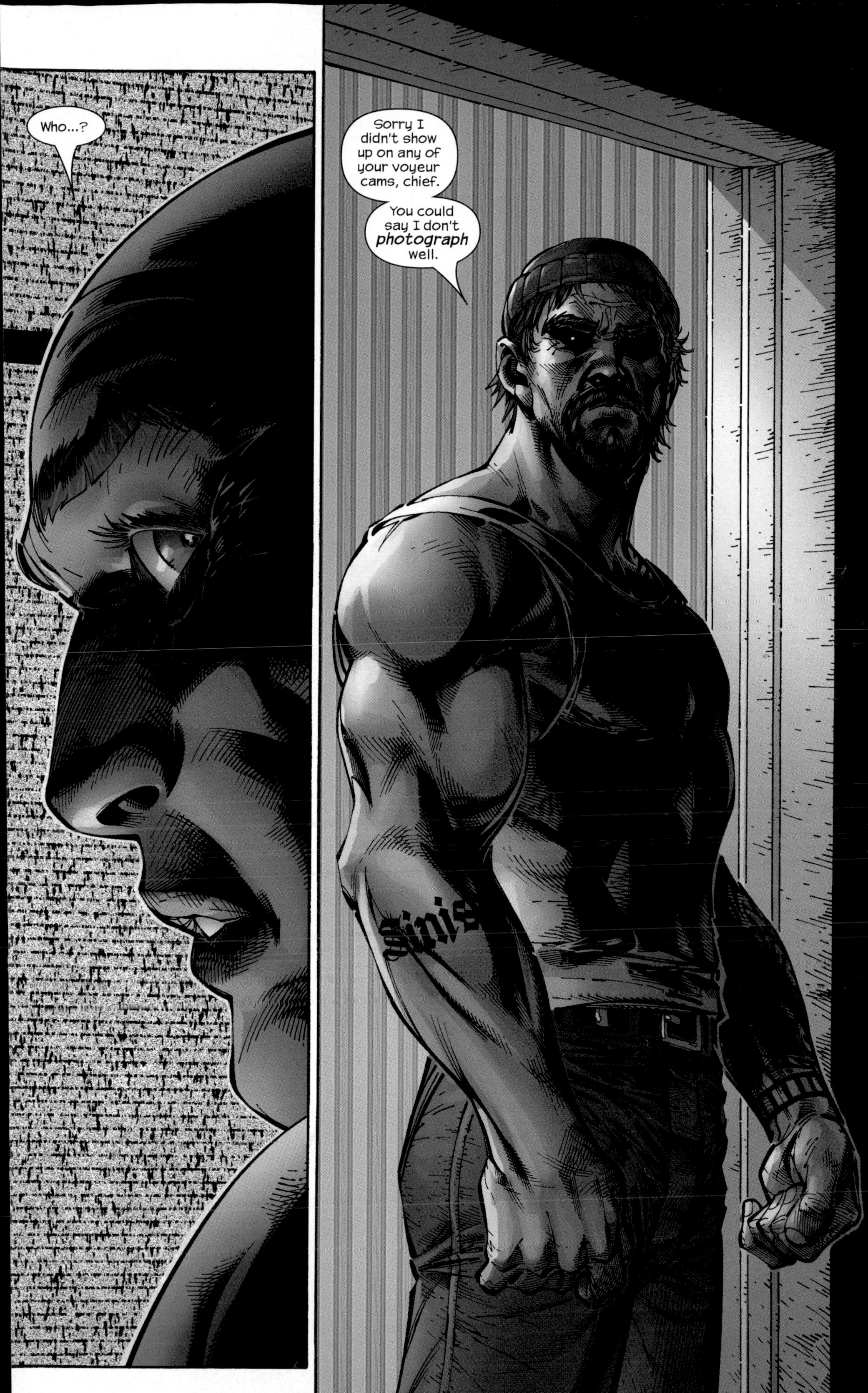

Who...?
Sorry I didn't show up on any of your voyeur cams, chief.
You could say I don't *photograph* well.

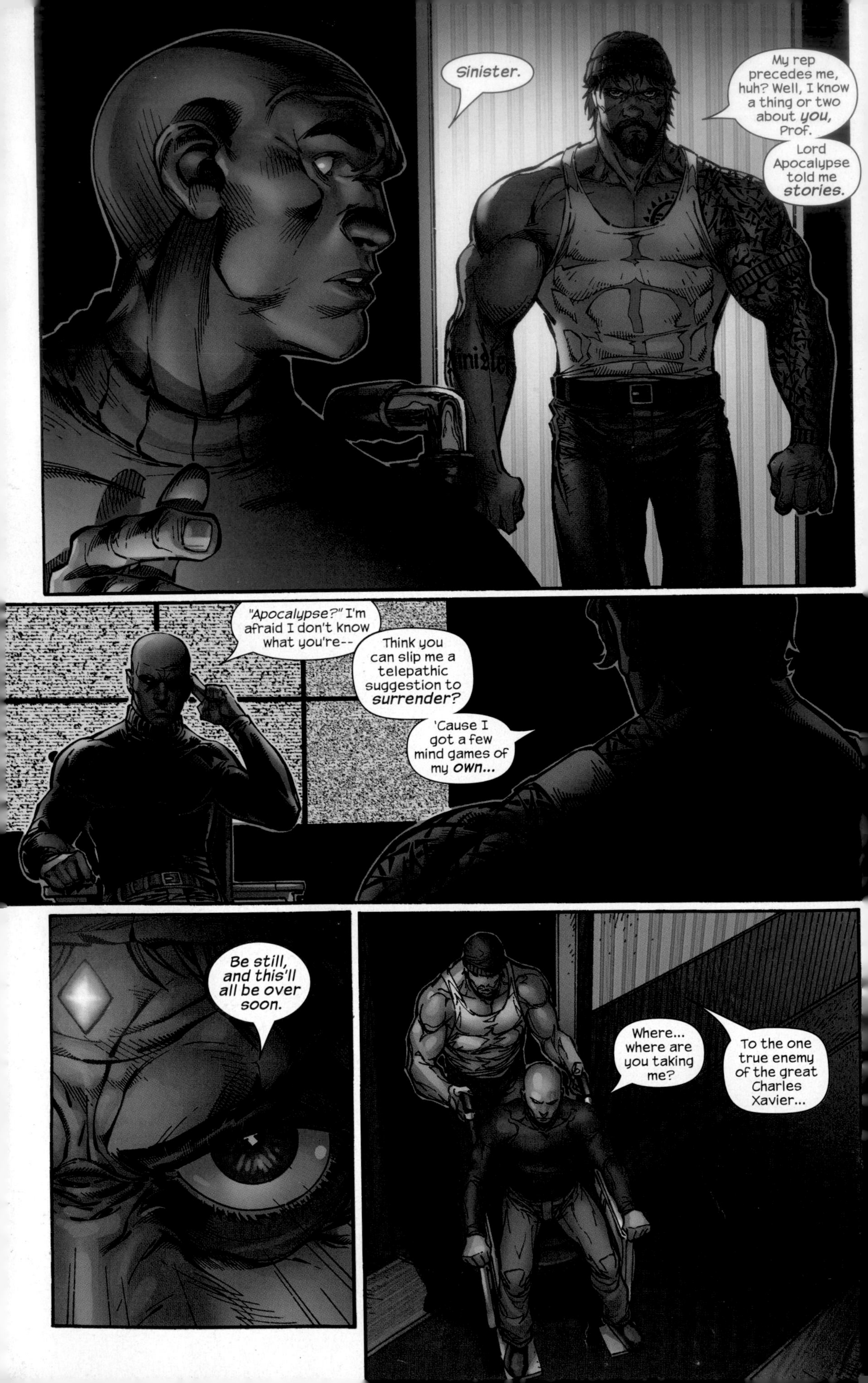
Sinister.
My rep precedes me, huh? Well, I know a thing or two about *you*, Prof.
Lord Apocalypse told me *stories*.
"Apocalypse?" I'm afraid I don't know what you're--
Think you can slip me a telepathic suggestion to *surrender*?
'Cause I got a few mind games of my *own*...
Be still, and this'll all be over soon.
Where... where are you taking me?
To the one true enemy of the great Charles Xavier...

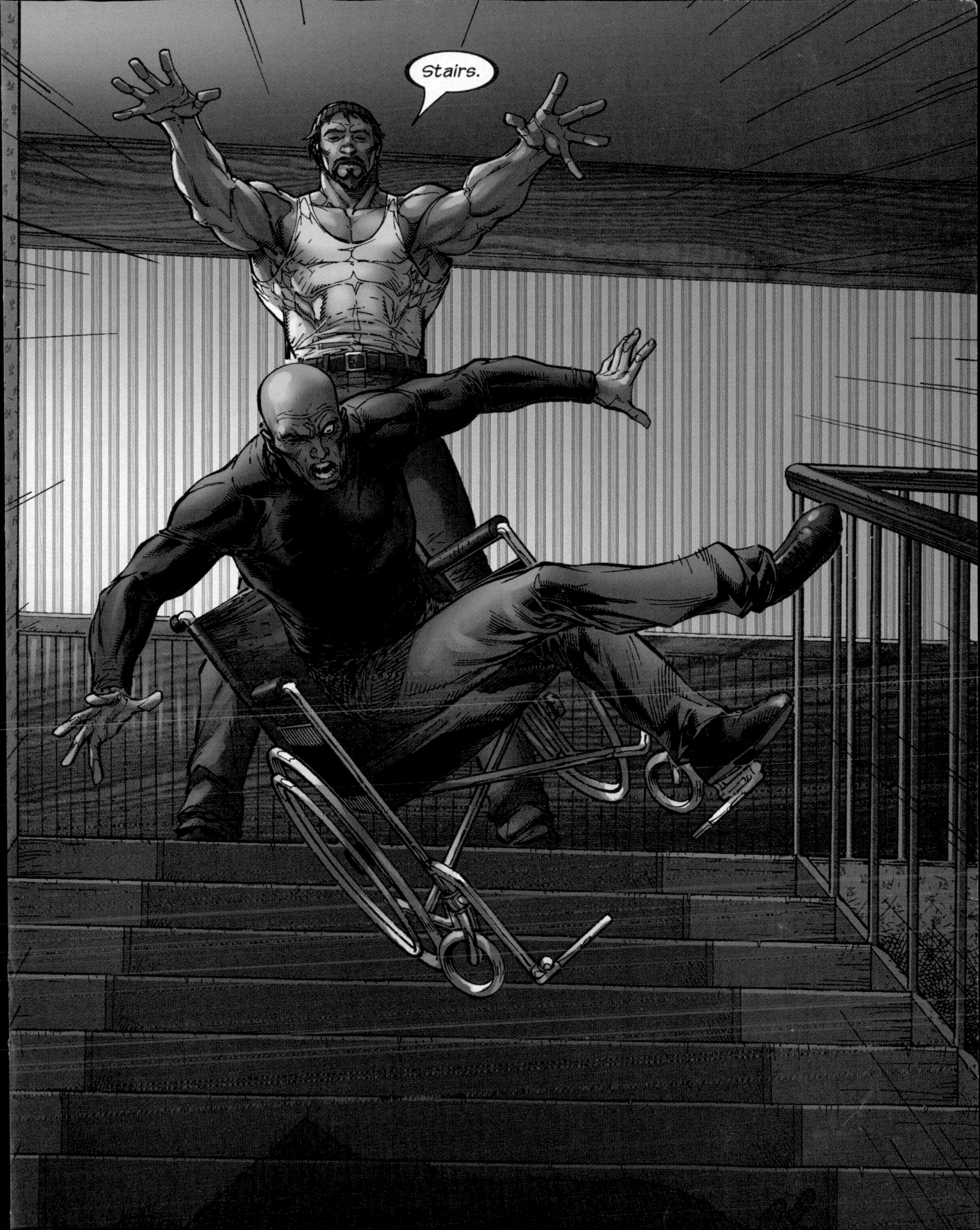
Stairs.

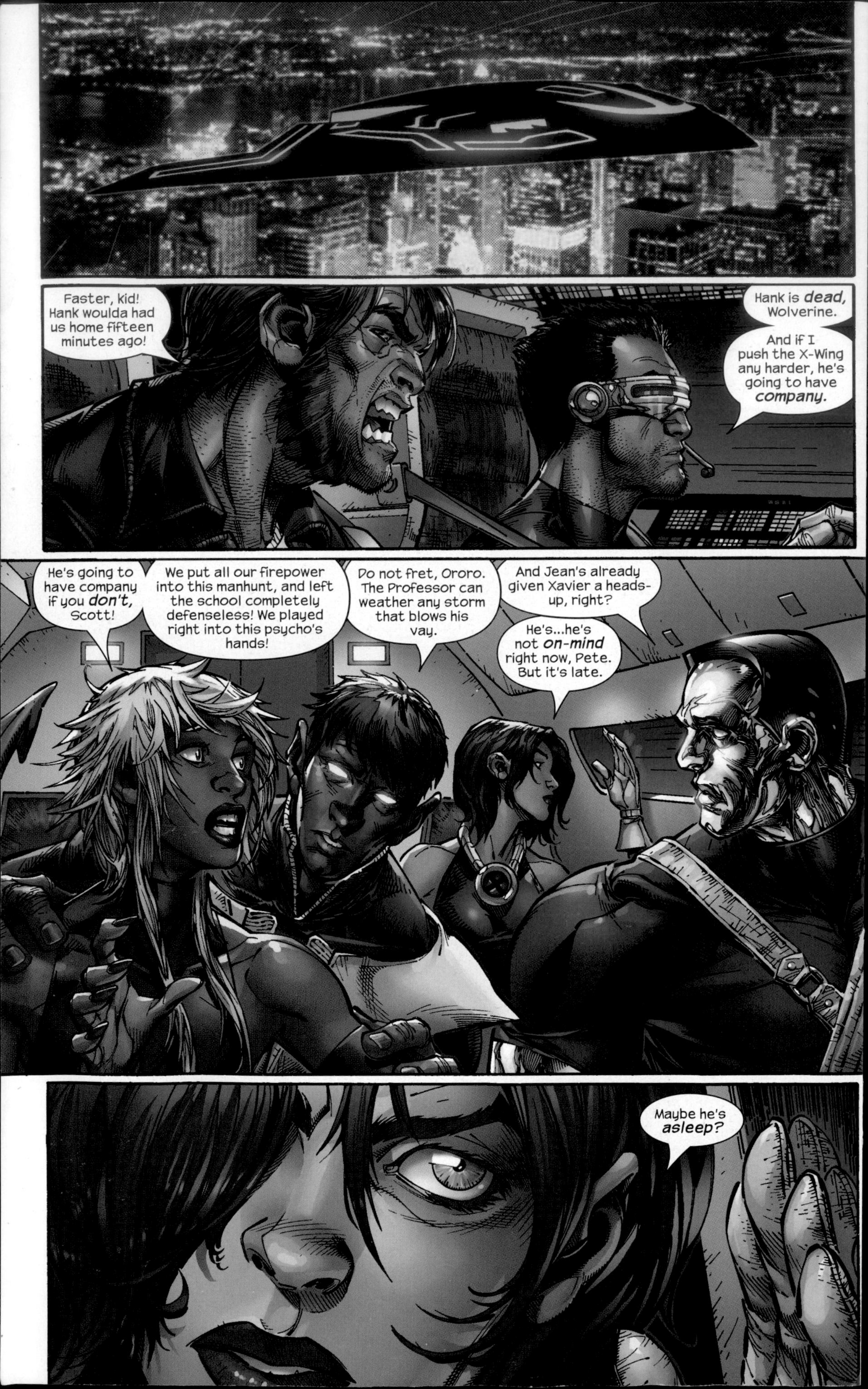

Faster, kid! Hank woulda had us home fifteen minutes ago!
Hank is *dead,* Wolverine.
And if I push the X-Wing any harder, he's going to have *company.*
He's going to have company if you *don't,* Scott!
We put all our firepower into this manhunt, and left the school completely defenseless! We played right into this psycho's hands!
Do not fret, Ororo. The Professor can weather any storm that blows his vay.
And Jean's already given Xavier a heads-up, right?
He's...he's not *on-mind* right now, Pete. But it's late.
Maybe he's *asleep?*

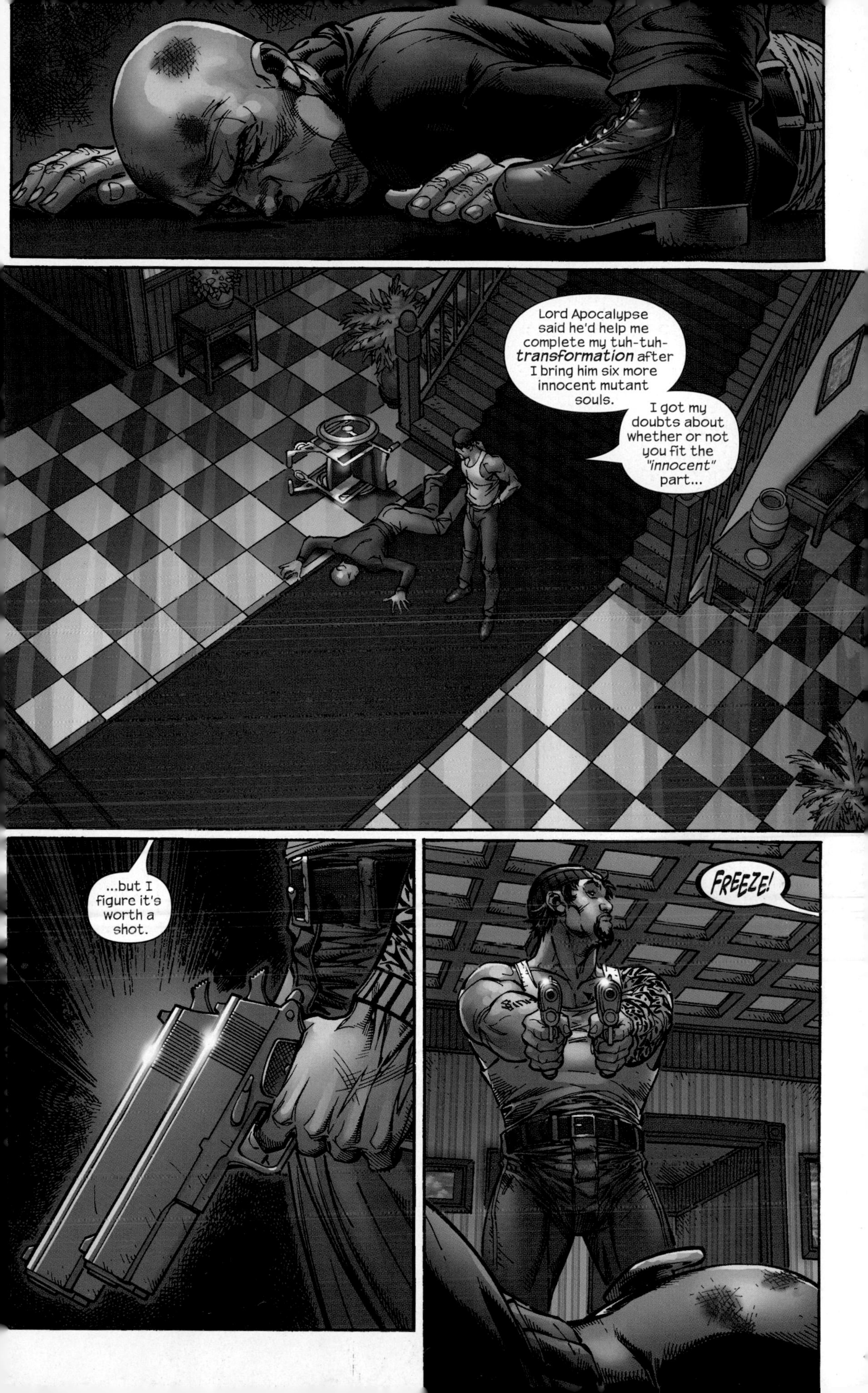
Lord Apocalypse said he'd help me complete my tuh-tuh-*transformation* after I bring him six more innocent mutant souls.
I got my doubts about whether or not you fit the *"innocent"* part...
...but I figure it's worth a shot.
FREEZE!

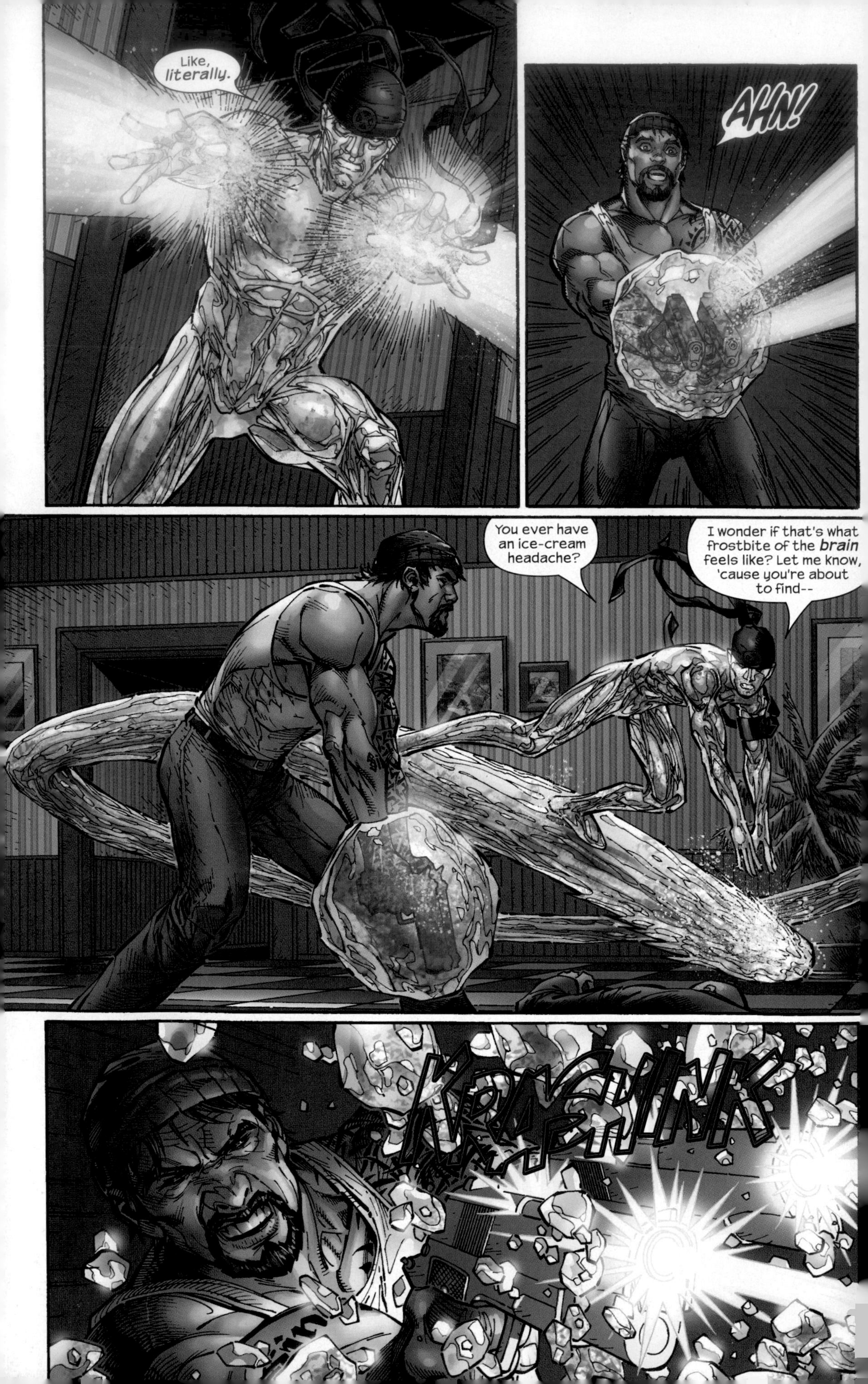

Like, *literally.*
AHN!
You ever have an ice-cream headache?
I wonder if that's what frostbite of the **brain** feels like? Let me know, 'cause you're about to find--
KRUNCHINK

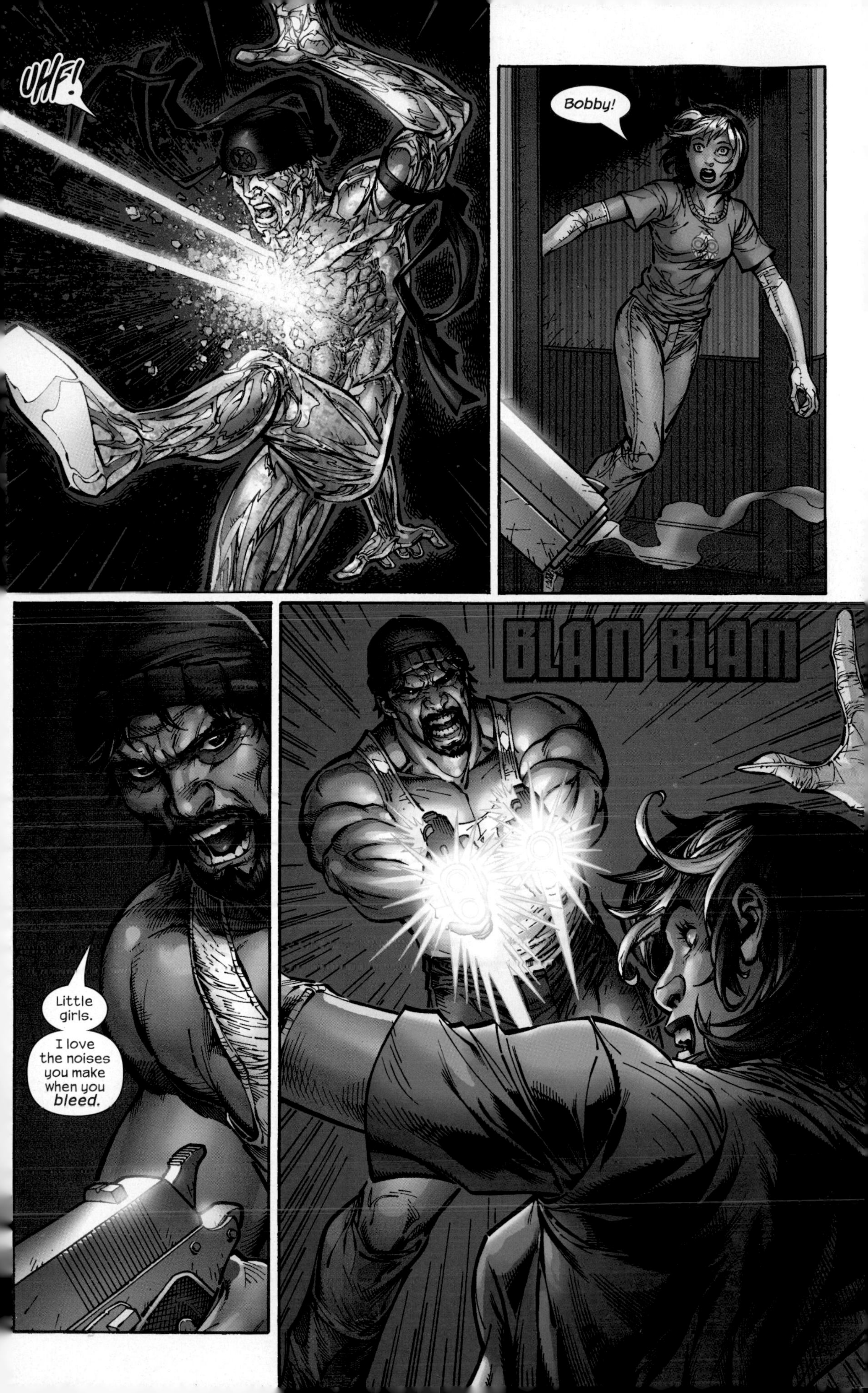
UHF!
Bobby!
Little girls.
I love the noises you make when you *bleed.*
BLAM BLAM

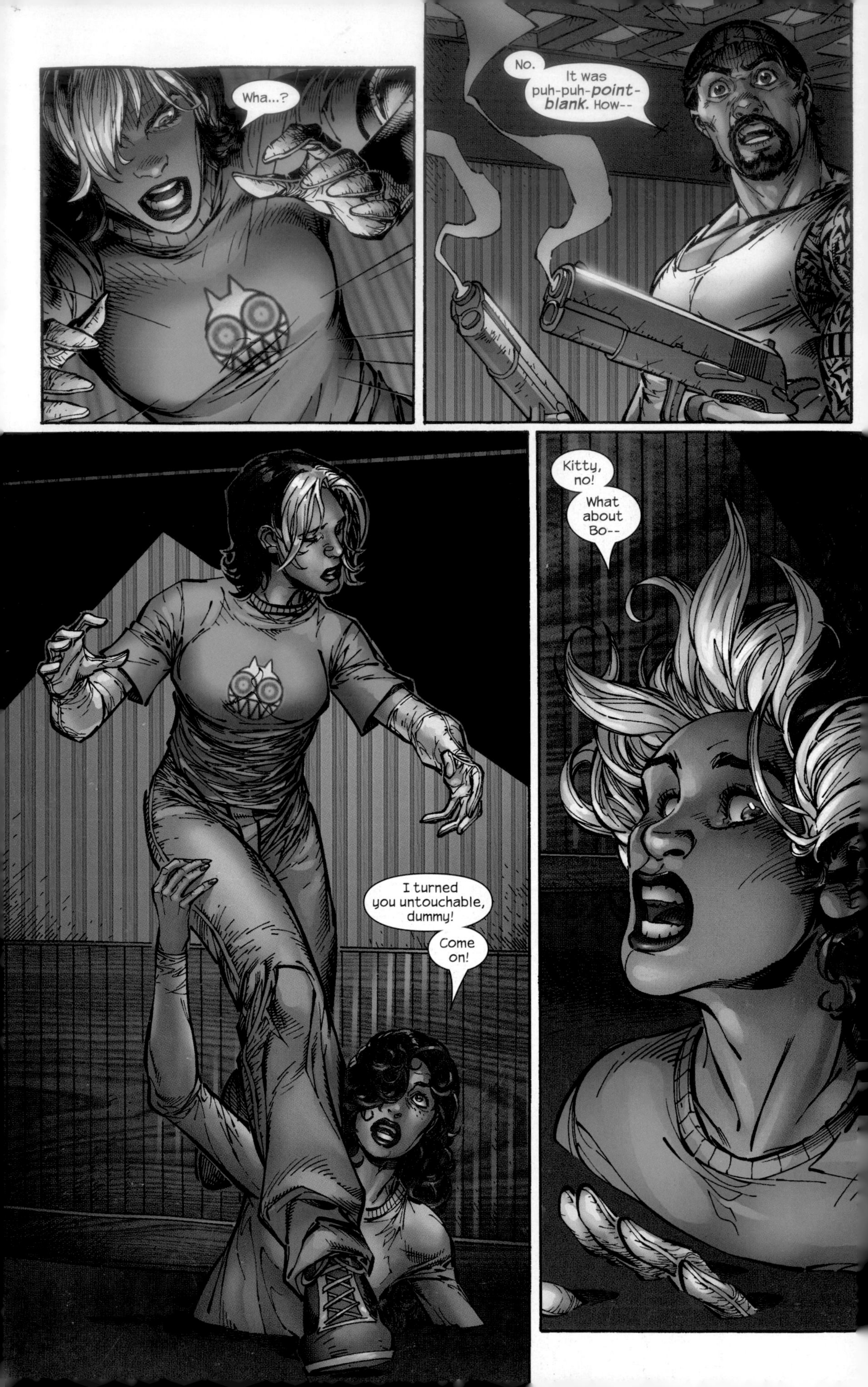
Wha...?
No.
It was puh-puh-*point-blank*. How--
I turned you untouchable, dummy!
Come on!
Kitty, no!
What about Bo--

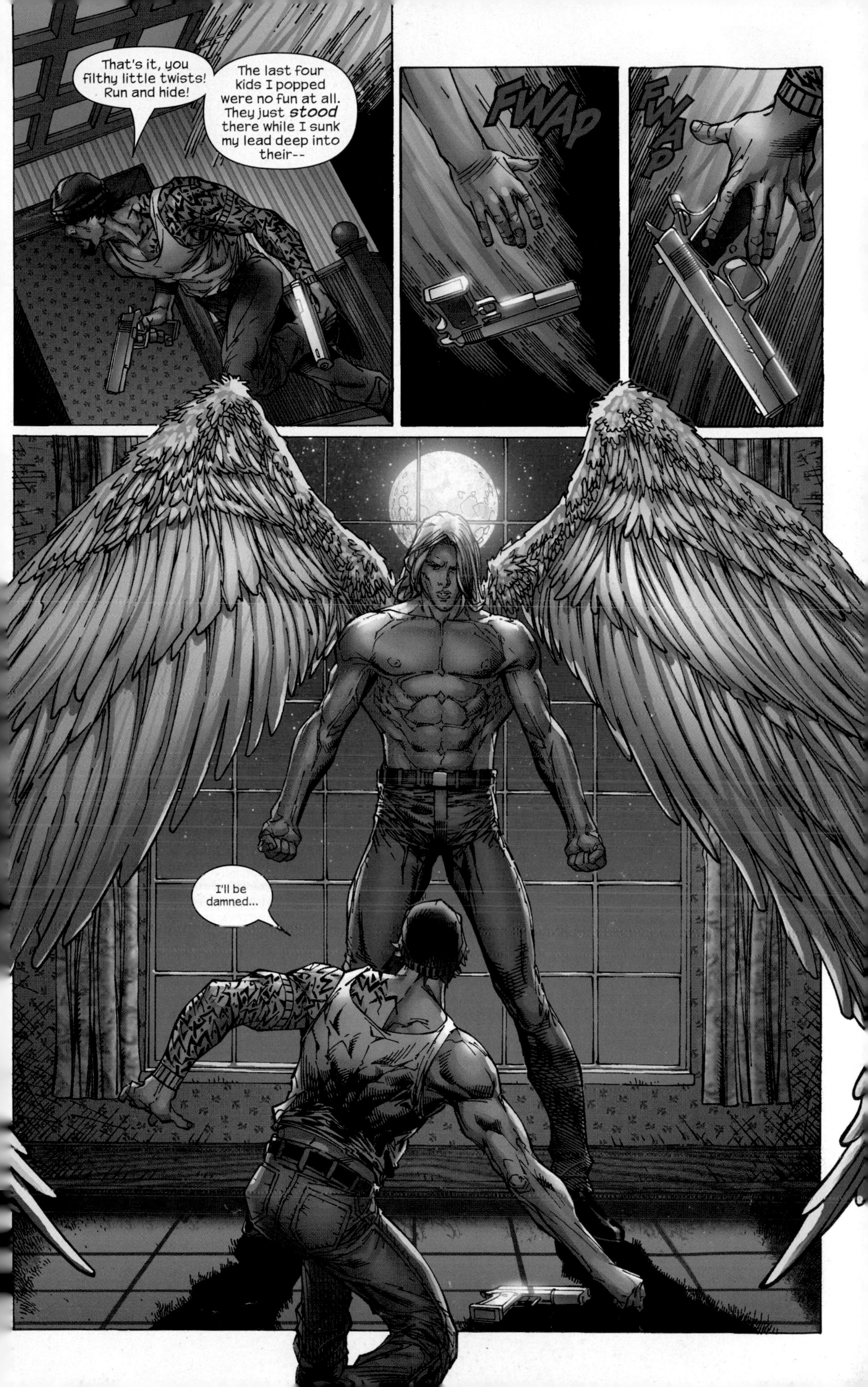
That's it, you filthy little twists! Run and hide!
The last four kids I popped were no fun at all. They just *stood* there while I sunk my lead deep into their--
FWAP
FWAP
I'll be damned...

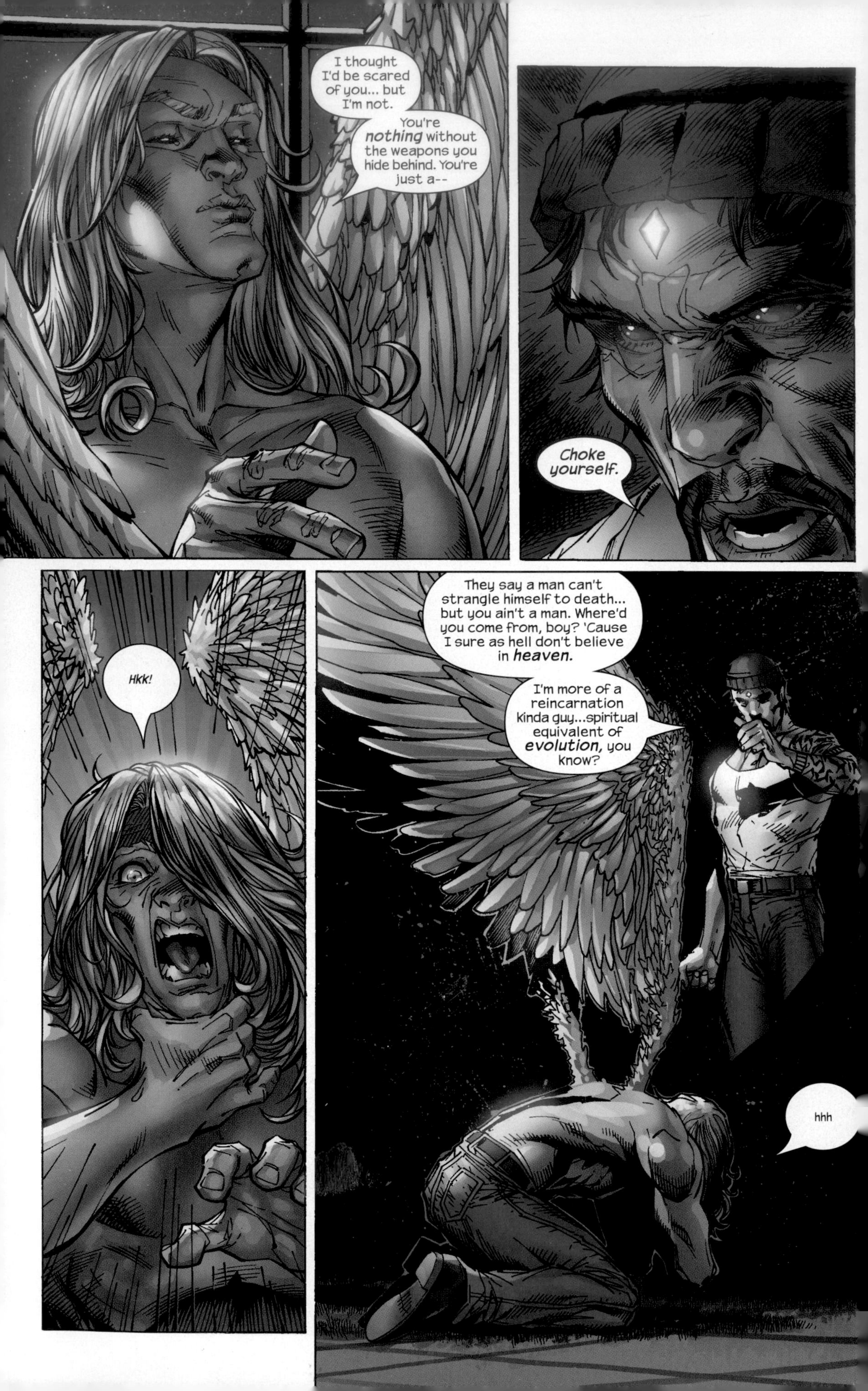
I thought I'd be scared of you... but I'm not.
You're *nothing* without the weapons you hide behind. You're just a--
Choke yourself.
Hkk!
They say a man can't strangle himself to death... but you ain't a man. Where'd you come from, boy? 'Cause I sure as hell don't believe in ***heaven.***
I'm more of a reincarnation kinda guy...spiritual equivalent of ***evolution,*** you know?
hhh

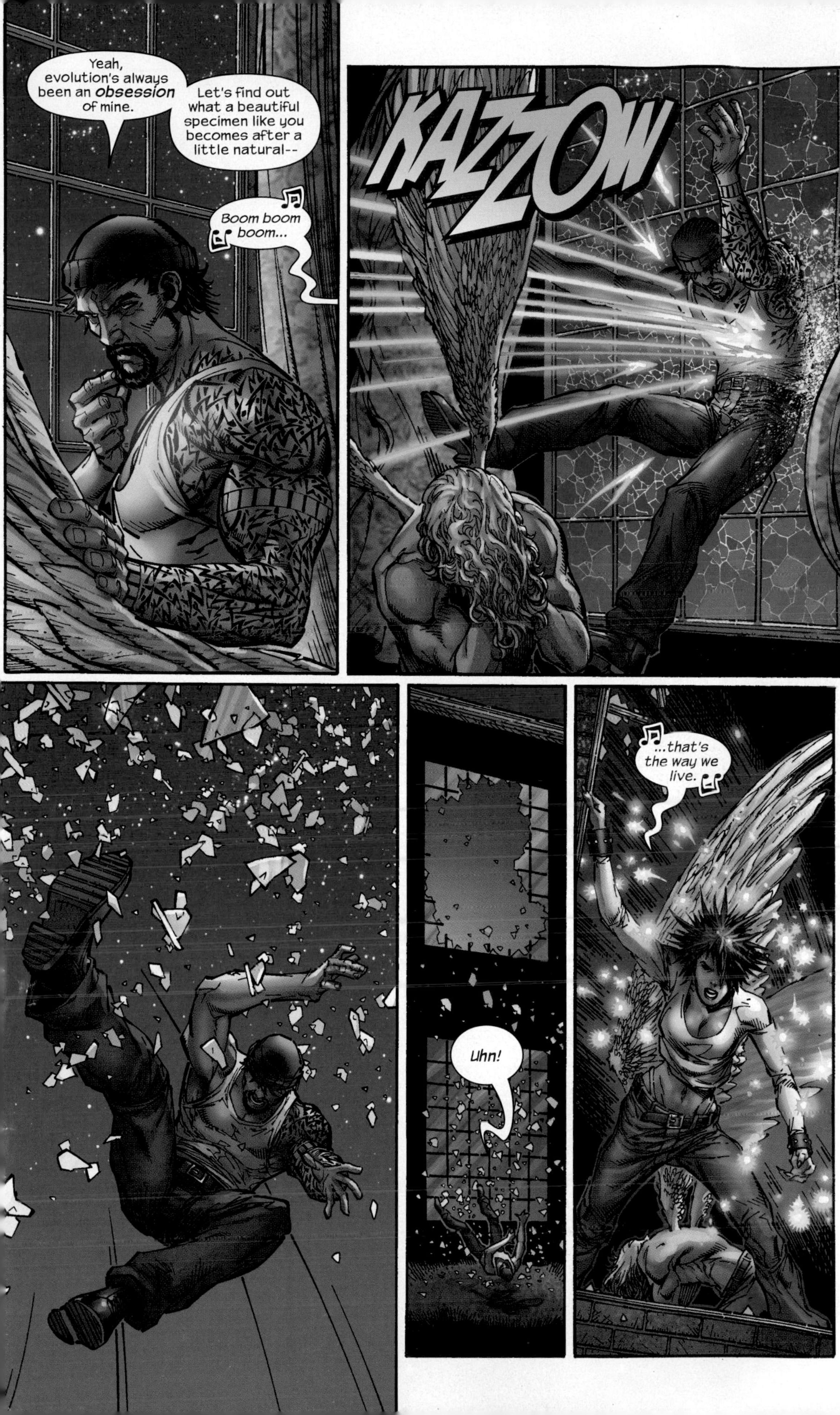
Yeah, evolution's always been an *obsession* of mine.
Let's find out what a beautiful specimen like you becomes after a little natural--
Boom boom boom...
KAZZOW
Uhn!
...that's the way we live.

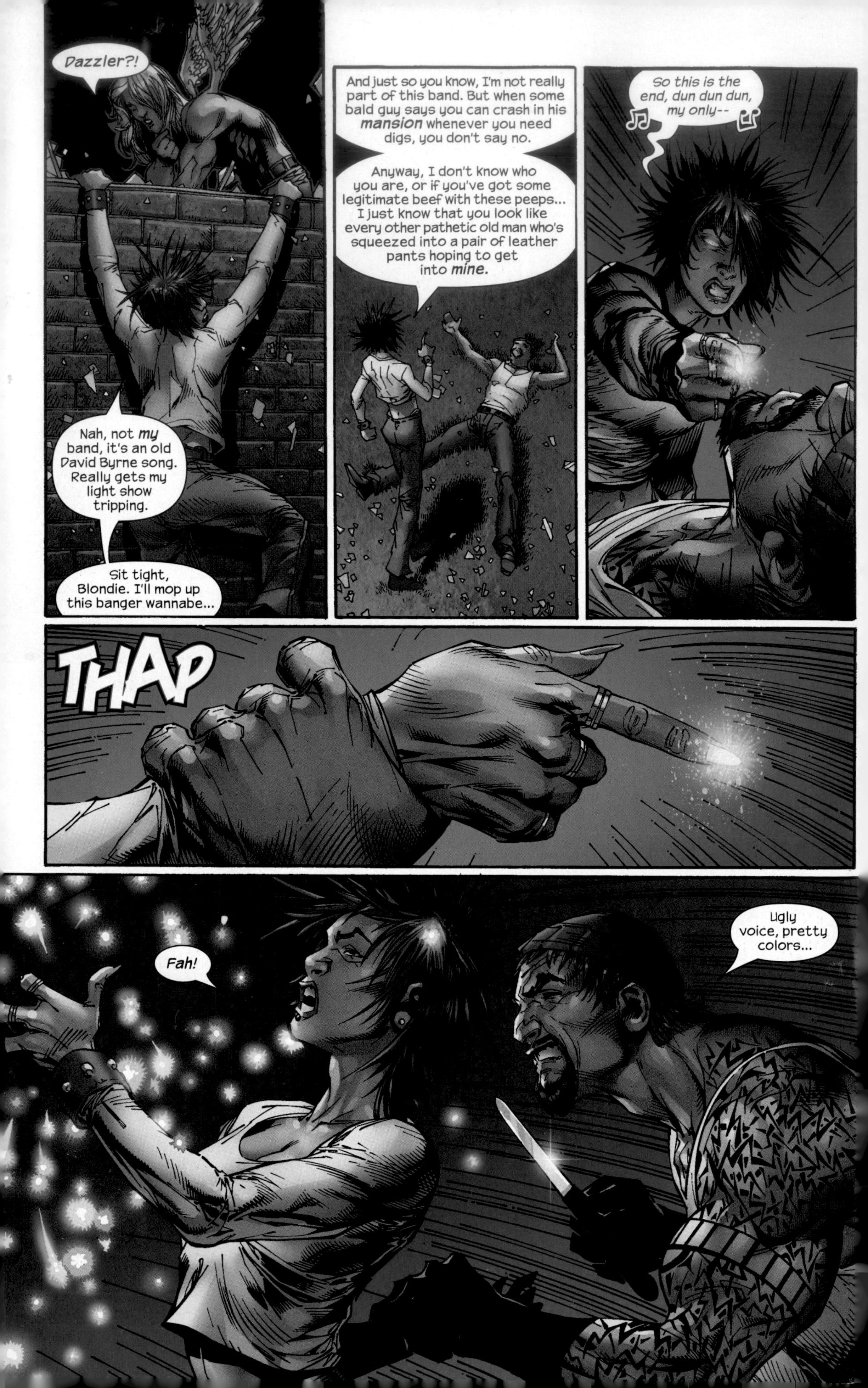
Dazzler?!
Nah, not *my* band, it's an old David Byrne song. Really gets my light show tripping.
Sit tight, Blondie. I'll mop up this banger wannabe...
And just so you know, I'm not really part of this band. But when some bald guy says you can crash in his *mansion* whenever you need digs, you don't say no.
Anyway, I don't know who you are, or if you've got some legitimate beef with these peeps... I just know that you look like every other pathetic old man who's squeezed into a pair of leather pants hoping to get into *mine.*
So this is the end, dun dun dun, my only--
THAP
Fah!
Ugly voice, pretty colors...

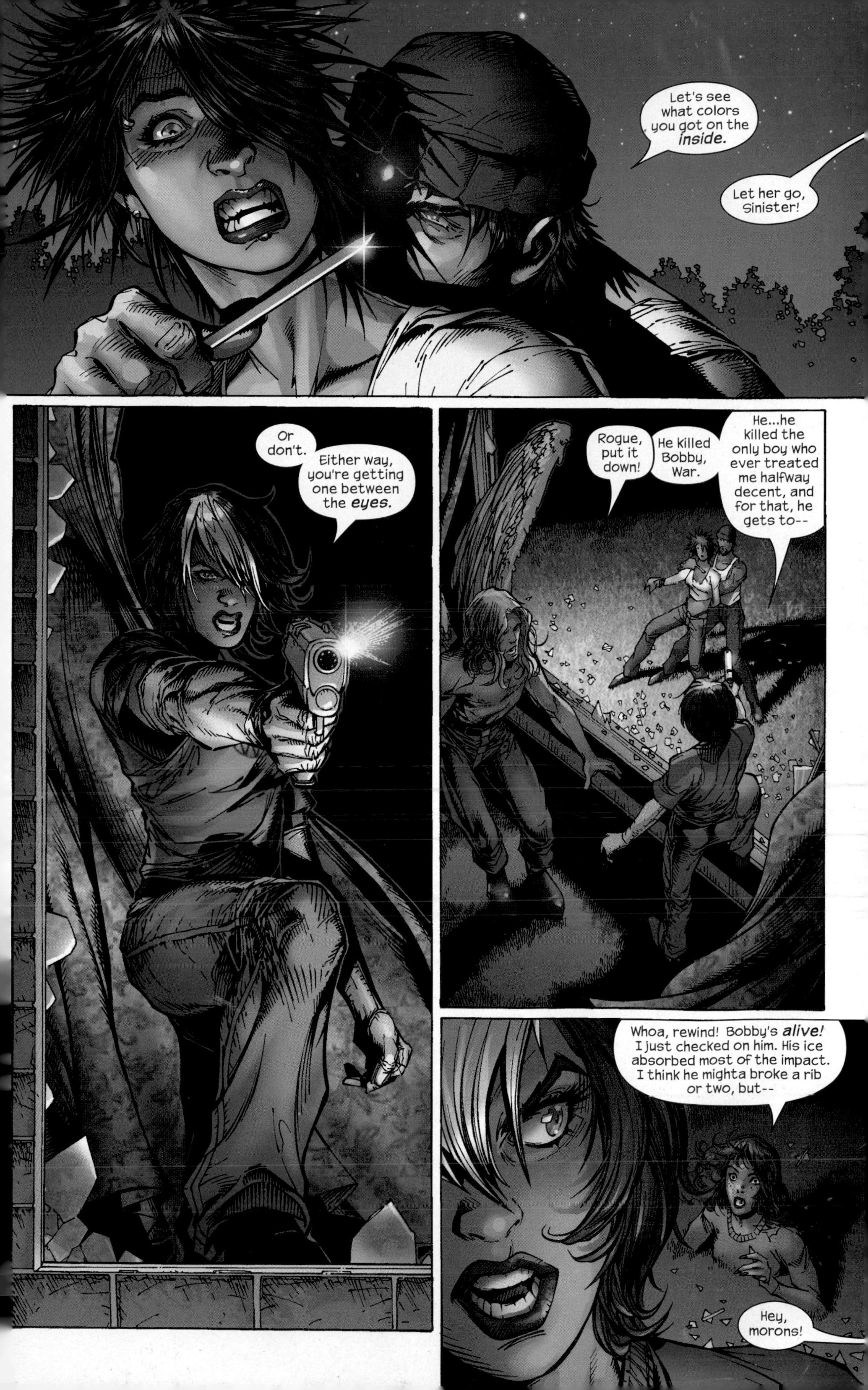
Let's see what colors you got on the *inside.*
Let her go, Sinister!
Or don't.
Either way, you're getting one between the *eyes.*
Rogue, put it down!
He killed Bobby, War.
He...he killed the only boy who ever treated me halfway decent, and for that, he gets to--
Whoa, rewind! Bobby's *alive!* I just checked on him. His ice absorbed most of the impact. I think he mighta broke a rib or two, but--
Hey, morons!

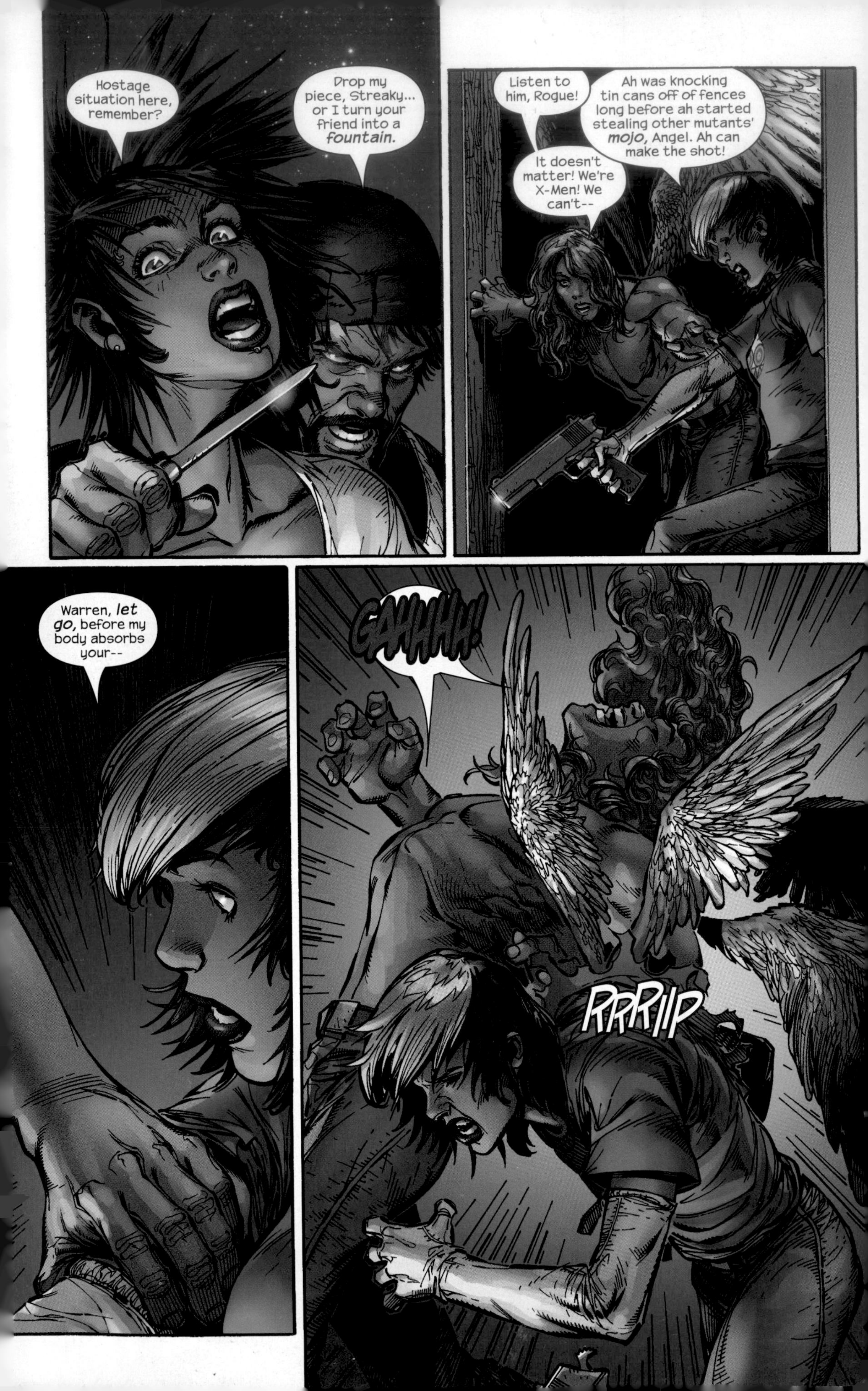
Hostage situation here, remember?
Drop my piece, Streaky... or I turn your friend into a *fountain*.
Listen to him, Rogue!
Ah was knocking tin cans off of fences long before ah started stealing other mutants' *mojo,* Angel. Ah can make the shot!
It doesn't matter! We're X-Men! We can't--
Warren, *let go,* before my body absorbs your--
GAHHHH!
RRRIIP

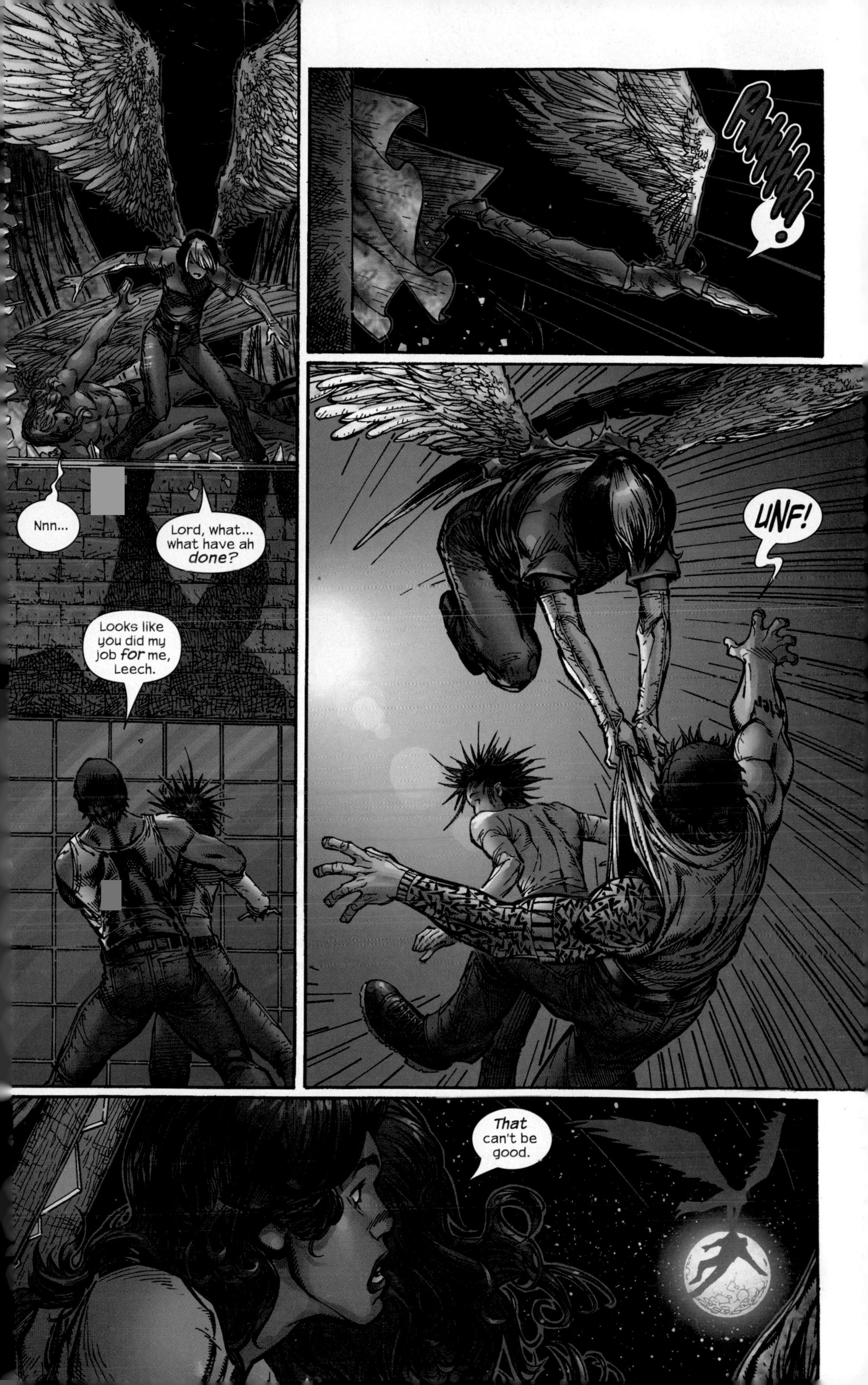
RAHHHH!
Nnn...
Lord, what... what have ah *done*?
Looks like you did my job *for* me, Leech.
UNF!
That can't be good.

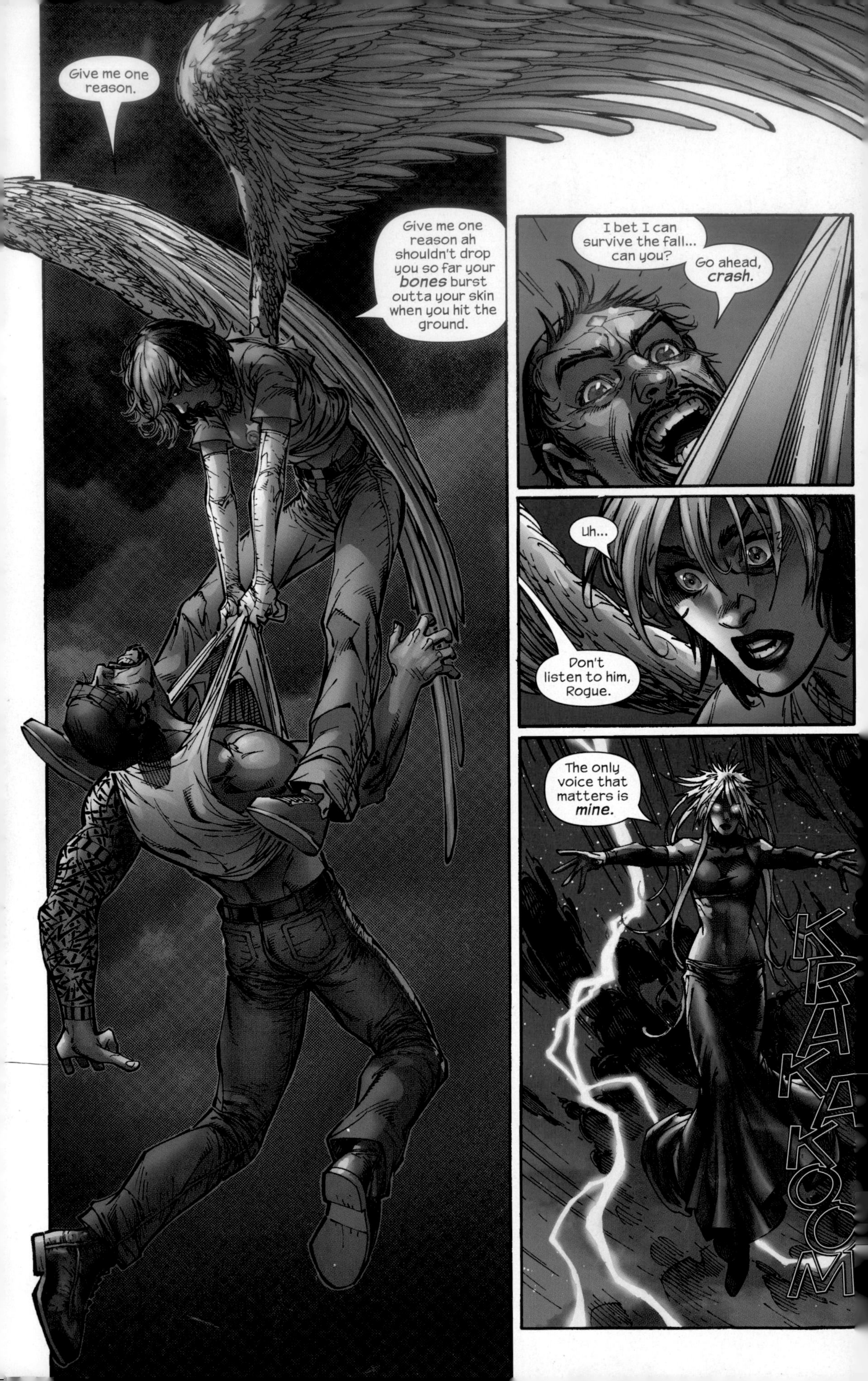
Give me one reason.
Give me one reason ah shouldn't drop you so far your bones burst outta your skin when you hit the ground.
I bet I can survive the fall... can you?
Go ahead, crash.
Uh...
Don't listen to him, Rogue.
The only voice that matters is mine.
KRAKAKOOM

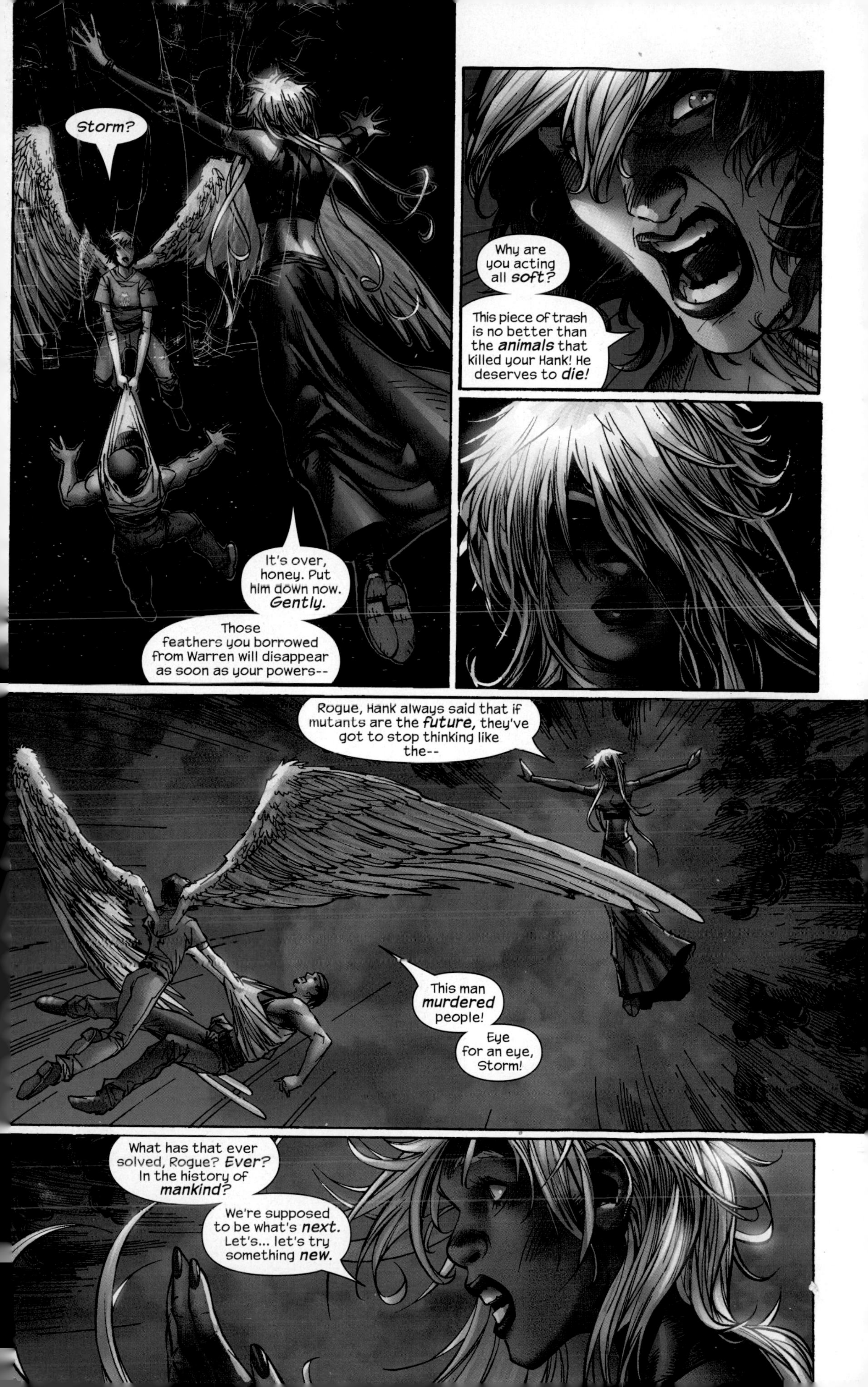
Storm?
Why are you acting all soft?
This piece of trash is no better than the animals that killed your Hank! He deserves to die!
It's over, honey. Put him down now. Gently.
Those feathers you borrowed from Warren will disappear as soon as your powers--
Rogue, Hank always said that if mutants are the future, they've got to stop thinking like the--
This man murdered people!
Eye for an eye, Storm!
What has that ever solved, Rogue? Ever? In the history of mankind?
We're supposed to be what's next. Let's... let's try something new.

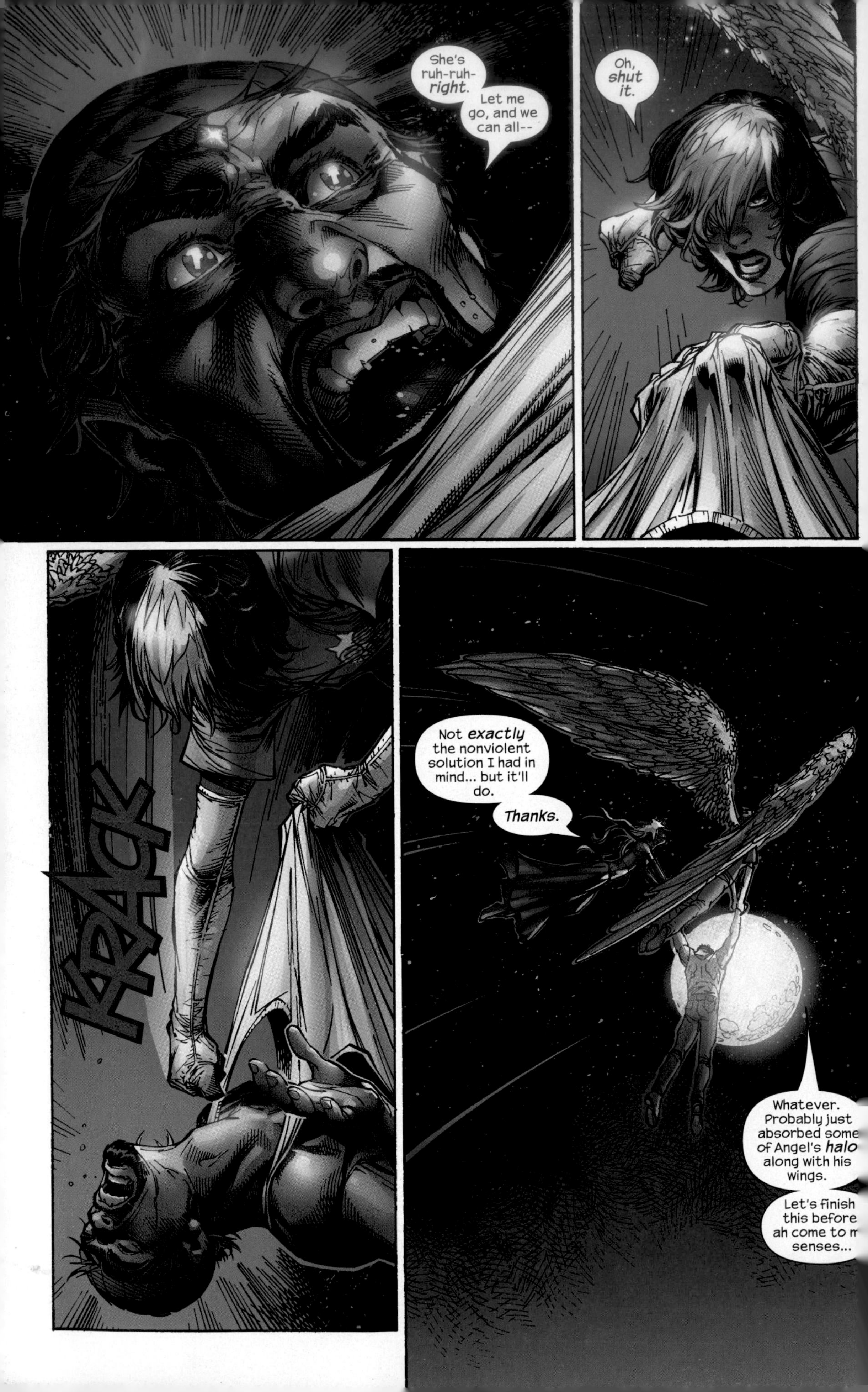
She's ruh-ruh-right.
Let me go, and we can all--
Oh, shut it.
KRACK
Not exactly the nonviolent solution I had in mind... but it'll do.
Thanks.
Whatever. Probably just absorbed some of Angel's halo along with his wings.
Let's finish this before ah come to m senses...

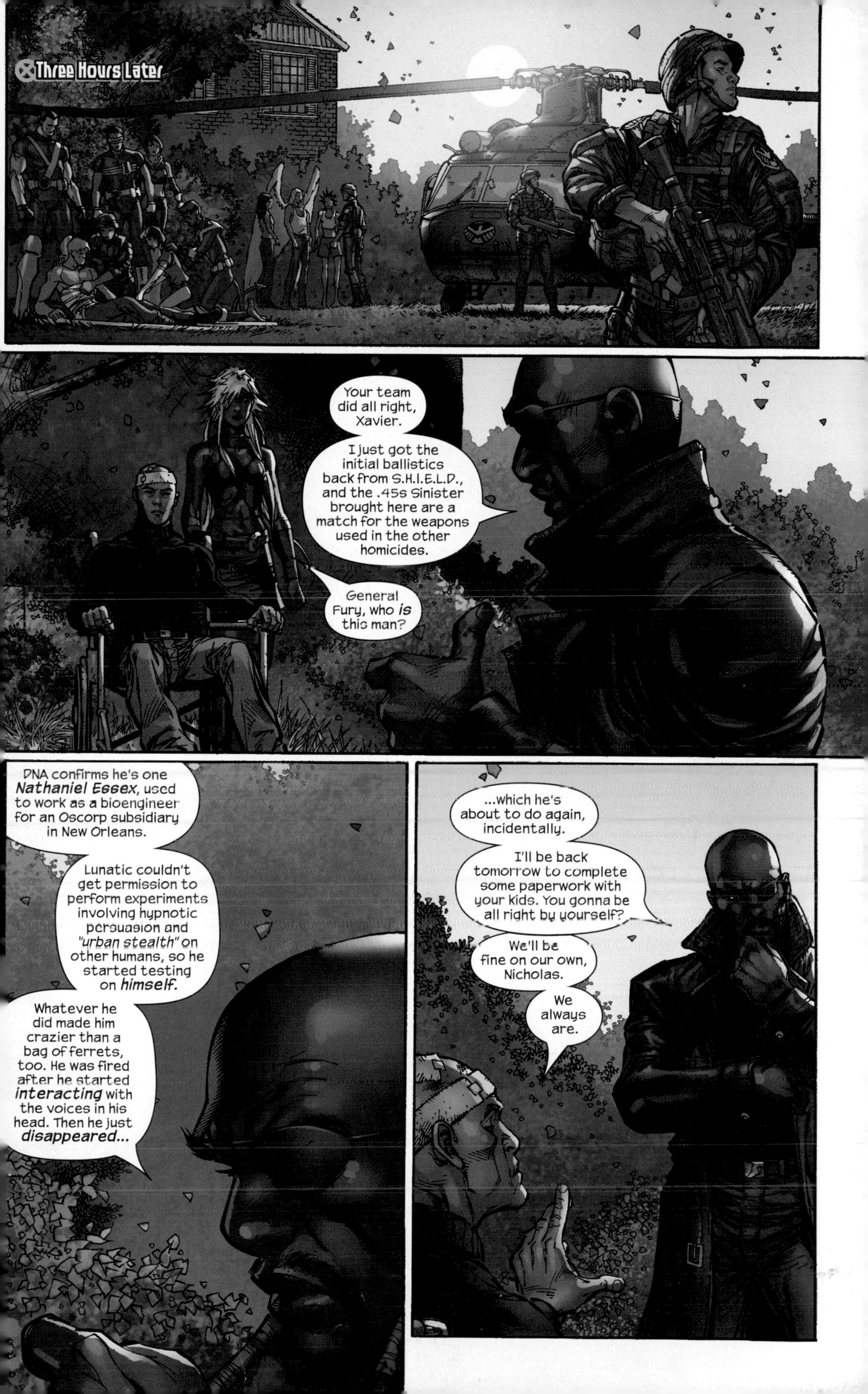
Three Hours Later
Your team did all right, Xavier.
I just got the initial ballistics back from S.H.I.E.L.D., and the .45s Sinister brought here are a match for the weapons used in the other homicides.
General Fury, who *is* this man?
DNA confirms he's one *Nathaniel Essex*, used to work as a bioengineer for an Oscorp subsidiary in New Orleans.
Lunatic couldn't get permission to perform experiments involving hypnotic persuasion and *"urban stealth"* on other humans, so he started testing on *himself.*
Whatever he did made him crazier than a bag of ferrets, too. He was fired after he started *interacting* with the voices in his head. Then he just *disappeared...*
...which he's about to do again, incidentally.
I'll be back tomorrow to complete some paperwork with your kids. You gonna be all right by yourself?
We'll be fine on our own, Nicholas.
We always are.

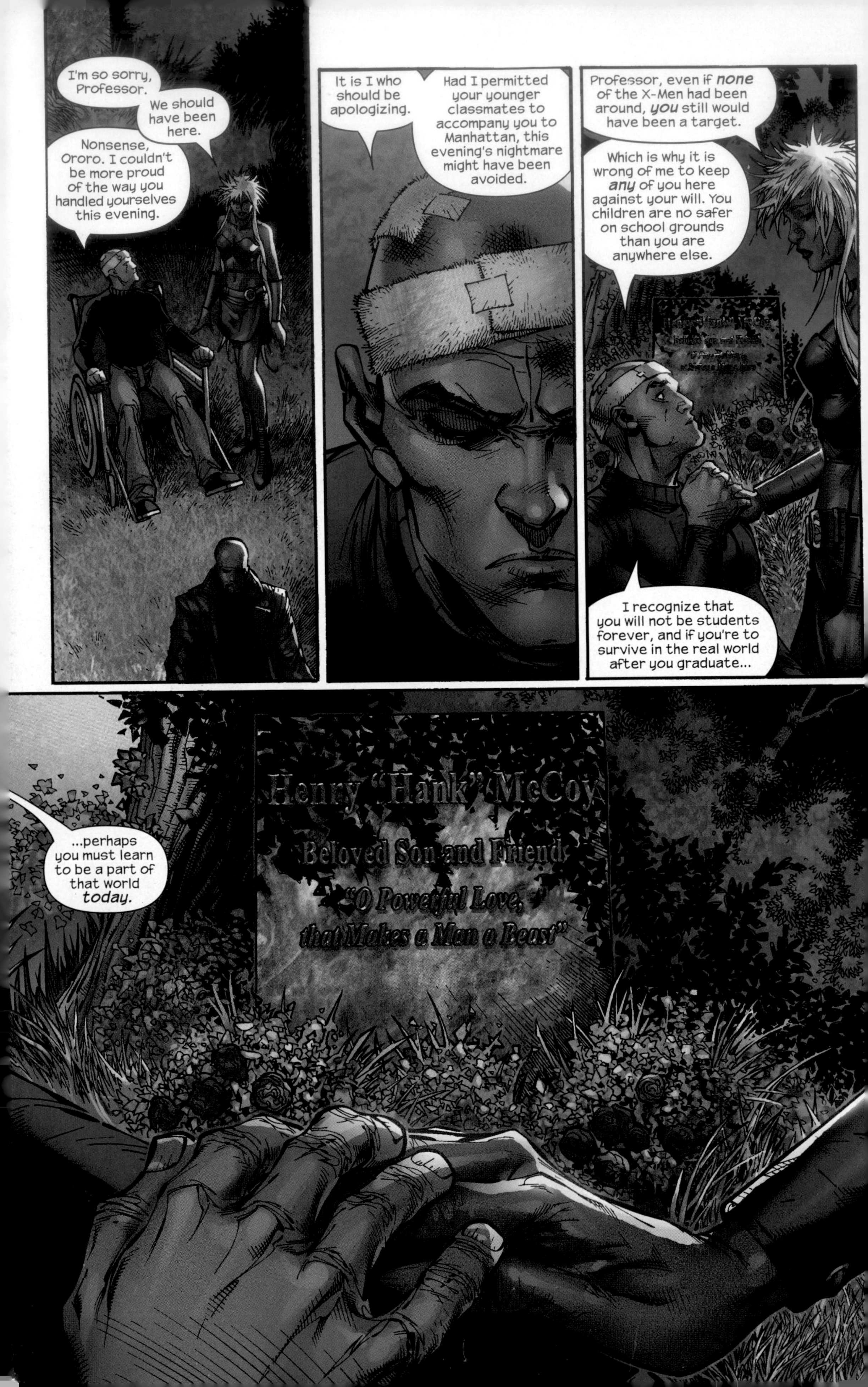

I'm so sorry, Professor.
We should have been here.
Nonsense, Ororo. I couldn't be more proud of the way you handled yourselves this evening.
It is I who should be apologizing.
Had I permitted your younger classmates to accompany you to Manhattan, this evening's nightmare might have been avoided.
Professor, even if *none* of the X-Men had been around, *you* still would have been a target.
Which is why it is wrong of me to keep *any* of you here against your will. You children are no safer on school grounds than you are anywhere else.
I recognize that you will not be students forever, and if you're to survive in the real world after you graduate...
Henry "Hank" McCoy
Beloved Son and Friend
"O Powerful Love, that Makes a Man a Beast"
...perhaps you must learn to be a part of that world *today*.

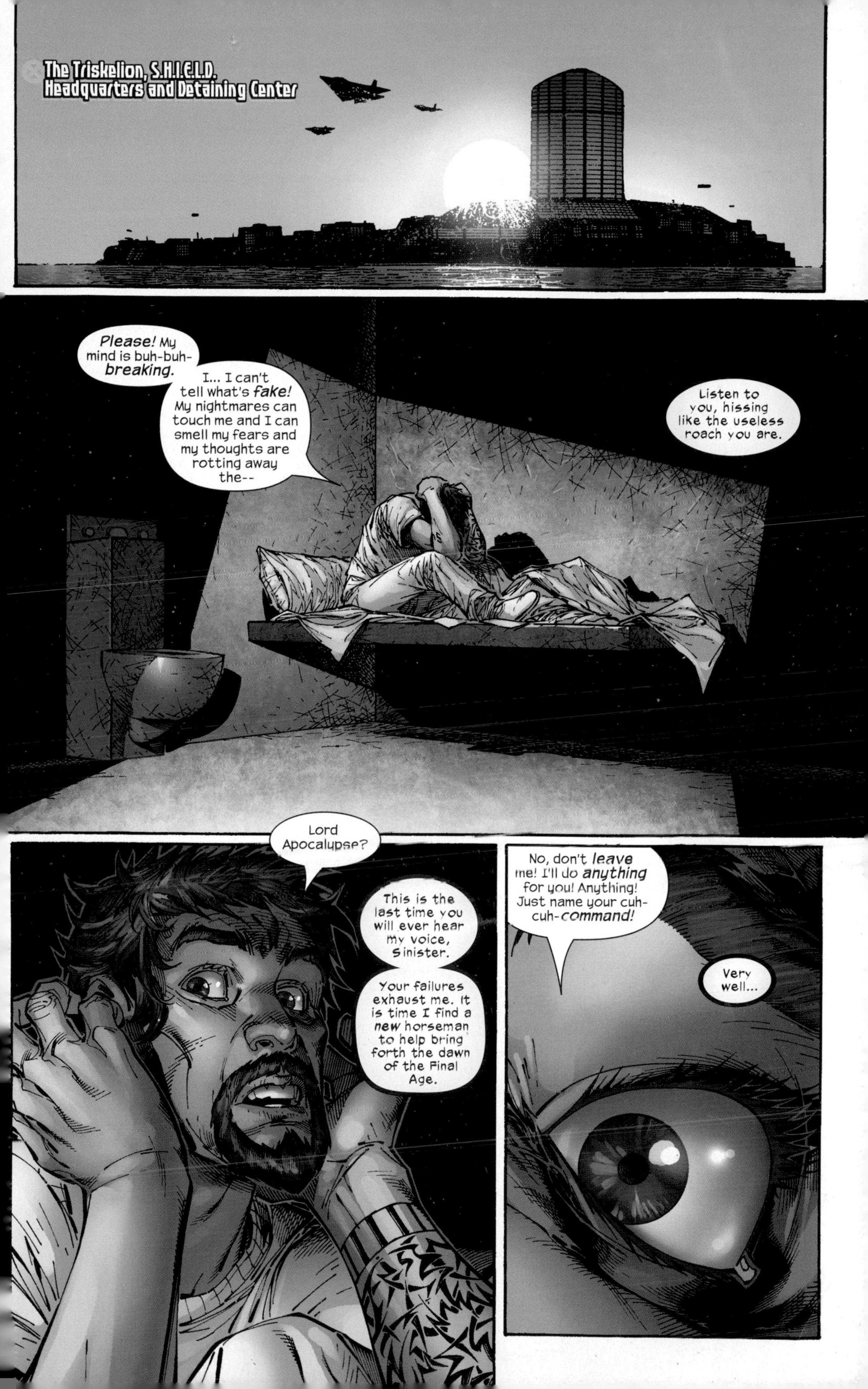
The Triskelion, S.H.I.E.L.D. Headquarters and Detaining Center
Please! My mind is buh-buh-breaking.
I... I can't tell what's fake! My nightmares can touch me and I can smell my fears and my thoughts are rotting away the--
Listen to you, hissing like the useless roach you are.
Lord Apocalypse?
This is the last time you will ever hear my voice, Sinister.
Your failures exhaust me. It is time I find a new horseman to help bring forth the dawn of the Final Age.
No, don't leave me! I'll do anything for you! Anything! Just name your cuh-cuh-command!
Very well...

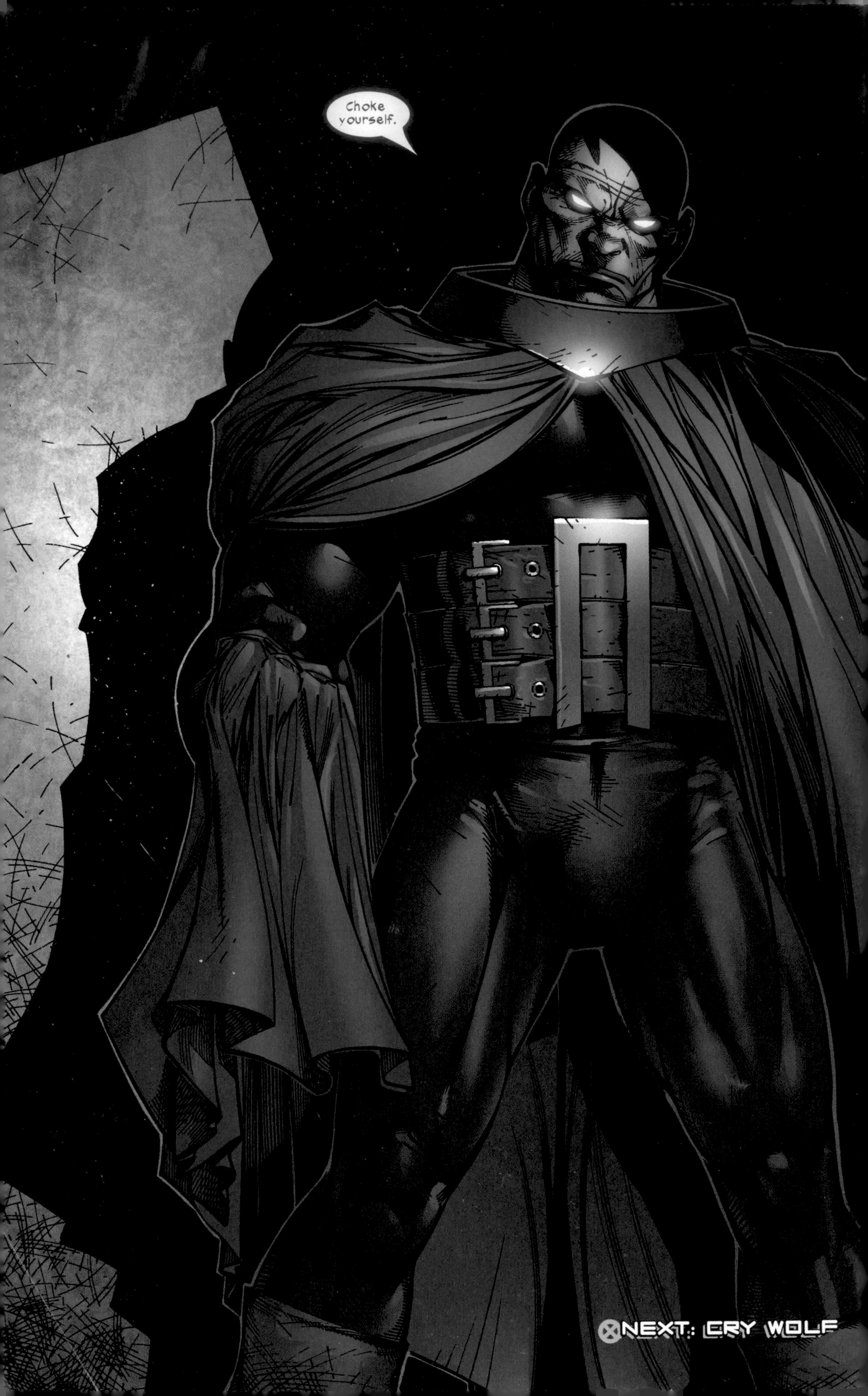
Choke yourself.
NEXT: CRY WOLF

ULTIMATE X-MEN

A Brief Outline by
Brian K. Vaughan

SINISTER

I'd like to accomplish three things with my four-issue arc:

1) Take an existing villain who never quite worked in the Marvel Universe, throw away almost everything except for his cool name, and turn him into the scariest character in the Ultimate Universe.

2) Remind readers why Ultimate X-Men is different from other X-books: it's a story about YOUNG men and women living in a world that fears and hates them. The X-Men can be grown-up celebrities over in the post-modern Marvel Universe, but our book should be a place where younger fans can read about freaks, outcasts and misfits... the kind of characters we identified with when we fell in love with the X-Men as awkward, brooding adolescents (or am I the only one?).

3) Tell a self-contained adventure that will also help bridge the gap between Bendis' action-packed Sentinel storyline and Mack's presumably more character-driven upcoming issues. Oh, and it would also be nice if I could convince a few thousand readers to follow me back to Runaways after they enjoy the hell out of my arc!

ISSUE ONE: We open in a public school somewhere in Manhattan, where a new young mutant has just been outted by his cruel classmates. We'll quickly establish mutants' place in the Ultimate Universe, as this young man's principal encourages him to matriculate to Xavier's School for Gifted Youngsters, where he can safely be with his "own kind." Much to our surprise, the young mutant chooses to stay at his public school, saying that he would rather suffer in a normal school than thrive in a "special" one (maybe subtly mirroring the debate that's going on about gay students at Harvey Milk High in the real world). We then cut to Xavier's, where the X-Men are all dealing with the recent death of one of their classmates in different ways (Storm shaves a mohawk into her hair and retreats to her room, Angel and Kitty turn to the Professor for answers, and Wolverine and Colossus hide from their feelings in the Danger Room). Eventually, we'll cut back to Manhattan, where the new young mutant from the beginning of our story is confronted outside of his family's apartment by a creepy older man. The startled young mutant asks about a word he sees tattooed on this shadowy figure's arm, "Sinister?" The man smiles as he pulls a handgun from his coat and says, "That's Mister Sinister to you, kid." He then fires a single shot at the off-panel young mutant!

SINISTER...

ISSUE TWO: Mercifully, we learn that this young mutant used his powers at the very last second to partially deflect Sinister's attack. Visiting this boy in the hospital, Cyclops and Jean explain that he was lucky... three other young mutants were shot and killed in Manhattan last night. The boy has already told the authorities what he remembers about the man named Sinister, but the bigoted NYPD is in no hurry to solve these homicides, and S.H.I.E.L.D. has more important things to worry about than one lowly serial killer. The X-Men vow to bring this murderer to justice themselves, but Professor X is hesitant to let his young students go, as he still feels responsible for Hank's recent death. But when Sinister is unable to be located with Wolverine's uncanny tracking abilities, Xavier realizes that this serial killer may himself be a mutant, born with the ability to live completely off the grid, invisible to all forms of detection (even Cerebro). Unwilling to see any more young mutants die, Xavier reluctantly allows his five oldest students to hunt for Sinister, while the enraged younger students are forced to stay back in the mansion (we'll play up the seniors vs. freshmen dynamic that I think will work well for our newly enlarged cast of young characters). At the end of this issue, we cut to a dark apartment somewhere in Manhattan, where Sinister is speaking to an invisible figure he addresses as "Apocalypse." Sinister promises his master that he won't stop killing until he's sacrificed twelve innocent young mutants. (Ralph reminded me how much X-readers love a little mystery, so we'll let fans decide whether this villain is insane, or if he's really an agent of the unseen Ultimate Apocalypse).

ISSUE THREE: Arriving in Manhattan, the "senior class" of the X-Men breaks up into smaller search parties. Though they all manage to prevent some anti-mutant crimes, Cyclops, Jean, Wolverine, Colossus, and Storm are unable to find Sinister. As we follow the action of these older X-Men, Sinister secretly travels to Westchester, and eventually breaks into the X-mansion! We end with the undetectable villain aiming his gun at the back of an unsuspecting Xavier's head...

ISSUE FOUR: Back in Manhattan, Wolverine screams for Jean to get them back to the mansion; he's just realized what a sick hunter like Sinister would do. But it's too late, as Sinister brings the barrel of his weapon crashing into Xavier's head (Sinister decides not to kill the Professor, as Apocalypse told him to slay only innocent mutants, and Xavier is apparently anything but). It's now up to the younger, less experienced kids like Kitty, Rogue, Iceman and Angel to stop this deadly mutant. Working together, the freshman class eventually manage to barely take down Sinister. In the end, the older mutants arrive, and a furious Storm flies the now-unconscious Sinister high into the air, planning to drop the villain to his death. Angel flies after the young woman, and begs her not to execute Sinister, saying that doing so won't bring Hank back. Ultimately, Storm relents and lets Sinister live. As S.H.I.E.L.D. arrives to cart Sinister off to prison, Xavier comes to and commends his youngest students for their heroism. The Professor realizes that it would be wrong to keep these kids constantly confined to the mansion. If they're going to learn how to survive in the real world, they should occasionally be permitted to be a part of it.

Anyway, those are the very basic beats I have planned, and like all of my proposals, I'm sure the story will evolve and improve as I begin working on the individual issues. But I'm open to any and all suggestions, so please let me know what you think!

Ultimate X-Men #48 Cover Pencils

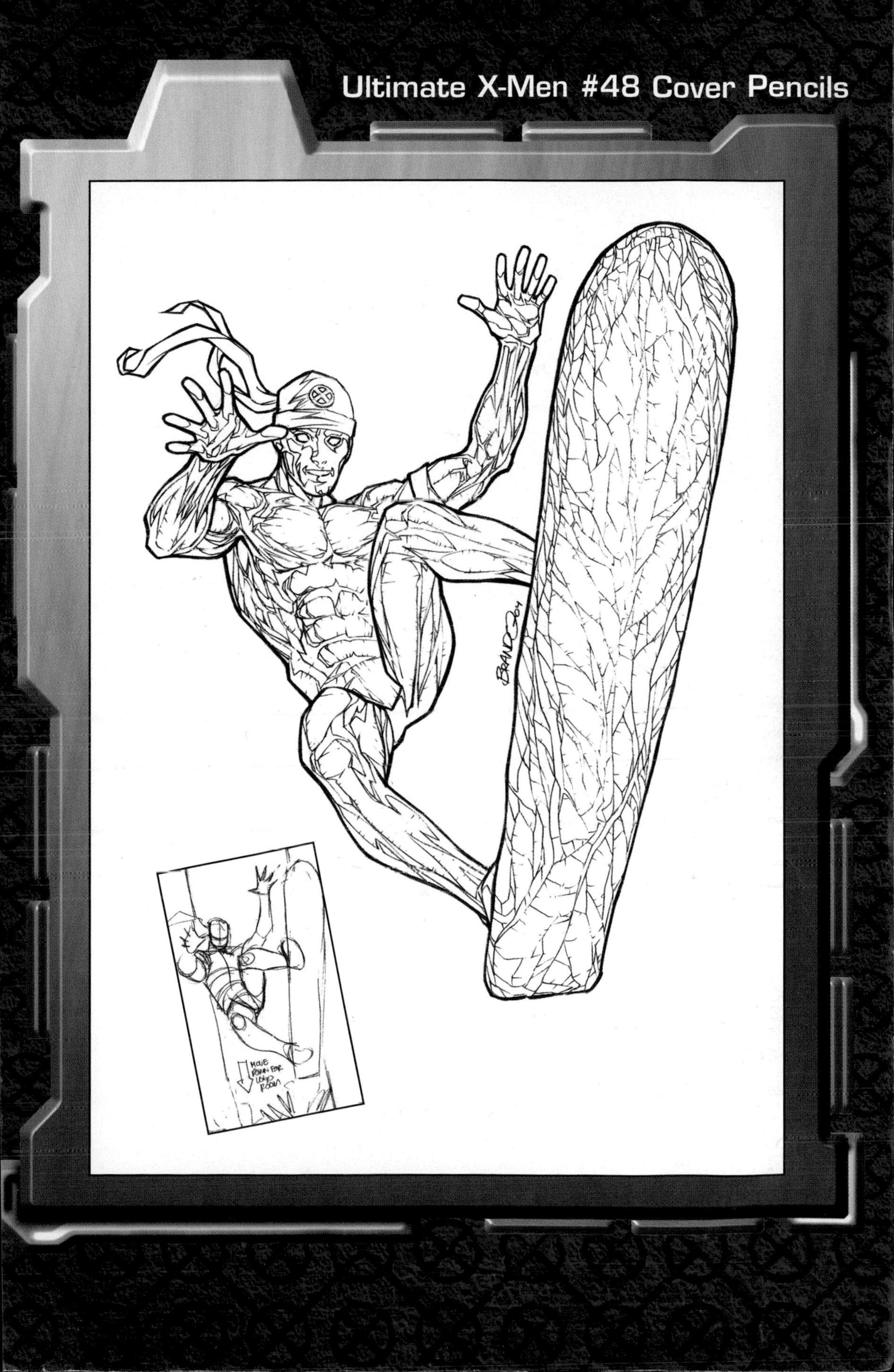
MOVE DOWN FOR LOGO ROOM

Ultimate X-Men #49 Cover Pencils

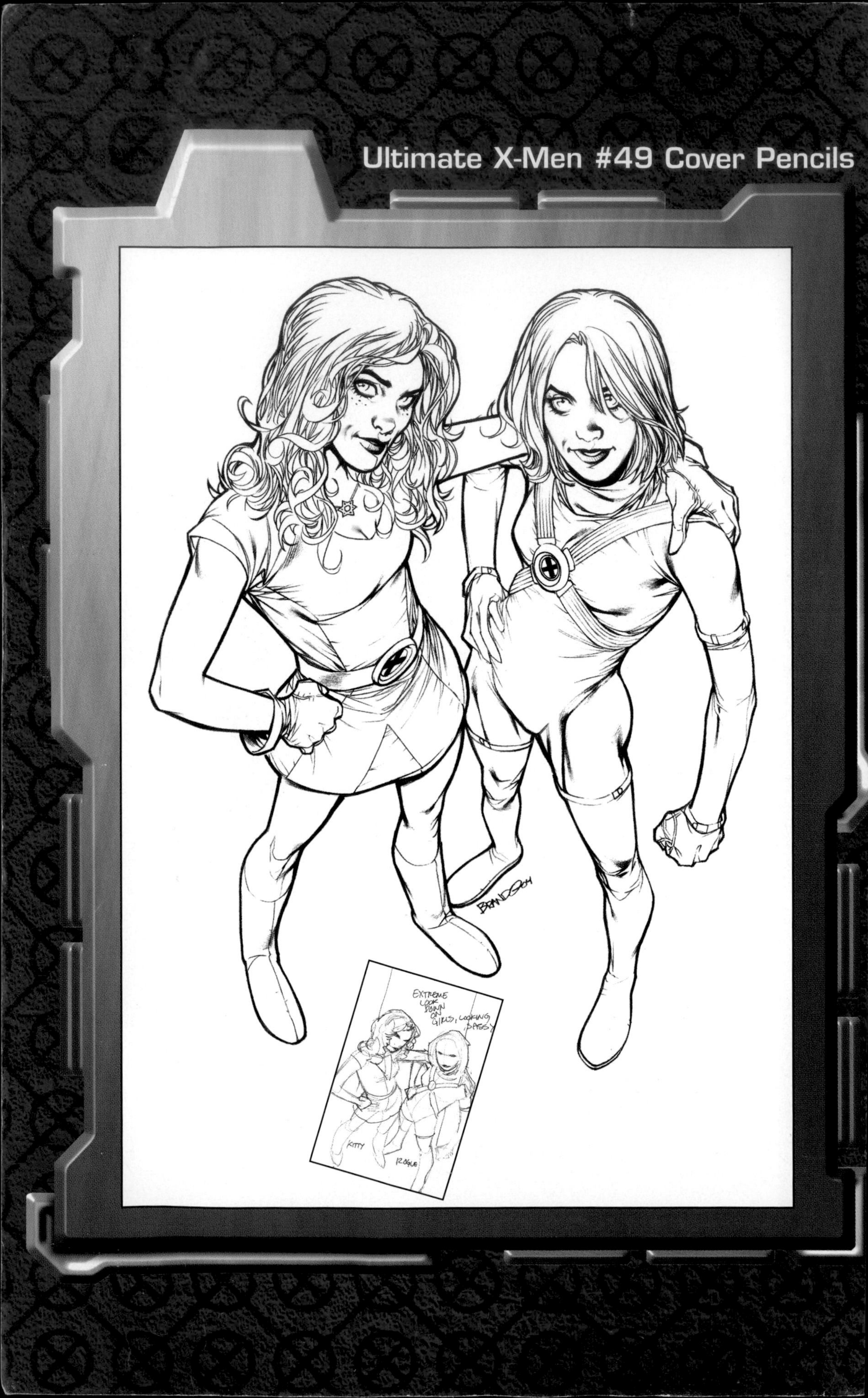
EXTREME LOOK DOWN ON GIRLS, LOOKING SASSY
KITTY
ROGUE

Ultimate X-Men #49 Page 14 Pencils

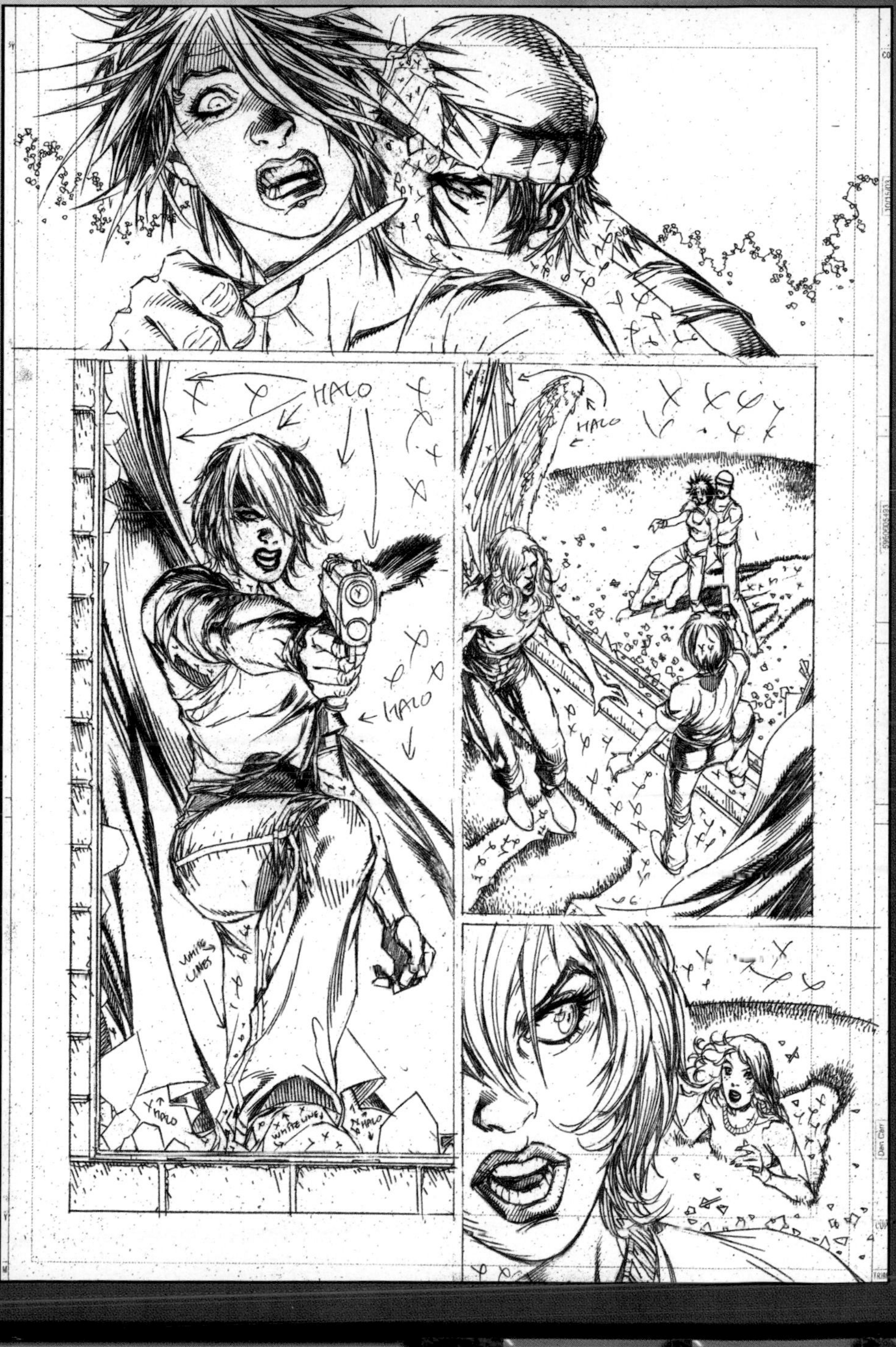
HALO
HALO
HALO
WHITE LINES
WHITE LINES

Ultimate X-Men #49 Page 14 Layout

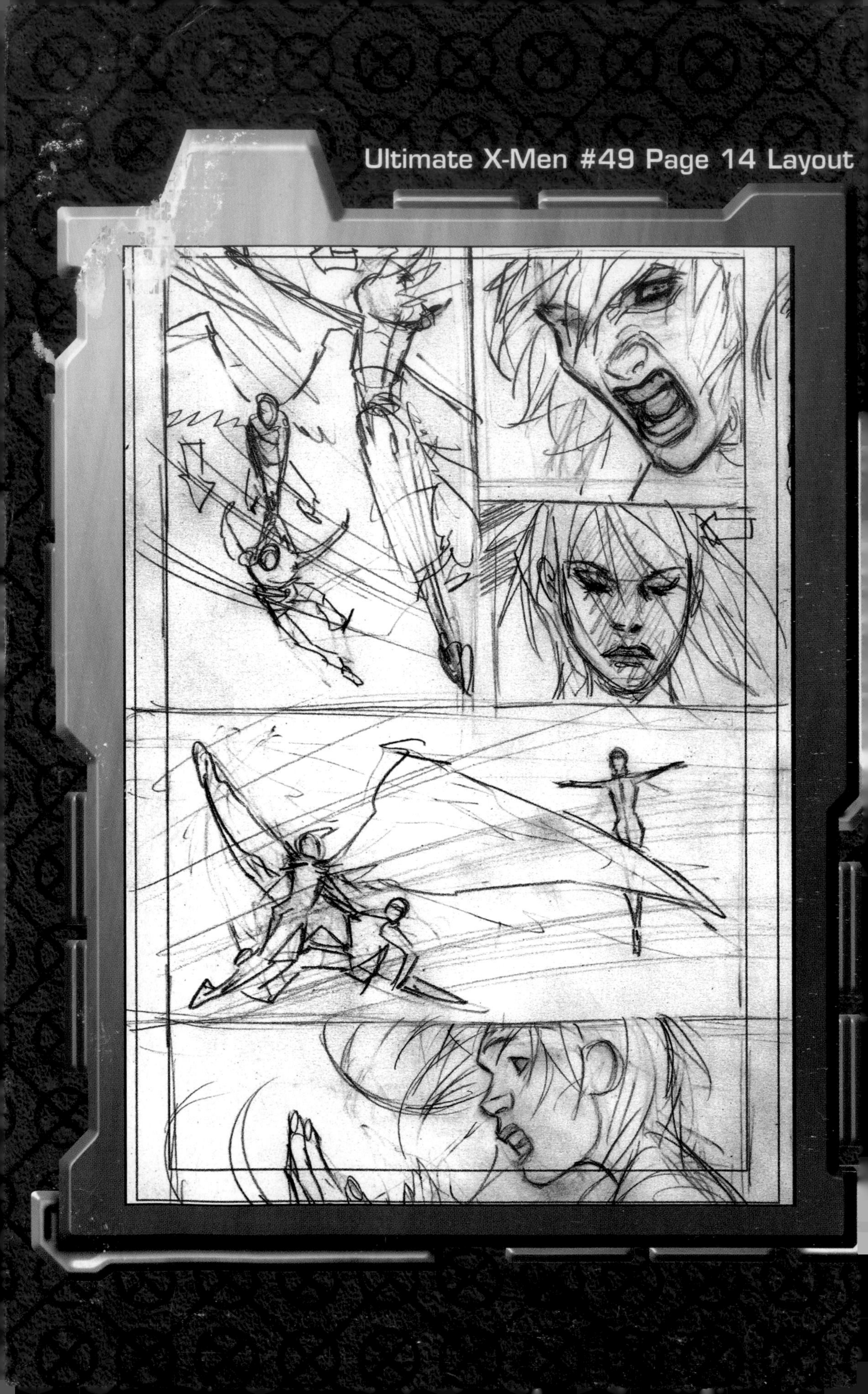